The Falkland Islands,
South Georgia and The
South Sandwich Islands

WORLD BIBLIOGRAPHICAL SERIES

General Editors:
Robert G. Neville (Executive Editor)
John J. Horton

Robert A. Myers   Hans H. Wellisch
Ian Wallace   Ralph Lee Woodward, Jr.

John J. Horton is Deputy Librarian of the University of Bradford and currently Chairman of its Academic Board of Studies in Social Sciences. He has maintained a longstanding interest in the discipline of area studies and its associated bibliographical problems, with special reference to European Studies. In particular he has published in the field of Icelandic and of Yugoslav studies, including the two relevant volumes in the World Bibliographical Series.

Robert A. Myers is Associate Professor of Anthropology in the Division of Social Sciences and Director of Study Abroad Programs at Alfred University, Alfred, New York. He has studied post-colonial island nations of the Caribbean and has spent two years in Nigeria on a Fulbright Lectureship. His interests include international public health, historical anthropology and developing societies. In addition to *Amerindians of the Lesser Antilles: a bibliography* (1981), *A Resource Guide to Dominica, 1493-1986* (1987) and numerous articles, he has compiled the World Bibliographical Series volumes on *Dominica* (1987), *Nigeria* (1989) and *Ghana* (1991).

Ian Wallace is Professor of German at the University of Bath. A graduate of Oxford in French and German, he also studied in Tübingen, Heidelberg and Lausanne before taking teaching posts at universities in the USA, Scotland and England. He specializes in contemporary German affairs, especially literature and culture, on which he has published numerous articles and books. In 1979 he founded the journal *GDR Monitor*, which he continues to edit under its new title *German Monitor*.

Hans H. Wellisch is Professor emeritus at the College of Library and Information Services, University of Maryland. He was President of the American Society of Indexers and was a member of the International Federation for Documentation. He is the author of numerous articles and several books on indexing and abstracting, and has published *The Conversion of Scripts and Indexing and Abstracting: an International Bibliography*, and *Indexing from A to Z*. He also contributes frequently to *Journal of the American Society for Information Science*, *The Indexer* and other professional journals.

Ralph Lee Woodward, Jr. is Professor of History at Tulane University, New Orleans. He is the author of *Central America, a Nation Divided*, 2nd ed. (1985), as well as several monographs and more than seventy scholarly articles on modern Latin America. He has also compiled volumes in the World Bibliographical Series on *Belize* (1980), *El Salvador* (1988), *Guatemala* (Rev. Ed.) (1992) and *Nicaragua* (Rev. Ed.) (1994). Dr. Woodward edited the Central American section of the *Research Guide to Central America and the Caribbean* (1985) and is currently associate editor of Scribner's *Encyclopedia of Latin American History*.

VOLUME 184

The Falkland Islands, South Georgia and The South Sandwich Islands

Alan Day

Compiler

CLIO PRESS

OXFORD, ENGLAND · SANTA BARBARA, CALIFORNIA
DENVER, COLORADO

British Library Cataloguing in Publication Data

The Falkland Islands, South Georgia and the South Sandwich Islands. – (World Bibliographical Series;
Vol. 184)
I. Day, Alan Edwin   II. Series
016.99711

ISBN 1–85109–236–6

ABC-CLIO Ltd.,
Old Clarendon Ironworks,
35A Great Clarendon Street,
Oxford OX2 6AT, England.

———

ABC-CLIO Inc.,
130 Cremona Drive,
Santa Barbara,
CA 93116, USA.

Designed by Bernard Crossland.
Typeset by Columns Design and Production Services Ltd., Reading, England.
Printed and bound in Great Britain by Bookcraft (Bath) Ltd., Midsomer Norton.

THE WORLD BIBLIOGRAPHICAL SERIES

This series, which is principally designed for the English speaker, will eventually cover every country (and many of the world's principal regions), each in a separate volume comprising annotated entries on works dealing with its history, geography, economy and politics; and with its people, their culture, customs, religion and social organization. Attention will also be paid to current living conditions – housing, education, newspapers, clothing, etc. – that are all too often ignored in standard bibliographies; and to those particular aspects relevant to individual countries. Each volume seeks to achieve, by use of careful selectivity and critical assessment of the literature, an expression of the country and an appreciation of its nature and national aspirations, to guide the reader towards an understanding of its importance. The keynote of the series is to provide, in a uniform format, an interpretation of each country that will express its culture, its place in the world, and the qualities and background that make it unique. The views expressed in individual volumes, however, are not necessarily those of the publisher.

VOLUMES IN THE SERIES

'This was a colony which could never become independent; for it never could be able to maintain itself. The necessary supplies were annually sent from England, at an expence which the Admiralty began to think would not quickly be repaid. . . That of which we were almost weary ourselves, we did not expect any one to envy; and therefore supposed that we should be permitted to reside in Falkland's Islands, the undisputed lords of tempest-beaten barrenness'.

Samuel Johnson, *Thoughts on the late transactions respecting Falkland's Islands* (1771).

Contents

Contents

Introduction

Situated in the South Atlantic, 480 kilometres (300 miles) from the southern coast of Argentina, the Falkland Islands comprise two main islands, East and West Falkland, and some 746 others of which 372 are unnamed (see item no. 98). Covering an area of 12,173 square kilometres, roughly equivalent to the size of Wales, the Islands are sparsely populated, with a total number of just 2,206 inhabitants in July 1993 (ninety-six per cent of British descent); 1,560 of these reside in Stanley on East Falkland, the Islands' capital and only town. The remainder live in the 'Camp', a local term derived from the Spanish word 'campo' meaning countryside, elsewhere on the two main islands.

Politically the Falkland Islands form a Dependent Territory of the United Kingdom, administered by a Governor, who is the personal representative of the monarch. Under the terms of the current Falkland Islands Constitution, which came into force in 1985, he is assisted by an Executive Council, which comprises two ex-officio members, the Chief Executive, who is responsible for the management of the Public Service and the economic development of the Islands, the Financial Secretary, and three annually-elected members from the Legislative Council. In addition, the Commander British Forces Falkland Islands, and the Islands' Attorney General, may attend the monthly Council meetings and are entitled to speak on any matter under discussion.

Based on English Common Law, the Falklands' judicial system consists of a Supreme Court, a Magistrate's Court, presided over by the senior magistrate, and a court of summary jurisdiction presided over by at least two magistrates. The Court of Appeal may hear appeals from the Supreme Court and, in certain circumstances, there is a final appeal to the Privy Council in London.

Traditionally the Islands' economy relies on sheepfarming which directly, or indirectly, is the main source of employment. Increasingly in recent years the rich fisheries in the surrounding seas have also provided many jobs; their potential was signified by the declaration of a Falklands Outer Conservation Zone of 200 kilometres from the Islands coastal baselines, and the establishment of a South Atlantic Fisheries Commission, involving Britain and Argentina in exploring ways and means of improving the conservation of migrating and straddling fish resources. The economy also benefits from an appreciable return from postal and philatelic services. In June 1984 the Falkland Islands Development Corporation was established 'to encourage and assist in the economic development of the Falkland Islands'.

Renowned for their wildlife, the Falklands boast of five breeding species of penguins, unique species of other breeding birds, and three species of seals, whilst the surrounding waters of the South Atlantic teem with marine life. Increasingly, however, the Islands' ecology is under threat from uncontrolled stock farming, and from the burgeoning fishing industry, both of which consume vital natural resources at an alarming rate. Conservation issues currently occupy much of the Islanders' attention although the interests of various groups cannot easily be reconciled.

The Falklands have experienced a short but controversial and momentous history which has exploded at intervals onto a world not always absolutely certain of where they are located. Even the date of their discovery, and by whom, is the subject of fierce debate. In 1502, three storm-driven Portuguese ships, with Amerigo Vespucci on board one of them, reported an unknown coast, between 52° and 53° latitude south, and some believe this to have been the first European sighting of the Islands. The British mariners, John Davis and Sir Richard Hawkins, separately reported the discovery of the Islands, ninety years later, although not every Hispanic cartographer or historian accepts their claims. In January 1600, Seebald de Weert, captain of one of three ships on a Dutch voyage to the South Seas, sighted three small islands, now identified as the Jason Islands, the furthermost North-western islands of the Falklands archipelago. What is certain is that the first European to set foot on the Islands was Captain John Strong, on a voyage to the South Seas at the end of January 1690; he named the sound between the two main islands 'Falkland's Sound' in honour of the Treasurer of the Navy. Soon afterwards, in 1701, the French mariner, Gouin de Beauchêne, discovered the island that now bears his name.

The crucial period in the history of the Falklands was 1764-70. Antoine Louis de Bougainville, sailing from St Malo, established a settlement at Port Louis in 1764, shortly followed by a British settlement at Port Egmont in 1765. It was the transfer of the French settlement to Spain in 1766 and the expulsion of the British from Port Egmont by a Spanish expedition from Buenos Aires, that led to a sovereignty dispute which almost dragged Britain and Spain into war, and ultimately resulted in the South Atlantic War between Argentina and Britain 200 years later. After the Spanish withdrawal from the Islands in 1811 a period of confusion followed, during which time a United States warship evicted the Argentine Governor. Britain revived its claims to the Islands, establishing a colony there in 1833. Since then they have been under British control and administration, although Argentina has retained a sense of grievance and has reasserted its sovereignty from time to time. Inconclusive negotiations after the Second World War dragged on until 2 April 1982 when the Argentine government, misled by an apparent British withdrawal of its armed forces from the South Atlantic, except for a token Royal Marine presence in Stanley, invaded and occupied the Islands. Diplomatic efforts by the United States and by the United Nations failed to halt a British Task Force being despatched to repossess the Islands for the Crown.

Life for the Islanders has changed irrevocably since the Argentine surrender. Reconstruction and rehabilitation, a more democratic constitution, a second Shackleton Report on the Islands' economy, the building of a garrison airport complex thirty miles from Stanley, the establishment of the Falkland Islands Development Corporation, and the imposition of the fishing zone round the Islands, have all had an incalculable effect. There is still unease about the future, since Argentina has shown no signs of renouncing its claims and in their hearts the Islanders must realize that things cannot remain as they are forever. Moreover, there is a lingering sense of distrust over the attitude of future British governments despite the huge sums of money that have poured into Stanley in the last ten years.

South Georgia

Captain James Cook was the first to land on South Georgia, which lies 1,290 kilometres east-south-east of the Falklands, when he displayed his colours and 'took possession of the Country in his Majesty's name under a discharge of small Arms', 17 January 1775. During the nineteenth century this mountainous island, which extends for some 160 miles, became a centre for sealing and whaling, lasting until December 1965 when the shore-based industry ceased operations. In 1908 Britain formally annexed the Island which, together with the South Sandwich Islands, South Shetlands, South

Orkneys, and Graham Land, formed the Falkland Islands Dependencies. It was not until 1985 that its political status altered, when it was declared the Territory of South Georgia and the South Sandwich Islands. This latter group was circumnavigated by Captain Cook, and also in January 1820 by Captain Fabian Gottlieb von Bellinghausen, of the Imperial Russian Navy, who named several of the islands. A small military detachment has been stationed on South Georgia since the 1982 war but the South Sandwich group remains unpopulated.

The bibliography

This volume follows the normal pattern of the World Bibliographical Series except that entries within the various sections are arranged in chronological order, usually by date of publication, but where necessary, according to the period covered by the books or articles in question. The History section is sub-divided into Eighteenth century and Nineteenth century but not Twentieth century. Apart from the Battle of the Falklands in the First World War, and the South Atlantic War of 1982, both of which obviously demanded separate sections of their own, there is remarkably little twentieth-century history to record. In order that the 1982 War should not dominate the bibliography in terms of the number of items cited, it was decided that only the actual invasion, and the war itself, on, over and around the Falklands would be covered, thus excluding material describing and explaining the turmoil at the United Nations, the political situation in Argentina, and the controversy aroused in Britain. Less than a handful of items relating to these political and diplomatic aspects of the war are included because of their overview nature and their bibliographical apparatus. Similarly, very few defence journal articles are entered.

A few items which appeared in previous World Bibliographical Series titles, Alan Biggins' *Argentina* (1985), H. G. R. King's *Atlantic Ocean* (1991), and Janice Meadows, William Mills and H. G. R. King's *The Antarctic* (1994) also appear here although their descriptive annotation is slanted appropriately. It seemed profitless to omit crucially important titles simply because they had been included elsewhere in the Series. The material selected for this bibliography encompasses books, maps, conference papers, bibliographies, and also a higher proportion than usual of journal articles, reflecting the sources of so much of the Falklands printed literature. To offset charges of national bias in the high-profile issue of sovereignty a small number of Spanish-language publications from the very large, but often repetitious, corpus of Argentine literature relating to this contentious, perplexing, and apparently insoluble topic, has also been included. Some recent articles from *The Times* find a place on the grounds that so many academic and large public libraries now hold long runs of this newspaper on microfilm that these articles would be accessible to most students and researchers.

Acknowledgements

As always a volume of this nature could not possibly be compiled without the co-operation and interest of many professional colleagues. The compiler is indebted to William Mills and his staff at the Scott Polar Research Institute in Cambridge; to the library of the Royal Geographical Society; to Chris Perkins at the Department of Geography, University of Manchester, who struggled valiantly to explain the mysteries of GEOBASE to a technologically challenged bibliographer; and to Alan Barlow, David Tuxford, and Stephen Witkovski at the Social Sciences Library, Manchester City Council Libraries & Theatres Department, whose combined experience in locating uncatalogued source material was much appreciated and shamefully exploited. A particular debt is owed to Ewa Cadwallader and her colleagues in the inter-library loans office of Manchester Metropolitan University Library, for their endless patience and forbearance.

Alan Day
Manchester
July 1995

The Islands and Their People

1   **Letter from Capt. Hunt of H.M.'s frigate Tamar dated from the New Exchange Coffee House.**
In: *Calendar of Home Office Papers of the reign of George III 1770-1772 preserved in Her Majesty's Public Record Office.*   Edited by Richard Arthur Roberts.   London: Longmans, 1881, p. 84.

'Near the seashore the soil is of a black spongy nature, and in general not above 18 inches deep, and then you come to a cold yellow clay. The valleys, when it is swampy, we found good turf: the other parts of it, and the side of the hills, afforded good herbage; and we found the sheep, goats, and hogs that we put on shore to thrive very well upon it, tho' the surface is much like our heaths and moors. . . There is no wood growing upon the Islands; but a few shrubs and a kind of brushwood, and great plenty of sedge growing near the seashore, which give the cattle good shelter in the bad weather. There is but two sorts of fish – the mullet and the smelt. At our first coming to Port Egmont, we found great plenty of wild geese. . .'.

2   **A description of Patagonia and the adioyning parts of South America . . . and some particulars relating to the Falkland Islands.**
Thomas Falkner.   Hereford, England: C. Pugh, 1774. 143p. 2 pull-out maps.

Falkner's particulars, which are limited to three pages, consist of descriptions of the Islands given to him by a number of Spanish officers who took over Port Louis from the French settlers, and by a French gunner who sailed with him from the River Plate to Cadiz. A facsimile edition was published in Chicago by Armann & Armann in 1935.

3 **A short description of Falkland Islands, their produce, climate and natural history.**
S. W. Clayton.   *Philosophical Transactions of the Royal Society*, vol. 66 (1776), p. 99-108.

Captain William Clayton RN commanded the small British garrison stationed at Port Egmont, Saunders Island, West Falkland, in 1773-74. His account of the Islands was the first to be published in English. He concludes: 'these are all the remarks I made while I commanded on that barren, dreary, desolate, boggy, rocky spot, in 1773 and 1774'. A modern transcription is printed as 'Clayton's account of the Falkland Islands, 1774', edited by F. C. Stott, in *Polar Record*, vol. 23, no. 144 (September 1986), p. 351-56.

4 **Account of East Falkland Island.**
Woodbine Parish.   *Journal of the Royal Geographical Society*, vol. 3 (1833), p. 94-99. folded map.

Drawn up for the author by Louis Vernet, the Argentine Governor of the Islands between 1829 and 1832, this early account of the Falklands' deep harbour facilities, climate, topography, soil, vegetation and animal life, together with sailing directions into Berkeley Sound, East Falkland, is of immense historical interest.

5 **Despatch from Lieutenant Governor Moody to Lord Stanley.**
Falkland Islands Journal, no. 3 (1969), p. 2-33.

Dated 14 April 1842, this despatch provides a full description of the islands' rivers and harbours, geology and soil, climate and temperature, prevailing winds, vegetation, prospects for hardy fruit trees, export prospects, necessary staple imports, the price of land to settlers, and the site for a new town, all of which information was designed for 'British subjects desirous of emigrating'.

6 **Falkland heritage: a record of pioneer settlement.**
Mary Trehearne.   Ilfracombe, England: Stockwell, 1978. 201p. 7 maps.

Based on letters and diaries only recently brought to light, this book is the story of two early settlers in West Falkland, Ernest Holmested and Robert Blake, who joined forces to start a large sheepfarm at Hill Cove in 1874. The narrative brings alive, as no 'outsider' account or official report could possibly emulate, the life of the islands in the latter half of the nineteenth century. Such events and features as the mission station on Keppel Island, the Easter races at Hill Cove, cookhouse dances, the privations and hardships endured by newly arrived colonists from Britain, and the opening of the Falkland Islands Government Savings Bank in 1888, are all concisely detailed at first hand.

7 **Falkland Islands South-America.**
Gustav Schulz.   London: C. Gross, 1890. 24p. bibliog.

Every aspect of contemporary Falklands life is briefly sketched in this handsome boxed volume. It covers: the history; size; coasts; interior; climate; government; Port Darwin; Goose Green; Port Louis; agriculture; sheepfarming; houses; peat; geology; rivers of stone; botany; Balsom bogs; tussock (tussac) grass; kelp; zoology; birds; reptiles; insects; fish; rabbits; wild horses; cattle; and seals. Twenty photographs of views, birds and other subjects mounted on 28cm x 23cm cards, accompany the text.

8   **The Falkland Islands.**
    R. M. Routledge.   *Scottish Geographical Magazine*, vol. 12, no. 5 (May 1896), p. 241-52.

A description of Port Stanley, the Falkland's climate, churches, education, the government dockyard, engineering works and carpentry shops, law, social life and recreation, sheepfarming, employment, husbandry, and travel within the Islands, are all encompassed in this sketch of the life and habits of the islanders.

9   **The wilds of Patagonia: a narrative of the Swedish expedition to Patagonia Tierra Del Fuego and the Falkland Islands in 1907-1909.**
    Carl Skottsberg.   London: Edward Arnold, 1911. 336p. 3 maps.

A member of the Swedish South Polar Expedition of 1901-03, the author began preparations to go back to the Antarctic soon after he returned in January 1904. This book constitutes a record of the Swedish Magellanic Expedition, which consisted of Skottsberg himself, Percy D. Quensel, and Thore G. Halle, whose main interests were botanical and geological. The first two chapters form an excellent travelogue of the Falklands, encompassing: Port Stanley and its social life; the landscape around the town; Cape Pembroke lighthouse; West Falkland; the wild cattle; the Falklands fox; life on the more remote islands; Westpoint Island; bird life; Hill Cove settlement; the life of the shepherds; an ascent of Mt. Adam; Saunders Island; the valley of the Warrah River; Port Howard; geological notes; Lafonia and Port Darwin; San Carlos; and Port Louis and its history. A later chapter describes a winter in South Georgia and includes information on its nature and geographical location, its climate, its flora and fauna, and on the whaling industry there.

10 **The Falkland Islands and Dependencies.**
    William S. Bruce.   In: *The Oxford survey of the British Empire: vol. 4 America*.   Edited by A. J. Herbertson, O. J. R. Howarth.   Oxford: Clarendon Press, 1914, p. 430-49.

The precise location of the Falklands, South Georgia and the South Sandwich group; their early settlement; their physical features; their geology, climate, hydrography, vegetation, and animal life, are some of the topics explored in this brief survey. Economic and social conditions, agriculture, fishing, whaling and sealing, transportation and shipping, and postal and telecommunications, are also treated. At the time this was as thorough a survey as could be expected.

11 **Falkland Islands: Kerguelen.**
    Foreign Office.   London: HMSO, 1920. 62p. (Handbooks Prepared Under The Direction of the Historical Section of the Foreign Office).

The Foreign Office handbooks were originally published to provide British delegates to the Versailles Peace Conference after the First World War with useful background information on the various territories they might find themselves discussing. The Falkland Islands (p. 1-43) deals with the colony's physical and political geography, its political history, social and political conditions, and its economy. It remains a mystery why the Foreign Office should imagine the Falklands would be a subject of discussion.

12   **The Falkland Islands.**
V. F. Boyson.   Oxford: Clarendon Press, 1924. 414p. 4 maps. bibliog.

Boyson has divided this study into twenty-two detailed chapters arranged in four parts: history (ten chronological chapters); industries (cattle and sheep, whales and the whaling industry, seals and sealing); geophysical notes (climate, stone rivers, flora); zoology (by Robert Vallentin); and a statistical appendix. This was the definitive work on the Falklands until Ian J. Strange's *The Falkland Islands* (item no. 38), which was first published in 1972. Even now it is essential reading for any serious study of the Islands.

13   **Falkland Islands centenary 1833-1933 a short notice, historical and descriptive, in regard to the Falkland Islands prepared on the occasion of the centenary of the colony in 1933.**
J. M. Ellis.   Stanley: Government Printing Press, 1933. 16p.

In this celebratory booklet Ellis, who was Colonial Secretary in the' Falklands at the time, briefly outlines the Islands' location, their early history and settlement, the establishment of the Colony, and its modern history. He ends with a description of Stanley.

14   **Falkland Islands interlude.**
Tom Beaty.   Oswestry, England: Anthony Nelson, 1991. 50p.

In 1939, at the age of twenty-four, the author went to the Falklands as a stock inspector. From 1944 to 1953 he was Farm Manager at Port Stephens. This autobiographical account describes a way of life that has long passed, 'a class-ridden, feudal and dependent but often caring society'.

15   **British Islands in the Southern Hemisphere 1945-1951.**
London: HMSO for the Colonial Office, 1951. 127p. 2 maps. (Cmnd. 8230).

The section on the Falkland Islands (p. 79-92) outlines the Colony's historical background, its development as a Crown Colony, and its role in the two World Wars. It also details its constitution; local government; commerce; internal air service; posts and telegraphs; health and medical service; education; social services; social amenities and social activities; living conditions; labour and wages; economy; and public finance. Falkland Islands Dependencies (p. 93-98) is concerned with their economy, public finance, and foreign relations. This report was presented to Parliament in May 1951.

16   **The Falkland Islands to-day.**
Forrest McWhan.   Stirling, Scotland: Stirling Tract Enterprise, 1952. 88p. pull-out maps. bibliog.

A brief history of the Islands, and a description of Port Stanley and the Camp, the government and economy of the Colony, its natural history, and that of the Falkland Islands Dependencies, are the main topics covered in this guide. The author spent seventeen years on the Falklands including a spell as editor of *Falkland Islands Weekly News*.

17   **The other side of the Falklands: the lion and the lamb.**
   Roger M. Edwards.   Waterlooville, England: Drift Publications, 1993.
   170p. map.

In the 1950s Roger Edwards answered an advertisement in the *Portsmouth Evening News* and went to work on a large sheep station at Fox Bay, West Falkland. When his five-year contract was up he took a land drainage job at Chartres. This delightful, nostalgic, and zestful little book offers a personal and sympathetic glimpse of the life and people of West Falkland before the twentieth century finally engulfed them.

18   **Christmas in the Falklands.**
   Sir Miles Clifford.   *Geographical Magazine*, vol. 27, no. 8 (December
   1954), p. 423-30.

Governor of the Falkland Islands for seven years, Clifford reminisces about a typical Islands' Christmas, both in Stanley, and in the Camp, which culminates in the two-day race-meeting, 'the real business of the holiday'. Boxing Day saw the serious racing, with the day after given over to gymkhana events. 'This is an article which should be read and pondered in those "other quarters" whence come the "persistent claims" on the Falklands'.

19   **The Falkland Islands and their Dependencies.**
   Sir Miles Clifford.   *Geographical Journal*, vol. 121, no. 4 (December
   1955), p. 405-16. 2 maps.

Opening with some authoritative historical notes, Clifford then turns his attention to the Falkland Islands economy and administration in the years immediately after the Second World War when he was Governor. In 1946 the Colony had no form of political representation, no social security, and no communications. By 1952, however, the Falkland Islands Government Air Service had been established, an old-age contributory pension scheme for all males had been set up, an up-to-date hospital opened, and arrangements made for scholarship pupils to attend schools in England.

20   **The Falkland Islands.**
   M. A. Willis.   *Corona: The Journal of Her Majesty's Overseas
   Service*, vol. 9, no. 11 (November 1957), p. 416-18.

Based on a three-week visit to the Islands, this article is redolent of the downbeat Colonial Office attitude towards the Falklands. Willis notes the terrible climate, and 'the general air of desolation in Stanley', but reports on the introduction of the Government seaplane service and the two-way radio telephone link with Stanley, both innovations of great service to farmers in the Camp. He ends by remarking that the Colony offers only limited opportunities to Overseas Service members.

21   **Lonely Falkland Islands.**
   Ian J. Strange.   *Geographical Magazine*, vol. 40, no. 12 (April 1968),
   p. 1065-72. map.

A brief illustrated overview of life on the Falkland Islands, touching upon the climate, soil, farm settlements, economy, internal air services, education, and the wool industry.

22 **Whose flag over the Falklands?**
Ian Jack, Philip Jones Griffiths. *Sunday Times Magazine* (13 August 1978), p. 14-19, 21, 23-24.

In this 'colour supplement' feature on life in Stanley and in the Camp, a Sunday morning in Stanley, the cinema, shops, the radio transmitting station, life on a sheepfarm, the games at Darwin, the Falklands' tangled history, and the problem of emigration and a declining population all come under close scrutiny. Similar features include Marion Morrison's 'The little bit of Empire at the end of the world', *Observer Magazine* (31 August 1969), p. 16-22, and Joseph Lucas' 'The islands Argentina wants to swallow', *Daily Telegraph Magazine*, no. 190 (May 1968), p. 22-27.

23 **The Falkland Islands.**
Ian J. Strange. Newton Abbot, England: David & Charles, 1983. 3rd ed. 328p. 6 maps. bibliog.

Without doubt the standard work on the Falklands for many years to come, this book was first published in 1972, with a second edition in 1981. This third edition was revised to include two new chapters on the impact of the 1982 war. It encompasses the Islands' geographical features, their people, communications, natural history, fisheries, future and development, and their post-war reconstruction and rehabilitation. Ian Strange has lived in the Islands since the early 1960s; he is an active conservationist, a wildlife artist and photographer, a Crown Agents stamp designer, and a prolific author and contributor to a wide range of journals and periodicals.

24 **Antarctica and the South Atlantic: discovery, development and dispute.**
Robert Fox. London: British Broadcasting Corporation, 1985. 336p. map. bibliog.

Especially valuable for its critical discussion on the Falklands' way of life in the post-1982 war period, this definitive study is divided into two distinct parts. The first is an account of a voyage in *HMS Endurance*, the Royal Navy's ice-patrol ship, to South Georgia, the South Sandwich Islands, South Orkneys, and Graham Land, whilst part two, 'The Falklands dimension', comprises an evaluation of the effect of the military presence on the islands. It also provides a study of the development and land reform on which the future viability of the Falklands so crucially depends, as well as a detailed examination of the circumstances surrounding the King Edward Memorial Hospital fire, 16 April 1984, and the administrative confusion over the building of a new hospital. Finally, it covers the Colony's future educational, medical and hospital prospects, which were all excluded from the second *Shackleton report*.

25 **The Falkland Islands: the ideal Antarctic base.**
A. R. Michaelis. *Interdisciplinary Science Reviews*, vol. 13, no. 1 (1988), p. 1-4.

'The time has come to make a strong case for the Falkland Islands to become the forward base for international scientific research in the Antarctic. . . It will be the one function which brings to the islands a meaningful future' (preamble). This editorial considers the various factors which together add up to a strong argument for establishing the islands as a base for international research. Among them are the new international airport at Mt. Pleasant; the strong probability of coal and oil in the

Antarctic region, and perhaps even uranium; the need for ski landing aircraft; the slowness of sea transport; and the international aspect. The benefits to the Islands' economy are also well to the fore.

26 **Unspoilt beauty of the Falkland Islands.**
Algernon Asprey, Phyllis Rendell.   Oswestry, England: Anthony Nelson, 1988. 64p.

Twenty-two of Asprey's watercolours depicting Stanley and the Camp, including some of the outer islands, are reproduced here, each supported by Rendell's text describing the heritage and features of each locality. In some instances the text provides historical detail and relevance to the 1982 war.

27 **An introduction to the Falkland Islands.**
London: London Office Falkland Islands Government, [1988].

Filed together in a laminated folder (16 cm × 22 cm) are twenty-seven constantly updated information sheets on a variety of topics: Geography and climate; Natural resources; Population; Government; Economy; Communications; Wages, labour and employment; Taxes and duties; Education; Health services; Philatelic and postal services; Transport; Recreation; Wildlife; Tourism; Travel; and Falkland Islands Development Corporation agricultural and industrial services. A book list and a list of useful addresses are also supplied. A remarkably complete picture of life on the Islands is presented.

28 **Those were the days: a miscellany of reflections on the life and times in Stanley as it used to be.**
John Smith.   Bluntisham, England: Bluntisham Books for the Falkland Islands Trust, Stanley, 1989. 48p.

Five engaging nostalgic cameos are collected in this attractive little booklet: The cemetery at Stanley; The peace celebrations of 1919; the Globe store; Dances and other entertainments; and Ready for the off (that is, on board *Fitzroy* and *Darwin* on voyages home). 'The purpose has been to set down those little bits and pieces of the Falklands way of life which, though small and not really relevant to any particular part of history, do not find their way into the books written about the Islands'.

29 **The Falkland Islands.**
Paul Morrison.   Bourne End, England: Aston Publications, 1990. 96p.

Notes on the Islands' early history, settlement, economy, tourism, flora and fauna, the 1982 conflict, and Port Stanley, are accompanied in this splendid pictorial volume by a superb collection of colour photographs.

30 **Old Falklands photographs: a view of life 1880-1940.**
Compiled by Shane Wolsey.   Bangor, Northern Ireland: Peregrine Press, 1990. 92p.

A selection of ninety black-and-white photographs illustrating Stanley, camp life, the Falkland Islands Defence Force, leisure, transport, shipping, and other miscellaneous aspects. 'Some are familiar ... but many are unique and quite remarkable' (*Falkland Islands Newsletter,* no. 47 [May 1991], p. 14).

31   **Falkland people.**
     Angela Wigglesworth.   London: Peter Owen, 1992. 138p. maps on
     endpapers.
With contributions from over seventy individuals, including some fifth- and sixth-
generation Islanders, reflecting on their lives and everyday work, their hopes and fears
for the future, and relating their experiences during the 1982 conflict, this pleasant
book is as much a social study as a geographical description.

32   **The Falklands.**
     Tony Chater.   St. Albans, England: Penna Press, 1993. 168p. maps.
Essentially this is a large-page collection of over 300 of the author's own spectacular
colour photographs, including many of the 1982 conflict never published before, with
a few older in black and white borrowed from the albums of his friends. An
accompanying text is arranged in two sections, covering: Les Iles Nouvelles
(Discovery); seabirds; Stanley; predators and passerines; ships and shorelines; waders
and wildfowl; camp and the Campers; marine mammals; war; and the future. In the
words of Patrick Watts, Station Manager, Falkland Islands Radio, this is 'quite simply
the finest book about the Falklands ever produced'.

33   **Diary of a farmer's wife: an everyday story of a Falkland Islands
     farm.**
     Rosemary Wilkinson.   Dunnose Head Farm, West Falkland: Published
     by the author, 1992. 57p. map.
An account of life on a 'small' sheepfarm over the past ten years. 'If you want to
know what really goes on in the Falklands Camp these days then you must read this
book' (*Falkland Islands Newsletter*, no. 52 [August 1992], p. 12). A second booklet
with the same title was published in 1993.

34   **Britain and the Falkland Islands.**
     London: HMSO, 1993. 53p. map. (Aspects of Britain).
Researched and written by Reference Services, Central Office of Information, this
short book outlines the history of the Falkland Islands and the dispute over
sovereignty between Argentina and Britain. It also provides information on the
Islands' government, economy, social welfare, communications, South Georgia, and
the South Sandwich Islands. In effect, this title is an updated version of *The disputed
islands: the Falkland crisis: a history and background* (HMSO, 1982).

Penguin News.
See item no. 541.

Discovery and Early Voyages

35   **The voyages and works of John Davis the navigator.**
Edited by Albert Hastings Markham.   London: Hakluyt Society, 1880.
392p.

Captain John Davis of the ship, *Desire*, was Rear Admiral to Thomas Candish on a voyage to the South Sea, the Philippines, and the China Coast, which sailed 26 August 1591. Separated in a storm, Davis related: 'The seventh of August [1592] towards night wee departed from Penguin-isle, shaping our course for The Streights, where wee had full confidence to meete with our General. The ninth wee had a sore storme, so that wee were constrained to hull, for our sailes were not to indure any force. The 14 wee were driven in among certaine Isles never before discovered by any knowen relation, lying fiftie leagues or better from the shoare East and Northerly from The Streights'. Markham pointed out in his introduction (p. 108-09): 'These were undoubtedly the Falkland Islands. The credit of discovering this group has been divided between Davis and Richard Hawkins; the latter navigator, however, did not sight them until 1594, or two years after they had been seen by Davis. In spite of the claims put forward by the supporters of these navigators, there is very conclusive evidence to prove that the Falkland Islands had been discovered long before the time of either Davis or Hawkins, and called the Ascension Islands, but by whom it is difficult to decide. Their discovery can hardly be ascribed to Vespucius, who, even if he made a voyage at all, which is by no means certain, does not pretend to have sailed further south than the River Plate. Magellan, during his voyage round the world in 1519 and 1520, makes no mention of having seen the group; thus the honour of their discovery must belong to some unknown foreign navigator, for they appear, as the Ascension Islands, on the two charts constructed for Charles V, one (anonymous) in 1527, and the other by Diego Ribero in 1529'.

36 **The observations of Sir Richard Hawkins Knt. in his voyage into the South Sea in the year 1593.**
Edited by C. A. Drinkwater Bethune. London: Hakluyt Society, 1847. 246p.

First published in London by John Jaggard (1622), these observations are also included in *The Hawkins' voyages during the reigns of Henry VIII, Queen Elizabeth and James I* (London: Hakluyt Society, 1878. 453p.). Section thirty reads: 'All this coast, so farre as we discovered, lyeth next of anything east and by north, and west and by south. The land, for that it was discovered in the raigne of Queene Elizabeth, my soveraigne lady and mistres, and a maiden Queene, at my cost and adventure, in a perpetual memorie of her chastitie, and remembrance of my endeavours, I gave it the name of Hawkins maiden-land'. According to Hawkins the land he sighted on 2 February 1594, was in latitude 49° 30'S. But, as Markham noted, 'Hawkins wrote from memory, and fortunately he is corrected, as regards his latitude, by one of his officers named Ellis, who tells us that the land was in 50°S and about fifty leagues off the Straits of Magellan. Without doubt they sighted the Falkland Islands, but the group had already been discovered by John Davis'.

37 **Can Hawkins' 'Maiden Land' be identified as the Falkland Islands?**
B. M. Chambers. *Geographical Journal*, vol. 17, no. 4 (April 1901), p. 414-23. 2 maps.

By comparing Hawkins' description of 'Maiden Land' printed in *The Hawkins' voyages during the reigns of Henry VIII, Queen Elizabeth and James I* (Hakluyt Society, 1878), and his own on-the-spot observations, Chambers proposed 'to show that the evidence of Hawkins having ever visited the Falklands is entirely insufficient'. H. Henniker-Heaton's 'Did Sir Richard Hawkins visit the Falkland Islands?', *Geographical Journal*, vol. 67, no. 1 (January 1926), p. 52-56, refutes Chambers' conclusions and asserts that Hawkins' account was the first ever to be published of the Islands. See also M. B. R. Cawkell's 'The curious case of Sir Richard Hawkins', *Falkland Islands Journal*, no. 22 (1988), p. 7-9, which demands 'how could a man who not only sailed into the Falklands but identified well-known land-marks continue to be regarded as an also-ran in the story of Falkland discovery?'. She also refers to Goebel's zest to dispose of any British connection with the discovery.

38 **A new voyage round the world.**
William Dampier. London: A & C Black, 1937. 376p. 3 pull-out maps. (The Pioneer Histories).

In an adventurous life William Dampier (1652-1715) spent many years at sea, including some as a pirate. In 1697 he published *A new voyage round the world describing particularly the Isthmus of America, several coasts and islands in the West Indies, the isles of Cape Verd, the Passage by Terra del Fuego . . . their soil, rivers, harbours, plants, fruits, animals, and inhabitants, their customs, religion, government, trade etc.* This was a summary of his diaries and journals. One entry, dated 28 January 1684, remarks 'we made the Sibbel de Wards, which are 3 islands lying in the latitude of 51d. 25m. South, and longitude West from the Lizard in England. . . These islands of Sibbel de Wards were so named by the Dutch. They are all three rocky barren islands without any tree, only Dildoe-Bushes growing on them. And I do believe there is no water on any one of them, for there was no appearance of any water'. This edition includes an introduction by Sir Albert Gray who narrates what is known of Dampier's life.

39 A voyage to the South-Sea, and along the coasts of Chili and Peru, in the years 1712, 1713 and 1714 . . .
Amadee Frézier. London: Jonah Bowyer, 1717. 344p. 37 maps and charts.

This voyage was an intelligence reconnaissance lest war should break out between France and Spain. Engineer Ordinary to the King, Frézier was given command because of his ability to make hydrographic charts, and to plot the ports, fortresses, and harbours, along the west coast of South America. Only four pages relate to the Falklands (p. 287-90) but a pull-out map 'Carte réduite de l'extrémité de l'Amérique Meridionnale dans la partie du Sud ou sont comprises les nouvelles isles descouvertes par les vaisseaux de St Malo depuis 1700 dont la partie de l'ouest est encore inconnue', which shows the routes of various St Malo ships between 1706-13, is of prime historical interest. Frézier remarks that 'these islands are certainly the same which Sir Richard Hawkins discovered in 1593'. First published as *Relation du voyage de la Mer du Sud aus côtes du Chily et de Pérou et du Brésil, fait pendant les années 1712- 14* (Paris, 1716), this English-language edition includes a postscript by Edmond Halley pointing out some errors of geography.

40 Anson's voyage.
In: *Documents relating to Anson's voyage round the world 1740-1744*. Edited by Glyndwr Williams. London: Navy Records Society, 1967, p. 231.

Anson's voyage round Cape Horn in *HMS Centurion*, to attack Spanish ports in the Pacific led him to consider two possible locations for a British base. One was the mythical Pepys Island, whilst 'The second place, of Falkland's Isles, have been seen by many ships both French and English, being the land laid down by Frezier, in his chart of the extremity of South America under the title of the New Islands. It is true, they are too little known to be at present recommended as the most eligible place of refreshment for ships bound to the southward: But if the Admiralty should think it advisable to order them to be surveyed . . . it is scarcely to be conceived of what a prodigious import a convenient station might prove . . . even in time of peace, might be of great consequence to this nation: and, in time of war, would make us masters of those seas' (Extracted from *A voyage round the world in the years MDCCXL, I, II, III, IV by George Anson . . . compiled from papers and other materials of the Rt. Hon. George Anson, and published under his direction by Richard Walter MA. Chaplain of His Majesty's ship Centurion, in that expedition* [1748]).

41 A journal of a voyage round the world in His Majesty's Ship the Dolphin . . . commanded by the Honourable Commodore Byron . . . by a Midshipman on board the said ship.
London: M. Cooper, 1767. 75p. folded map.

'On the thirteenth of January we espied the land, which at first view appeared as a considerable number of islands. Here we sent our boats on shore, where they found a safe and convenient bay, sheltered from the fury of the winds. To this port we gave the name of Port Egmont, in honour of Lord Egmont. This harbour is of such extent as to receive the whole navy of England'. It is striking that both a junior Midshipman and his Commodore (see item no. 42) both immediately appreciated the harbour's potential as a naval station.

42　**Byron's journal of his circumnavigation 1764-1766.**
　　Edited by Robert E. Gallagher.　Cambridge, England: Cambridge
　　University Press for the Hakluyt Society, 1964. 230p. maps. bibliog.

A 'Letter from Byron to the Earl of Egmont sent via Florida Storeship 24 February 1765' (p. 153-60) describes Falkland Harbour as one of the world's finest and reports plenty of good water, wild fowl in abundance, a profusion of wood sorrel and wild sellary 'which are the best anti-scorbuticks in the world', and reports that he has formally taken possession in the name of the King. 'Voyages and journals whence the extracts relative to Falkland's Islands. . .' and 'Extracts from journals and accounts and voyages so far as they relate to Falkland's Islands and Pepys Island' (p. 162-75) provide a good bibliographical guide to printed sources of information to that time.

43　**Early voyages to the Falkland Islands, 1769-1850.**
　　A. G. E. Jones.　*Falkland Islands Journal*, vol. 6, no. 2 (1993),
　　p. 18-40.

Although it is virtually impossible to determine with any accuracy the number of voyages made to the Falklands in this early period, Jones does as well as any research scholar could by combing the files of *Lloyd's List*, *Lloyd's Register*, the *Register of the Society of Merchants, Shipowners and Underwriters*, the *Navy list*, the Admiralty Protections, and HM Custom Bills of Entry.

44　**Some American visitors to the Falkland Islands 1788-1795.**
　　Andrew C. F. David.　*Falkland Islands Journal*, vol. 5, no. 5 (1991),
　　p. 18-26. bibliog.

David records the activities of two Boston merchantmen engaged in the sea otter trade bound for the north-west coast of America in 1787; the *Columbia* and *Lady Washington*, 16-22 February 1788; *Columbia*, 21 January-2 February 1791; *Hope*, 4-13 January 1791; and *Union*, 2-24 January 1795. Copious use is made of extracts from contemporary accounts and narratives.

45　**Alejandro Malaspina's visits to Port Egmont in 1789 and 1794.**
　　Lola Manterola Jara, Andrew David.　*Falkland Islands Journal*, vol. 6,
　　no. 2 (1993), p. 1-17. 3 maps. bibliog.

On Malaspina's first visit to the Falkland Islands, 18-24 December 1789, he made an hydrographic survey of the Islands to provide Spanish navigators with a reliable guide to previously uncharted waters notably in the immediate vicinity of Puerto Soledad. Whilst at Port Egmont a second time, 2-20 January 1794, he had occasion to 'persuade' two American sealers to leave the Islands, remarkably foreshadowing similar events nearly forty years later.

46 **Voyages and discoveries in the South Seas 1792-1832.**
Edmund Fanning. Salem, Massachusetts: Marine Research Society, 1924. 335p.

First published as *Voyages round the world; with selected sketches of voyages to the South Seas, North and South Pacific Oceans, China etc.* (New York: Collins & Hannaway, 1833), with London and Paris editions following in 1834, Fanning's narrative includes details of hunting for seals in Stanley Harbour in September 1792. It also covers another visit to the Falklands in 1797, when he noted down observations on penguin and albatross rookeries, and other aspects of the Islands' wildlife, and mentioned an organized sealing voyage to South Georgia in the 1800-01 season.

47 **A chronological history of the voyages and discoveries in the South Seas or Pacific Ocean.**
James Burney. London: G. & W. Nicol, 1803-17. 5 vols.

This renowned collection of Spanish, English, French and Dutch voyages of discovery in the Pacific Ocean, either via the South Atlantic, or Indian Oceans, includes many references. At times these consist of only a brief report of the sixteenth-century voyages, and at others more expansive accounts of seventeenth- and eighteenth-century landings on the Falklands. Volume four gives the full circumstances of the voyage of Captain John Strong, who sighted the islands on 27 January 1690, and was the first European navigator known to have landed on the Islands. The same volume also provides details of the voyage of M. Gouin de Beauchêne who discovered the island named after him 19 January 1701, and of subsequent French mariners from St. Malo who frequented the islands in the first decade of the eighteenth century, naming them Les îles Malouines.

48 **Realms and islands: the world voyage of Rose de Freycinet in the corvette Uranie 1817-1820: from her journal and letters and the reports of Louis de Saulces de Freycinet Capitaine de Corvette.**
Marnie Bassett. London: Oxford University Press, 1962. 275p. bibliog. 3 maps.

Louis de Freycinet was appointed commander of the *Uranie* and leader of a French scientific expedition around the world. His wife Rose was smuggled aboard at Toulon in 1817 disguised in men's clothing. The *Uranie*'s voyage took them to South America, South Africa, Mauritius, Timor, the Moluccas, New Guinea, the Carolines, Guam, the Sandwich Islands and Australia, until disaster struck in the Falklands in February 1820 when the ship was pierced by a submerged rock whilst entering French Bay. Three chapters, covering the period February to April 1820, tell how she was eventually beached after ten hours hard pumping, and of the negotiations with various American whaling skippers to return the ship's company to Montevideo or Rio de Janeiro.

49 **Narrative of the surveying voyages of His Majesty's ships Adventure and Beagle between the years 1826 and 1836, describing their examination of the southern shores of South America and the Beagle's circumnavigation of the globe.**
Robert Fitzroy.   London: Henry Colburn, 1839. 3 vols. appendix.

Robert Fitzroy RN (1805-65), a hydrographer and meteorologist, commanded the *Beagle* on her circumnavigation of the world. Volume two of this work, *Proceedings of the Second Expedition*, includes: chapter eleven, a historical sketch of the Falklands, discovery and pretended discoveries by Spanish, British and French mariners (p. 228-40); chapter twelve which covers topics such as tides, the climate, winds, seasons, settlements, animals, seals and whales, fish and fishery, birds, peat, pasture, grazing, fruit and vegetables, plants, Vernet's establishment, and prospective advantages (p. 241-68); chapter thirteen, at anchor in Berkeley Sound, British flag hoisted (p. 269-79); and chapter fifteen, the second visit in March 1834 and an account of the murders of 26 August 1833 (p. 327-35). Chapter twelve of volume three, *Journal and Remarks 1832-1836* (by Charles Darwin), covers an excursion round the island, cattle, horses, rabbits, the wolf-like fox, hunting wild cattle, geology and fossil shells, penguins, geese and zoophytes (p. 245-62), whilst the appendix includes papers relating to the Falklands, notably Bougainville's instructions to deliver the French colony to the Spaniards, the diplomatic correspondence relating to the Spanish restoration of the British settlement at Port Egmont, and Fitzroy's instructions to Lieutenant J. C. Wickham of HBM Sloop *Adventure* to survey the Islands in 1834.

Travellers' Accounts

50 A visit to the Falkland Islands - 1832.

Anonymous. *Falkland Islands Journal*, vol. 6, no. 2 (1993), p. 41-49.

Reprinted from the *United Services Journal and Naval and Military Gazette*, part 3 (1832), p. 309-16, this anonymous article was written by a passenger on *The Thomas Lawrie* which visited the Islands, 22 October 1831. It consists mainly of 'remarks which I was enabled to make during my stay at Port Louis, my researches extending to a few miles in every direction round the settlement'. The author describes the tense situation in the settlement in the aftermath of Vernet's run-in with the United States vessels as well as detailing the climate, vegetation, and wildlife of the Islands, their cattle hides, and agricultural production, and the prospects for new settlers and immigrants.

51 Extracts from the diary of Admiral The Honourable George Grey.

Falkland Islands Journal, no. 3 (1969), p. 54-68; no. 13 (1980), p. 4-9.

In a tour of duty between 30 November 1836 and 4 January 1837, Captain George Grey inspected the main islands on horseback and completely circumnavigated the archipelago. These extracts from his diary include an historical review of the British, French and Spanish occupations.

52 Atlantic and transatlantic.

Lauchlan Bellingham Mackinnon. New York: Harper, 1852. 324p.

Mainly consisting of essays on various aspects of the United States, this book concludes with four chapters under the general heading, 'Wild sports of the Falklands'. The first chapter takes the form of a 'brief summary of prominent circumstances connected with the Falkland Islands since they were first occupied by an English governor (Lieutenant Moody), whose appointment took place in 1842, to which year the birth of the colony may be consigned'. In the remainder are sketches extracted from a diary kept by the author while surveying the islands in 1838-39, many of which relate to the herds of wild cattle then to be found. A 'Supplement to the Falklands' (p. 295-302) recounts the events of 1769-71. 'Wild sports in the

Falklands: sketches during a survey of those islands' first appeared in *New Monthly Magazine*, vol. 87, no. 10 (October 1849), p. 139-56.

53   Cruise of HMS Dwarf amongst the Falkland Islands January 1882.
Falkland Islands Journal, no. 5 (1971), p. 32-36.

HMS Dwarf was sent to the Islands in response to a request by the Governor for a vessel to protect the seal fisheries. Whilst there she sailed from Stanley to Lively Island, Darwin, Bleaker Island, Point Shepherd Settlement, Beaver Island, Jason Island, Hope Harbour, Carcass Island and Keppel Island. Among the details recorded is a description of a New Years Day race meeting.

54   From Edinburgh to the Antarctic: an artist's notes and sketches during the Dundee Antarctic Expedition 1892-93.
W. G. B. Murdoch.   London: Longmans Green, 1894. 364p. map.

Descriptions of Port Stanley harbour and town, the bird life on the Islands, a visit to the Governor, wildfowling along the coast, and a discussion of whaling prospects, form the subject matter of chapter thirteen (p. 164-98) of this expedition narrative.

55   In the Falkland Islands.
James Buchanan.   *Chamber's Journal*, series 7, vol. 3, no. 111 (11 January 1913), p. 95-96.

'The colony is substantially one vast sheep-run . . . very much a slice of Scotland set in the South Atlantic'. Its population is recorded as numbering 2,365. This article is complemented by the Reverend A. Mackintosh's 'Memories of the Falkland Islands', *Chamber's Journal*, vol. 4, no. 166 (31 January 1914), p. 135-37, which vividly describes the capture of wild cattle and the breaking of wild horses.

56   The Falkland Islands.
Conor O'Brien.   *Blackwood's Magazine*, vol. 218, no. 1318 (August 1925), p. 199-209.

A discursive report on a brief visit to the Islands and the Dependencies where there is 'no Parliament and no press, no taxes, no trade-unions, no strikes, no unemployment – or as near as no matter'. The account is of value as an historical vignette of life on the Islands.

57   Travels in the Falkland Islands.
G. Hattersley-Smith.   *Canadian Geographical Journal*, vol. 76, no. 4 (April 1968), p. 140-49. map.

Hattersley-Smith spent three months on the Falklands in the summer of 1949-50 during which time he travelled extensively round the Islands by sea and on horseback. This is a well-illustrated record of a voyage northwards from Stanley round East Falkland, through Falkland Sound, south-westwards round West Falkland, to Weddell Island, New Island, Speedwell Island, Darwin, and back to Stanley.

58   **Focus on the Falkland Islands.**
        Margaret Stewart Taylor.   London: Robert Hale, 1971. 191p. map.
        bibliog.
The author's visit to the Falklands coincided with the Chalfont mission to consult the
islanders, at a time when Argentina was pressing its claims to the Islands. She
travelled extensively to East and West Falkland, Weddell Island, and to many of the
smaller islands, her itinerary taking her to many isolated settlements including twenty-
six sheep farms. This description of Margaret Stewart Taylor's visit contains a
discussion on the Islands' social and economic problems, the daily life of Port
Stanley, and a chronological list of significant dates in the Islands' history.

Geography and Geology

General

59   A historical geography of the British Colonies: vol. 2.

C. P. Lucas.   Oxford: Clarendon Press, 1890. 343p. 11 maps. bibliog.

Section three of this second volume of five, entitled 'The Falkland Islands and South Georgia' (p. 318-29), covers their discovery; attempts at settlement in the eighteenth century; occupation by the Buenos Aires government; the final occupation by Great Britain; government and administration; area and geography; climate; products, trade and finances; population; distances and general summary; and South Georgia. It is a reliable historical source.

60   The geography of the Falkland Islands.

Geographical Journal, vol. 149, no. 1 (March 1983), p. 1-21. 2 maps.

Covering the political and legal aspects of the British claim to sovereignty over the Falkland Islands, these papers were contributed to a symposium held at the Royal Geographical Society on 18 May 1982. Topics covered are: The Falkland Islands and their history (Lord Shackleton); The islands' resources (Richard Johnson); The Antarctic connection (Charles Swithinbank); Legal aspects (James Fawcett); The Falklands region (George Deacon); Sheepfarming in the Falklands (Huw W. Williams); The Falkland Islanders (Patrick Vincent); Conservation issues (Bernard Stonehouse); and Krill (Inigo Everson).

Geology and glaciology

61 On the geology of the Falkland Islands.
Charles Darwin. *Journal of The Geological Society*, vol. 2, no. 1 (1846), p. 267-74.
Darwin read this paper to the Geological Society on 25 March 1846. It comprises a short account of the Falklands' geological structure with special reference to their palaeozoic mollusca, stratified quartz rocks, and sandstone beds. It is directed at a specialist audience.

62 Notes on the Falkland Islands.
Rupert Vallentin. *Memoirs and Proceedings of the Manchester Literary & Philosophical Society*, vol. 48, no. 23 (1903-04), p. 1-48. 3p. of plates. bibliog.
Vallentin's paper was read to the Society on 15 March 1904. It describes his geological investigations of the 'stone rivers' near Stanley and his visits to West Falkland's Roy Cove and Whaler Bay in 1900. Much of the paper, which was issued as a separate publication in June 1914, is given over to his observations on the Islands' wildlife and there are lengthy notes on insects, butterflies, birds and mammals.

63 Solifluction, a component of subaerial denudation.
J. G. Andersson. *Journal of Geology*, vol. 14, no. 2 (February-March 1906), p. 91-112.
Based on earlier reports, notably on his own investigations in 1902, this influential paper explains the origins and processes which led to the formation of the Falkland stone rivers. Andersson studied and surveyed in detail the stone river south of Port Louis, which was probably the largest on the Islands and was originally described by Darwin.

64 Note on the geology of the Falkland Islands.
J. Halle. *Geological Magazine*, new series 5, vol. 5, no. 6 (June 1908), p. 264-65.
As geologist to the Swedish Magellanic Expedition the author's most important work during his short stay in the Falklands before proceeding to Tierra Del Fuego was to examine the supposed occurance of permo-carboniferous layers of Gondwana rocks. He concluded that the whole southern part of East Falkland, south of Wickham Heights, belonged to the Gondwana system.

65 Contributions to the geology of the Falkland Islands.
J. G. Andersson. In: *Wissenschaftliche Ergebnisse der Schwedishen Südpolar-Expedition 1901-1903: Band III: Geologie und Paläontologie*. Edited by Otto Nordenskjöld. Stockholm: Lithographisches Institut Des Generalstabs, 1916. 38p. 3p. of maps. 6p. of plates.
Written as a guide for Thore G. Halle who was returning to the Falklands to continue his geological exploration, this paper deals with stratigraphical and tectonic outlines,

the Archean basement of the sandstone formation, the stone rivers, and changes in the level of the Islands. It is not intended for the general reader.

66   On the geological structure and history of the Falkland Islands.
Thore G. Halle.   Uppsala, Sweden: Almquist & Wiksells, 1911. 117p. map. 5p. of plates. bibliog.

Also printed in *Bulletin Geological Institute, University of Uppsala*, vol. 11 (1912), p. 115-229, this influential academic dissertation covers previous explorations, the Devonian and Permo-Cartoniferous formations of the Falklands, the eruptive dykes, some remarks upon Permian geology and glaciation, the forest bed of West Point Island, and level changes in the Falklands. Halle was a member of the Swedish expedition in the Antarctic during 1907-08 and spent fifteen weeks on the Falklands.

67   On a collection of fossil plants from the Falkland Islands.
Albert Charles Seward, John Walton.   *Journal of The Geological Society*, vol. 79 (1923), p. 313-33. 4p. of plates. bibliog.

By permission of the Colonial Office, H. A. Baker's collection of permo-carboniferous plant fossils from the Falklands, mostly found off the southern extremities of East Falkland, was given to Seward for examination and description. This specialist paper presents his findings.

68   Final report on geological investigations in the Falkland Islands.
H. A. Baker.   Stanley: CSO, 1924. 48p.

Baker arrived in the Falklands to carry out his investigation on Christmas Day 1920 and left on 2 April 1922. In his introduction he remarks on the difficulties he encountered during his stay: climatic conditions; the frequency, suddenness, and violence of the winds, a real menace when travelling by sea in a sailing cutter; and the difficulties of travelling around the Islands. His report covers the Islands' rock-succession (lower crystalline rocks, Devono-carboniferous rocks, Gondwana rocks, and the later intrusive rocks) and remarks on the Falkland Islands in relation to other areas. Baker also discusses the 'stone-runs' or stone rivers, recent changes of level, the alleged forest-bed of West Falkland and the results of a comprehensive survey for coal, oil, and other minerals.

69   Stone runs of the Falkland Islands.
J. R. F. Joyce.   *Geological Magazine*, vol. 87, no. 2 (March-April 1950), p. 105-15. bibliog.

Investigating the stone rivers of the Falklands – or 'stone runs' as they are known – Joyce argues that they are largely an accident of the past climate and the structure and lithology of the Upper Quartzite Series rocks. 'Hill creep, freeze and thaw, frost heaving, and solifluction all contributed to the formation, but their importance must be kept in true perspective'.

70 **The position of the Falkland Islands in a reconstruction of Gondwanaland.**
Raymond J. Adie. *Geological Magazine*, vol. 89, no. 6 (November-December 1952), p. 401-10. map. bibliog.

Using structural, tectonic, and stratigraphical evidence, Adie contends that the Falkland Islands should be positioned due east of the Eastern Province coast, thus completing the truncated Karroo Basin. Only readers familiar with palaeontology, the permo-carboniferous glaciation, the lower Perminian coal measures, or the Karroo Dolomites, should attempt this paper.

71 **A magnetic survey in the vicinity of Port Stanley, Falkland Islands.**
J. Mansfield. *British Antarctic Survey Bulletin*, no. 7 (November 1965), p. 69-71.

A magnetic survey of the Port Stanley peninsula was carried out by J. Ashley of the Falkland Islands Dependencies Survey during December 1958. Tabulated here are observations of 160 magnetic stations at 600 yard intervals, providing their station numbers, latitude, longitude and magnetic field value.

72 **Evidence of cirque glaciation in the Falkland Islands.**
Chalmers M. Clapperton. *Journal of Glaciology*, vol. 10, no. 58 (1971), p. 121-25. map. bibliog.

After an examination of the Falklands' cirques, glaciated valleys, and moraines, and the significance of their periglacial landfiords, Clapperton concludes that 'the presence of 49 cirques . . . indicates that glacial conditions were prevalent during the Pleistocene. . . There appear to have been three phases: a period of cirque formation, the growth of local ice caps, and subsequent cirque development. Periglacial landforms such as stone runs, stone terraces and stone lobes also developed during the Pleistocene'.

73 **The geology of the Falkland Islands.**
Mary E. Greenway. London: British Antarctic Survey, 1972. 42p. 8p. of plates. 5 maps. bibliog. (Scientific Report, no. 76).

In this authoritative report Greenway provides a history of geological exploration, and detailed studies of the Islands' physiology, stratigraphy, ignaceous rocks, structural geology, and their regional and tectonic setting. Appendices deal with economic geology, palaeontology, map compilation, and a gravity survey. A two-sheet geological map, prepared by the Directorate of Overseas Surveys in 1972 on a scale of 1:250,000, and a twenty-one-page gazetteer, are accommodated in an end pocket.

74 **Scenery of the South: the Falkland Islands, South Georgia and other sub-Antarctic islands.**
Chalmers M. Clapperton, David E. Sugden. Aberdeen, Scotland: Sugden, 1975. 22p. 3 maps.

A geological history and description of the Falkland Islands, the Antarctic Peninsula, and the intervening chain of islands, this booklet blends genuine scholarship with superb illustrations.

75 **Peat: patterns and processes.**
Richard Clark. *Warrah*, no. 1 (November 1991), p. 4-5.

The author, the leader of the Cumbria and Lancashire Falklands Expedition, explains how climatic conditions favoured the formation of peat in the Falklands, describes how the present peat deposits have accumulated since the last ice age, and estimates the degree and extent of their subsequent degradation.

76 **Prince's Street: an East Falkland stone-run early descriptions and theories.**
Patrick Armstrong. *Falkland Islands Journal*, vol. 6, no. 1 (1992), p. 33-38. bibliog.

Surely one of the most distinctive land forms of the Falklands, the 'stone runs' have attracted continuous comment through the years. In this article Armstrong summarizes the accounts of early travellers in an attempt to show how successive generations have influenced the changing ideas about their origin. In particular the views of Sir C. Wyville Thompson (1876) and J. G. Andersson (1907) are noted.

Meteorology and climatology

77 **Journal of the winds and weather, and degrees of heat and cold by the thermometer, at Falkland Islands, from 1st February 1766, to 19th January 1767.**
John McBride. In: *A collection of voyages chiefly in the Southern Atlantick Ocean published from original manuscripts by Alexander Dalrymple.* London: Dalrymple, 1775. 13p.

Contains daily table of winds, weather, and temperature throughout the year.

78 **Annual reports on the state of the colonies 1876.**
In: *British parliamentary papers: colonies general 17*. Shannon, Ireland: Irish Universities Press, 1970, p. 52-54.

A summary of meteorological observations for 1875 at Stanley, which provided the maximum and minimum temperatures, the mean temperature, temperature in the shade, the dew point, rainfall etc., month by month, was included in Governor G. D'Arcy's despatch to the Earl of Carnarvon, dated 14 March 1876, along with a prevailing wind return for the months January-May. The *Annual report 1875* was first published by HMSO in 1876.

79 **Annual reports on the state of the colonies 1881-82.**
In: *British parliamentary papers: colonies general 21*. Shannon, Ireland: Irish Universities Press, 1970, p. 771-80.

This abstract of meteorological observations at Stanley, from February to December 1880, provided the air temperatures, the relative humidity, amount of cloud, and rainfall, together with a monthly table of wind directions. Compiled by F. E. Cobb, the Colonial Manager for the Falkland Islands Company, the abstract was included in Governor T. Kerr's despatch to the Earl of Kimberley dated 27 June 1881. *Annual Report 1880* was first published by HMSO in 1882.

80   **The climate and weather of the Falkland Islands and South Georgia.**
       C. E. P. Brooks.   London: The Meteorological Office, 1920. p. 95-146.
       3 maps. (Air Ministry, Meteorological Office, Geophysical Memoirs, no. 15).

Examining the general character of the climate and the pressure, temperature, relative humidity, cloudiness, sunshine, precipitation, fog, winds, and depressions of the Islands, this substantial study also includes tables of observations at Royal Bay, Grytviken, Port Louis, and Cape Pembroke.

81   **The meteorology of The Falkland Islands and Dependencies 1944-1950.**
       J. Pepper.   London: Falkland Islands Dependencies Survey, 1954. 249p.

Pepper's report is organized in three parts: Discovery, which deals with atmospheric pressure, temperatures, mist and cloud, precipitation and sunshine, humidity and visibility, the Antarctic convergence, and the distribution of pack-ice in the Southern Ocean; a Gazetteer of the general surroundings and sites of Falkland Islands Dependencies Survey bases 1944-50; and monthly and annual statistical tables of the Survey's meteorological observations.

82   **Weather stations of the Falkland Islands Dependencies.**
       D. J. George.   *Weather*, vol. 14, no. 1 (January 1959), p. 3-11. map.

At the time of writing twelve stations were conducting research programmes covering exploration, meteorology, geophysics, glaciology, ionospheric work, topographical and geological surveys, cold weather physiology, biology, and sea ice studies. This article describes life at the bases, the living conditions there, and work routines.

83   **Forecasting in the Falkland Islands and Dependencies.**
       S. D. Glassey.   London: HMSO for Air Ministry Meteorological Office, 1961. 30p. bibliog. (Scientific Paper, no. 7).

In drawing upon his five years experience as a weather forecaster in Stanley, Glassey hoped that some of his suggestions and conclusions would be of practical assistance in formulating a synoptic forecasting technique for the whole of the southern oceans and the Antarctic ice-cap. He studies the upper air, depressions, warm and cold anti-cyclones, the Antarctic front, the rejuvenation of an old front, the Trinity Peninsula eddy, and cloud structures.

84 **Tatter flags and climate in the Falkland Islands.**
   J. H. McAdam.   *Weather*, vol. 35, no. 11 (November 1980), p. 321-27.
   map. bibliog.

Experiments at three Falkland Islands sites indicated that wind factors rather than rainfall were the main contributors to Tatter. McAdam, an officer of the Grasslands Trials Unit, included a table of Stanley weather data between 1951 and 1965 in this highly specialist article.

Maps and charts

85 **Early charts of the Falklands: part 1 Passing contacts.**
   Terry G. Birtles.   *Cartography Journal of the Australian Institute of Cartographers*, vol. 13, no. 1 (March 1983), p. 35-48. bibliog.; *Part 2 The first settlements*, vol. 13, no. 2 (September 1983), p. 100-16. bibliog.

Birtles' purpose in this study of the early charts of discovery is 'to use cartographical information and associated records to review the background history of European knowledge of the Falklands'. He suggests that Portuguese knowledge of a south-west passage to the Pacific existed prior to the Spanish discovery of the Straits of Magellan but that Spain failed to capitalize on its knowledge. He adds that after Drake's circumnavigation, English, French and Dutch voyages resulted in a cartographic record of the Falklands. Birtles then pays attention to the French colony at Port Louis and the establishment of the Royal Navy outpost at Port Egmont, and proceeds to examine Spanish, British, and Argentine claims to sovereignty as evidenced in contemporary maps and charts.

86 **Falkland Islands: a bibliography of 50 examples of printed maps bearing specific reference to the Falkland Islands.**
   Angela Fordham.   London: Map Collectors' Circle, 1964. 32p. maps.
   (Map Collectors' Series, no. 11).

Arranged in chronological order, from 1597 to 1885, this bibliography contains descriptive notes on fifty important and significant maps, their dimensions, their geographical content, and their historical context.

87 **The early mapping of the Falkland Islands.**
   R. V. Tooley.   *Map Collector*, no. 20 (September 1982), p. 2-6.

Following an introduction on the discovery and history of the Islands up until 1833, Tooley lists and describes maps relating to that period. These range from 'Carte réduite de la partie du Sud où sont comprises les Nouvelles Isles découvertes par les Vaisseaux de St. Malo depuis 1700 dont la partie de l'Ouest est encore inconnue', published in Frézier's *Voyage au Mer du Sud* (Voyage on the South Sea) (Paris, 1716), to the first separate map of the Islands: Jacques Nicolas Bellin's *Carte des Isles Malouines ou isles nouvelles que les Anglais noment aujourd'hui Isles de Falkland* (1763). Aaron Arrowsmith's *A chart of the West Falkland from an actual survey by*

Lieutenant Thomas Edgar of the Royal Navy in the years 1786 and 1787 (1797), and John Tallis' popular and decorative mid-nineteenth century map are also included.

88 Falkland Islands cartographers.
Geoff D. Moir. *Upland Goose*, vol. 9, no. 3 (March 1988), p. 78-80; no. 4 (June 1988), p. 122-23; no. 5 (September 1988), p. 155; no. 6 (December 1988), p. 186.

In this series of articles Moir records the career biographies of four Royal Navy commanders who at different times mapped and charted the Islands, and who are commemorated on the 1985 Early Cartographers issues of postage stamps. They are Captain J. MacBride and *HMS Jason*, 1765; Commodore J. Byron and *HMS Dolphin* and *Tamar*, 1765; Vice-Admiral R. Fitzroy and *HMS Beagle,* 1831; and Admiral Sir B. J. Sullivan and *HMS Philomel*, 1842.

89 Five unusual maps of the Falklands.
Peter Barber. *Map Collector*, no. 20 (September 1982), p. 50-51. bibliog.

Five early maps of the British settlement at Port Egmont, drawn by Thomas Boutflower, the Purser of the *HMS Carcass* on her voyage to the Falklands in 1767-68, were acquired by the Department of Manuscripts at the British Library in 1978. The most important was *A draught of Falkland Islands in the latitude of 51° 22'S and longitude 64°W . . . about 90 leagues east from Cape Virgin Mary on the coast of Patagonia.* The others include *Representations of the mullet and trout fishing at the east end of Byron's Sound*; *The wild geese chase, or progging, on Keppel Island*; *A sea lion party on Burnt Island in Byron's Sound*; and *Pengwin and albitrose towns.*

90 The Falkland Islands surveyed by Captain Robert Fitz Roy, Commander William Robinson and Captain Bartholomew James Sulivan 1838-1845: with additions to 1883.
London: Hydrographic Office of the Admiralty, 1884. 2 sheets. 98cm × 65cm.

A large proportion of these two sheets was engraved before the triangulation of the whole archipelago was completed and some of the positions are therefore slightly incorrect.

91 Ports in the Falkland Islands as surveyed by Commander W. Robinson 1842.
London: Hydrographic Office of the Admiralty, 1884. 76cm × 51cm.

First published in 1846, this edition includes corrections and additions to the map published in December 1883. It provides hydrographic information on Port Edgar, Fox Bay, Port Howard, Port Albemarle, and Port Stephen, giving soundings and high water marks. The scale is eight inches and seven-eighths to nine sea miles.

92   A catalogue of Latin American flat maps 1926-1964: vol. 2.
      Palmyra V. M. Monteiro.   Austin, Texas: University of Texas, 1969.
      430p.

The section on the Falkland Islands, or Islas Malvinas, (p. 237-42) lists twenty-seven topographic, hydrographic, general and political maps published in England, Argentina, Chile, and Germany.

93   Mapping the Falklands.
      D. H. Maling.   Cartographic Journal, vol. 2, no. 1 (June 1965),
      p. 44-45.

Written by an expert on the Falkland Islands, this is a review article of the *Falkland Islands map, east sheet*, which has a scale of 1:250,000 and was published by the Directorate of Overseas Survey in 1964. Maling compares it to the Admiralty Chart used for the surveys of Captains Fitzroy, Sullivan and Robinson in the 1830s and 1840s, which remained the only document available to serve the needs of the Colony for 120 years.

94   Falkland Islands shores.
      Ewen Southby-Tailyour.   London: Conway Maritime, 1985. 270p.
      maps.

During his time as Officer Commanding the Royal Marine detachment in the Falklands, the author completed a thirteen-month survey of the Islands' coasts and beaches. Three years later his notes became the source of the detailed landing plans drawn up by the British Task Force. In this book, which is essentially a complete yachtsman pilot to the Islands, systematically covering the coastline in descriptive text, charts, and coastal profiles, he adds further observations made while a member of the landing force. Nautical mileages, windchill charts, weather data and tidal predictions are included as appendices. There is also an index to the unique collection of wrecks scattered around the Islands.

95   Admiralty charts.
      Taunton, England: Hydrographer Of The Navy, 1985. 176p. maps.

General and local Admiralty charts relating to the Falklands, South Georgia, and the South Sandwich Islands are listed in this catalogue. They include: chart no. 2505, *Approaches to the Falkland Islands* (November 1983) which was drawn on a scale of 1:1,500,000; no. 2512, *Falkland Islands* (July 1984), with a scale of 1:400,000; no. 3596, *Approaches to South Georgia* (March 1963), with a scale of 1:400,000; no. 3597, *South Georgia* (February 1972), on a scale of 1:250,000; and no. 3593, *South Sandwich Islands* (November 1968), with a scale of 1:500,000.

96   Maps on postage stamps as propaganda.
      Bruce Davis.   Cartographic Journal, vol. 22, no. 2 (December 1985),
      p. 125-30. bibliog.

The philatelic 'war' of 1933, the Antarctic claims by Argentina and Chile and Argentine propaganda since 1964, all figure prominently in this illustrated article which describes the stamps in question and their political significance.

97 **Falkland Islands.**
Southampton, England: Ordnance Survey for Government of Falkland
Islands, 1986. 50cm × 32cm. (DOS 96).
This post-war map, on a scale of 1:643,000, depicts such features as roads and tracks,
telephone lines, lighthouses and beacons.

98 **How many islands in the Falkland Islands?**
Robin Woods. *Falkland Islands Foundation Newsletter*, no. 5 (July
1986), p. 8-9.
Although various estimated numbers of islands in the Falklands group have been
bandied about in the literature, with 200 being the most widely accepted figure,
Woods states that the total number is in fact 746 offshore islands of which 372 are not
yet named. He outlines how he arrived at this figure and offers three main reasons for
the uncertainty and huge margin of error: the difficulties of landing on many of them
by small boat; the unpredictability of the weather; and the low human population.

99 **The Falkland Islands.**
Oswestry, England: Anthony Nelson, 1987. single sheet map.
550mm × 400mm.
Drawn on a scale of one inch to ten miles, this pictorial map shows settlements, roads
and tracks, airports and lighthouses, nature reserves and topographical features. Notes
on the Island's geography, climate, travel, wildlife and seven colour illustrations
occupy the margins.

100 **Falkland Islands.**
Southampton, England: Ordnance Survey for Government of Falkland
Islands, 1988. 28 sheets. 71cm × 103cm.
These large-scale maps (1:5,000) cover the whole of the Islands and depict such
features as heights, building roof lines, ruins, glasshouses, sloping masonry, gates,
concrete bases, bridges, tunnels, footpaths, slopes and cliffs, radio and television
masts, rivers and streams, ditches and culverts, and contours. Similar features are
shown on another series of twenty-six sheets at 1:2,500, also published by Ordnance
Survey (1988).

101 **Falkland Islands.**
Rolf Böhme. In: *Inventory of world topographic mapping: vol. 2
South America, Central America and Africa.* London: Elsevier
Applied Science Publishers on behalf of the International Cartographic
Association, 1991, p. 56-57. maps. bibliog.
Böhme provides concise information on national mapping organizations in the United
Kingdom, a brief mapping history, geodetic data, and map scales and map services.

102   **The maritime limits of the Falkland Islands.**
Patrick H. Armstrong, Vivian L. Forbes. *IBRU Boundary and Security Bulletin*, vol. 1, no. 1 (April 1993), p. 73-80. 3 maps.

Recent British and Argentine legislation establishing maritime jurisdictional zones is compared. The authors claim 'Both states appear to have acted within the limits of the law in defining their respective systems. However, the Argentine claim is more meticulous and conservative in that the segments between the chosen basepoints are relatively short. . . It is possible that the claim is designed to impress the international community in any future negotiations on the sovereignty issue'.

Gazetteers and place-names

103   **South Atlantic: official standard names approved by the United States Board On Geographic Names.**
Washington, DC: US Government Printing Office, 1957. 53p.
(Gazetteer no. 31).

Data provided in this gazetteer include name, date, designation (according to a list of eighty geographical or topographical features), and latitude and longitude co-ordinates.

104   **Place-names of the Falkland Islands.**
R. S. Boumphrey. *Falkland Islands Journal*, no. 1 (January 1967), p. 1-7. bibliog.

A chronological account of voyages to the Islands and the names given to various geographical features. 'Even a brief study of these place-names – some familiar to all, others familiar only to the inhabitants – discloses not only a succession of sea-farers and settlers, but recollections of stray, long-forgotten episodes in British and foreign colonial history'. The article was reprinted from *Durham University Journal*, vol. 55, no. 2 (March 1963), p. 60-64.

105   **Gazetteer of the Falkland Islands.**
London: British Antarctic Survey, [1972]. 21p.

The latitude and longitude co-ordinates for 2,895 place-names compiled from official maps published by the Directorate of Overseas Surveys, are included in this gazetteer which is housed in an end-pocket of Mary E. Greenway's *The geology of the Falkland Islands* (item no. 73).

Flora and Fauna

General

106 Journal of researches into the natural history and geology of the countries visited during the voyage round the world of HMS Beagle under command of Captain Fitzroy, R. N.
Charles Darwin.   London: John Murray, 1845. 2nd ed. 519p.

Chapter nine of this frequently reprinted classic work, 'Santa Cruz, Patagonia, and the Falkland Islands', describes *Beagle's* arrival in Berkeley Sound in March 1833, and relates Darwin's 'short excursion' round parts of East Falkland, during which he made observations on its horses and cattle, its large wolf-like fox, the absence of trees, its birds, and its geological structure. Comments on Darwin's letters and diaries insofar as they pertain to his visits to the Falklands in 1833 and 1834 are to be found in Richard Grove's 'Charles Darwin and the Falkland Islands', *Polar Record*, vol. 22, no. 139 (January 1985), p. 413-20. For Darwin's *Journal and Remarks 1832-1836* see item no. 49.

107 Darwin's desolate islands: a naturalist in the Falklands, 1833 and 1834.
Patrick Armstrong.   Chippenham, England: Picton Publishing, 1992. 147p. 3 maps.

Based on meticulous archival research, including access to Darwin's field notes, the log of *HMS Beagle* and Robert Fitzroy's manuscript charts, Armstrong reconstructs Darwin's two visits to the Falklands, with special emphasis on his biological, geological, and zoological studies. There are chapters covering Darwin's comparative and deductive techniques and on the chronology of his visits, his geological investigations, and the geographical distribution of Falklands flora and fauna. Although Darwin spent more time on the Falklands than on the Galapagos Islands, Armstrong remains unconvinced that his evolution and natural selection theories were greatly developed whilst he was there. See also Patrick Armstrong's 'Charles Darwin in the Falkland Islands', *Falkland Islands Journal*, vol. 5, no. 5 (1991), p. 1-6.

108 **Collecting zoological specimens and observations on wild-life in the Falkland Islands.**
Stanley W. Gorham. *Falkland Islands Journal*, no. 3 (1969), p. 48-51. bibliog.
Notes on a collection of fishes from the Falkland Islands.
Stanley W. Gorham. *Falkland Islands Journal*, no. 11 (1977), p. 43-57.

Gorham visited the Islands between 22 January and 20 February 1967, on behalf of the National Museum of Natural Science in Ottawa and the New Brunswick Museum, to collect fishes, invertebrates, and bird specimens. The second of these papers includes a catalogue of his collection and a comprehensive list of the fish of the Falkland Islands, family by family.

109 **Natural history of an unlikely battlefield.**
Olin Sewall Pettingill. *Audobon*, vol. 84, no. 4 (1982), p. 52-62.

Accompanied by magnificent photographs of Falkland birdlife, this essay is based on six visits to the Islands, at least two of which lasted for five or six months, in the period 1953-1979. The coverage ranges widely over the islands' landscape and topography, coastlines, climate and rainfall, settlements, sheep and cattle industries, vegetation, and wildlife. Writing during the course of the South Atlantic War, Pettingill ends: 'Regardless of how the armed conflict in the Falklands is resolved, steps must be taken at once to assure the survival and protection of the archipelago's natural and historical heritage'.

110 **The Falkland Islands and their natural history.**
Ian J. Strange. Newton Abbot, England: David & Charles, 1987. 160p. map. bibliog.

Separate chapters treat the coastal regions, the offshore islands, the lowlands and plains and island settlement, all splendidly illustrated with superb black-and-white and colour photographs. Strange covers the terrain of the whole Falklands archipelago in this contemporary guide to the Islands' topography, flora and fauna, which underlines the close connection between what is an essentially rural population and its rugged environment. Lists of Falklands' flora, kelps and seaweeds (Latin and English names) and checklists of breeding birds and mammals (English and Latin) are appended.

111 **The Cumbria and Lancashire Falklands expedition 1989.**
R. Clark, et al. *Falkland Islands Journal*, vol. 5, no. 4 (1990), p. 5-15. bibliog.

The purpose of the expedition, which spent seven weeks on East and West Falkland between 3 November and 20 December 1989, was to undertake ecological and earth sciences studies in a variety of terrain and habitat types. Marine and coastal ecology played no part in the programme. This short account contains a botanical report, other reports on freshwater ecology and on soil invertebrates, together with geological and geomorphological studies.

112   **A field guide to the wildlife of The Falkland Islands and South Georgia.**
Ian J. Strange.   London: Harper Collins, 1992. 188p. map. bibliog.

Profusely illustrated in the familiar Collins guides format, the main emphasis of this book is on the birds and mammals found in and about the Falkland Islands Archipelago. A very informative introduction (p. 17-43) focuses on the geography of the Islands, their climate, marine and terrestrial environment, the history of wildlife depredation (including an interesting speculation on the origins of the wolf-like fox on East and West Falkland), conservation laws and the country code, and a list of Falkland Islands Protected Areas. Separate sections follow on: Birds (checklists of breeding species, annual visitors, and vagrant species); Mammals; Fish; Marine and terrestrial invertebrates; and Plants, giving a full description, distribution pattern, breeding notes and food. There is also a botanical glossary. This definitive volume will remain the standard work for years to come. It is closely linked to the New Island Project in which the Island (in the extreme south-west of the Archipelago) became a base for studies in the management and control of wildlife and a site for scientific studies.

Flora

113   **The botany of the Antarctic voyage of HM Discovery Ships Erebus and Terror in the years 1839-1843 under the command of Captain Sir James Clark Ross.**
Joseph Dalton Hooker.   London: Reeve, 1847. 2 vols.

Volume two of this work, *Botany of Fuegia, The Falklands and Kerguelen's Land*, is the bedrock of Falkland Islands botanical studies. Over 300 pages are given over to expert and detailed botanical descriptions and collecting notes. Hooker was officially mustered as the Expedition's medical officer.

114   **Flora of the Falkland Islands.**
C. H. Wright.   *Journal of The Linnean Society (Botany)*, vol. 39, no. 273 (July 1909), p. 313-39.

'An enumeration of the plants of those islands with a view to show the changes which have taken place in the flora since the publication of *Flora Antarctica* by Sir J. D. Hooker in 1847, also to define more exactly the distribution of the plants in the islands'. This checklist, which is intended for specialist reference use, includes 156 species.

115   **Illustrations of the flowering plants and ferns of the Falkland Islands.**
Elinor F. Vallentin.   London: Reeve, 1921. 64 double-page plates.

Elinor Vallentin made many drawings of plants, with a view to compiling an illustrated flora of her native islands. However, her work was so seriously interrupted by a breakdown in health that her husband, Rupert Vallentin, decided to publish this incomplete volume. Each of sixty-four plants is allocated a double page: on the left there are very attractive colour drawings whilst on the right, notes on its family and genus are included, together with a brief description.

116 Plants which have flowered successfully in gardens of the Falkland Islands 1944.
H. R. Evans.   Stanley: Government Printing Office, 1944. 12p.

The object of this pamphlet compiled by the gardener at Government House was 'to acquaint would-be horticulturalists, and also newcomers entering the Colony, with the range of flowering plants, shrubs and climbers, which can be cultivated'. There are lists of hardy perennials, biennials and annuals, half-hardy annuals, bulbs, and shrubs and climbers. Each plant is given its Latin and vernacular name and a line or so of comment.

117 Some recent records of native and alien flowering plants from the Falkland Islands.
D. M. Moore, W. J. L. Sladen.   *British Antarctic Survey Bulletin*, no. 7 (November 1965), p. 29-35. map. bibliog.

A collection of plants made by Sladen on visits to the Islands in 1949-51 as a medical officer and biologist for the Falkland Islands Dependencies Survey 'contained a number of undoubtedly native species which are either new to the Falkland Islands or which represent interesting range extensions within the archipelago. In addition a large number of introduced species, many not recorded hitherto, are present'.

118 The natural vegetation of the Falklands.
C. D. Young.   *Falkland Islands Journal*, no. 1 (January 1967), p. 18-21.

'A number of species have been introduced either deliberately as crop for hay etc., or accidentally as impurities in seed. Most of the weeds are those common to Europe and most likely came in as impurities or stuck to potato tubers. . . It is now rather hard to say what has been introduced by man and what has not'. This refreshing, honest attitude to the subject is not always evident in exclusively scientific journals.

119 The vascular flora of the Falkland Islands.
D. M. Moore.   London: British Antarctic Survey, 1968. 202p. maps. 6p. of plates. bibliog. (Scientific Report, no. 60).

Following general descriptions of the Islands' topography, soils, climate, and geological structure, their botanical exploration, vegetation, and the geographical distribution of their flora, Moore provides a systematic account of all 163 species of native flowering plants and a further ninety-two introduced species. A glossary, a detailed bibliography of scientific reports and papers, and the East and West sheets of a 1:250,000 map of the Islands published by the Directorate of Overseas Surveys in 1967 complete this authoritative and comprehensive study.

120   **An extraordinary peat-forming community on the Falkland**
       Islands.
       R. I. Lewis-Smith, R. S. Clymo.   *Nature*, vol. 309 (14 June 1984),
       p. 617-20. bibliog.

Lewis-Smith made an ecological survey of Beauchêne Island in December 1980 for
the British Antarctic Survey. In this highly technical paper he reports that most of the
island is covered by tussac, the tussock-forming grass which has produced over a
12,500-year period a dense concentration of exceptionally deep peat.

121   **Wild flowers of the Falkland Islands: a fully illustrated**
       introduction to the main species and a guide to their identification.
       T. H. Davies, J. H. McAdam.   Bluntisham, England: Bluntisham
       Books for Falkland Islands Trust, 1989. 48p.

Intended for visitors and tourists, not for expert botanists, this is a compact descriptive
colour guide to sixty-one of the 163 native species recorded. It is arranged in seven
sections covering ferns, cushion plants, shrubs or bushes, flowering plants, grasses and
rushes. G. D. Moir's 'Some of the flora of the Falkland Islands', *Gibbons Stamp
Monthly*, vol. 26, no. 1 (June 1995), is of interest to both naturalists and philatelists.

Birds

122   **Catalogue of the birds of the Falkland Islands.**
       Philip Lutley Sclater.   *Proceedings of The Zoological Society*, pt. 38
       (1860), p. 382-91.

With full references to previous records this descriptive catalogue of fifty-seven
species, ordered by their scientific name, includes information on the circumstances of
their sighting and also, in some instances, of their capture. Taking advantage of
conversations with Captain Abbott, and of examinations of eleven further species he
brought with him from the Falklands, Sclater printed 'Additions and corrections to the
list of the birds of the Falkland Islands', *Proceedings of The Zoological Society*
(1861), p. 45-47.

123   **Notes on the birds of the Falkland Islands.**
       C. C. Abbot.   *Ibis*, vol. 3, no. 10 (April 1861), p. 149-67.

Notes on sixty-six birds, including their Latin-English names, habitat, plumage, and
laying habits, are 'the result of personal observations made during a residence of three
years, from February 1858 to October 1860 at Stanley . . . whilst I was in command of
the detachment of troops stationed there'.

124 **Bird photographing on the Falkland Islands.**
Rollo H. Beck. *American Museum Journal*, vol. 17, no. 7 (November 1917), p. 429-44.
A generously illustrated narrative of Beck's pioneering ornithological explorations on the Islands between October 1915 and February 1916.

125 **A list of birds of the Falkland Islands and Dependencies.**
A. G. Bennett. *Ibis*, series 12, vol. 2, no. 2 (April 1926), p. 306-33. bibliog.
These abbreviated notes on 121 species of birds found on the Islands are arranged by family and provide details of the first recorded sightings and distribution. Bennett printed updating amendments and revisions in his 'Additional notes on the birds of the Falkland Islands and Dependencies' *Ibis*, series 13, vol. 1, no. 1 (January 1931), p. 12-13. Thirty years later his list was revised in E. M. Cawkell and J. E. Hamilton's 'The birds of the Falkland Islands', *Ibis*, vol. 103a, no. 1 (January 1961), p. 1-27, bibliog. map, which provided population numbers of 127 breeding and migratory species.

126 **Birds of the Falkland Islands: a record of observation with the camera.**
Arthur F. Cobb. London: H. F. & G. Witherby, 1933. 88p.
From several years study, particularly on Bleaker Island, Cobb acquired an impressive file of notes and photographs on most Falklands species of birds.

127 **The effects of climate and weather on the birds of the Falkland Islands.**
Olin Sewall Pettingill, Jr. In: *Proceedings of the XIIth International Ornithological Congress, Helsinki (1958).* p. 604-14. bibliog.
The effects of the Falklands' climate and weather on the length of the breeding season of the fifty-one species known to breed in the Islands, on the variety of land birds, on bird populations, and on clutch and body size are the chief topics discussed in this conference paper.

128 **Penguin summer.**
Eleanor Rice Pettingill. London: Cassell, 1962. 167p. 3 maps.
Presents a personal record of the author's ornithological visit to the Falklands in the summer of 1953-54, accompanying her husband Olin Sewall, who was filming penguins for Walt Disney Productions. This excellent book opens with an account of the voyage from Montevideo to Stanley on board the *Fitzroy*. It is valuable not only for capturing the large penguin communities in endearing detail, but also for its portraits of the many Islanders who befriended the author and her photographer husband. An appendix lists the scientific names of animals and plants. The author's 'Bird finding in the Falkland Islands', *Falkland Islands Journal*, no. 6 (1972), p. 18-22, is also intended for the general reader.

129 **Penguins ashore at the Falkland Islands.**
Olin Sewall Pettingill. *Living Bird*, vol. 3 (1964), p. 45-64. bibliog.
During a five month's visit to the Falklands, from October 1953 to March 1954, the author and his wife, Eleanor Rice Pettingill, spent many hours watching and filming Gentoo, Rockhopper and Magellanic Penguins emerging from the sea. This detailed report on their nesting habits and behaviour ashore is the result. The author's 'People and penguins of the faraway Falklands', *National Geographic Magazine*, vol. 109, no. 3 (March 1956), p. 387-416, is a more general report, encompassing other bird species, sheepfarming, horse races, and carnival sports on the Islands.

130 **Kelp geese and flightless steamer ducks in the Falkland Islands.**
Olin Sewall Pettingill. *Living Bird*, vol. 4 (1965), p. 65-78. bibliog.
Pettingill's purpose here is to summarize his notes and impressions observing these birds and to confirm and add to previous information. 'Both species, while generally indifferent toward man when compared to most birds, frequently engaged in vigorous encounters with individuals of their own and other species. Pairs among either species were inseparable; the male was nearby while the female incubated and he assisted the female in attending the young'.

131 **The Falkland Islands: a South Atlantic bird haven.**
Ian J. Strange. *Animals*, vol. 6, no. 20 (1965), p. 554-60.
Nine especially superb photographs taken by the author illustrate this expert study of Falklands birdlife. At the time it was possible to write 'the remoteness of the Falkland Islands has meant that they have remained unspoilt and undisturbed'.

132 **The Avian ecology of a Tussock Island in the Falkland Islands.**
R. W. Woods. *Ibis*, vol. 112, no. 1 (January 1970), p. 15-24. bibliog.
Mature tussac (tussock) grass is a vitally important habitat to resident birds on Kidney Island (ten miles north-east of Stanley). It maintains a diverse number of bird species, offering abundant cover, nest-sites, nest-materials, and food. Woods, who spent a total of seven weeks on the Island between 1958 and 1963, noted twenty-eight species. Kidney Island is now a nature reserve.

133 **A breeding colony of *Pachyptila Turtur* in the Falkland Islands.**
Ian J. Strange. *Ibis*, vol. 110, no. 3 (July 1968), p. 358-59.
Strange discovered a breeding colony of Fairy Prions on Beauchêne Island (the southernmost outer Island of the Falklands) in January 1967. In this brief report he provides a physical description of the Island and describes the capture of adult birds and chicks for examination.

134 **Penguins of the Falklands.**
Ian J. Strange. *Falkland Islands Journal*, no. 8 (1974), p. 6-16.
An illustrated description of breeding and migratory species, rookeries, their location, plumage, and a useful discussion of the hazards penguins face at sea.

135   **Another Penguin summer.**
      Olin Sewall Pettingill.   New York: Charles Scribner's Sons, 1975.
      80p.

After Pettingill's visit to the Falklands in the summer of 1953-54 Walt Disney
Productions allowed him a selection of film sequences for a lecture-film, *Penguin
summer*. On a five month's return visit in 1971-72, he acquired footage for a new film,
Another penguin summer. This is the book of the film, a popular study with page after
page of photographs of the Gentoo, Rockhopper, Magellanic, King and Macaroni
Penguins.

136   **Geese in the Falkland Islands.**
      John Harradine.   *Falkland Islands Journal*, no. 10 (1976), p. 5-16.
      bibliog.

Included in this authoritative article is a general taxonomy and description of four
breeding species of geese, a documented historical record of their presence in the
Islands, and a discussion of why the sheepfarmers want their numbers reduced.

137   **Moult-skipping by Upland Geese Chloephraga Picta in the
      Falkland Islands.**
      R. W. Summers.   *Ibis*, vol. 125, no. 2 (April 1983), p. 262-66.
      **The life cycle of the Upland Goose Chloephraga Picta in the
      Falkland Islands.**
      R. W. Summers.   *Ibis*, vol. 125, no. 4 (October 1983), p. 524-44.
      2 maps. bibliog.

Upland geese are regarded by Falkland sheepfarmers as pests which compete with
sheep for grass. Over a period of seventy years they have therefore attempted to
control their numbers by shooting them. In 1977 the Overseas Development Agency
instigated a study to arrive at a more appropriate method of control based on geese
biology. These two scientific papers report on a breeding study of birds in the Ceritos
Arroyo valley, near Darwin, East Falkland, October 1977 to August 1980.

138   **A selected bibliography of Falkland Islands birds.**
      Barry Phillips.   Cambridge, England: International Council for Bird
      Preservation for the Falkland Islands Foundation, 1983. 80p.

A total of 269 entries are arranged in five categories in this definitive bibliography
which is printed on single-sided typescript pages. The categories are: References
specific to the Falklands relating to bird species regularly occurring in the Islands;
Birds of irregular or vagrant occurrence; References not specific to the Falklands but
which include important comments on bird species occurring in the Islands;
References to other topics of relevance to the conservation of Falkland Islands birds;
and Relevant legislation on the conservation of flora and fauna in the Falklands. The
data noted covers: date; author; article title; title of journal; volume and page number;
and a reference to the location of the item in one of nine London or Cambridge
libraries. The work was reproduced from typescript in spiral binding.

139   **Sheld-geese and man in the Falkland Islands.**
Ronald W. Summers, George M. Dunnet.   *Biological Conservation,*
vol. 30, no. 4 (1984), p. 319-40. map. bibliog.

This report on the findings of a study financed by the Falkland Islands Government
and by Overseas Development Administration carries information on the introduction
into the Islands of cattle, sheep, goats and pigs. Early references to geese from
Strong's 1690 landing onwards and the influence of sheep farmers convinced that
grazing by geese affected sheep numbers are also included along with details of goose
breeding, distribution and food and efficient control methods. Four million geese were
estimated to have been killed in a 100-year period.

140   **Birds of the South Atlantic.**
Gibbons Stamp Monthly, vol. 19, no. 6 (November 1988), p. 31-33.

Birds represented in this stamp-by-stamp examination of the South Georgia and South
Sandwich Islands birds issue of 1987, and the Falkland Islands geese stamps of 1988,
include the Dominican Gull, Blue-Eyed Cormorant, Wattled Sheathbill, petrels,
penguins, albatrosses, Kelp Geese, the Upland Goose, and the Ashy and Ruddy-
Headed Geese. P. J. Lanspeary's 'Birds of the Antarctic on stamps', *Gibbons Stamp
Monthly,* vol. 19, no. 10 (March 1989), p. 49-51, and Geoffrey Moir's 'The penguins
of the Falkland Islands', vol. 21, no. 4 (September 1990), p. 44-46, will also be of
interest to ornithologist-philatelists.

141   **Guide to the birds of the Falkland Islands.**
Robin W. Woods.   Oswestry, England: Anthony Nelson, 1988. 256p.
2 maps. bibliog.

A checklist to the identification of 185 species known to have been recorded on the
islands, or within a 200-mile zone of surface water around the archipelago, forms the
main part of this comprehensive guide. Twenty-one colour plates illustrating the
various species (such as: Penguins, shags and grebes; Storm petrels and diving petrels;
Sheathbills, gulls, terns and skua) are linked to the relevant text descriptions. An
introduction provides a historical summary of ornithological and conservation activity
in the Islands, an explanation of scientific classification, and general notes on the
distribution of breeding birds and the occurrence of vagrant species. The guide is an
expanded and revised version of Woods' *The birds of the Falkland Islands* (1975).

Mammals

142   **An account of the amphibious animals at Falkland's Islands.**
Annual Register 1771 (Natural History), p. 86-93.

Contains physical descriptions of sea-wolves, sea-lions and penguins, with notes on
their habitats and a narrative of a seal hunt, extracted from A. J. Pernetty's *The history
of a voyage to the Malouine (or Falkland Islands)* (item no. 204).

143 **On the seals of the Falkland Islands.**
C. C. Abbott. *Proceedings of the Zoological Society* (1868), p. 189-92.

Compiled at the request of the Secretary to the Zoological Society, these notes on the sea-elephant, the sea-lion, the fur-seal and the sea-leopard include a physical description of each species and an indication of their distribution.

144 **Rare animals in the Zoological Society's gardens.**
Falkland Islands Journal, no. 3 (1969), p. 52-53.

In its issue of 21 November 1868 the *Illustrated London News* reported the presence of some animals of unusual interest in the Society's zoological gardens, including four never brought to England before. One was the 'Falklands Wolf', (*Canis Antarcticus*) more recently known as *Dusicyon antarcticus – australis*. Reprinted here is its description and original drawing.

145 **History of the so-called Falkland Islands 'Wolf' *Dusicyon australis* (Kerr) 1792, (formerly *Dusicyon antarcticus Bechstein* 1799).**
Stanley W. Gorham. *Falklands Islands Journal*, no. 6 (1972), p. 23-35.

Becoming extinct in 1876, the so-called Falklands 'Wolf' was really a species of fox. Gorham reviews the principal literature written on the species and its synonomy and discusses the animal's taxonomy and its description as noted by various authors. The geological aspects of its presence in the Islands are examined: 'It would appear that the Falkland Islands "Wolf" reached the Falkland Islands from southern South America in recent or late Pleistocene time'.

146 **Sealion survey in the Falklands.**
Ian Strange. *Oryx*, vol. 15, no. 2 (1979), p. 175-84. map.

'In 1965 the author, a resident of the Falkland Islands, made an aerial survey of seal populations, concentrating mainly on sealions, because numbers appeared to be declining. . . In this article he surveys the history of sealing in the islands, describes his census, discusses results and the possible causes for the decline, and urges the need for a full official census' (Abstract).

147 **The southern elephant seal.**
Geoffrey Moir. *Gibbons Stamp Monthly*, vol. 20, no. 9 (February 1990), p. 48-49.

A physical description of the elephant seal, descriptions of the sometimes aggressive nature of the male seal, the breeding season, harems and pups, moulting, the elephant seals' natural enemies and the breeding population of the Falkland Islands are all encompassed in this illustrated essay.

148 **Where have all the sea lions gone?**
Falkland Islands Newsletter, no. 47 (May 1991), p. 6-7.

In the 1930s it was estimated that the sea-lion population on the rocks and beaches of the Falklands was 300,000; using aerial photography in the 1960s, Ian Strange calculated 30,000; a survey in January-March 1990 estimated only 3,500. This is an early report of a programme to explain the mystery of the disappearing sea-lion by

Dave Thomson and Callan Duck, of the Sea Mammal Research Unit in Cambridge, which is part of the Natural Environment Research Council. The programme is funded by the Falkland Islands Development Corporation, the World Wildlife Fund, and the NERC, through the Falkland Islands Foundation.

Spiders and insects

149   **Two spiders in subfamily Mynogleninae (Aranae: Linyphiidae) from the Falkland Islands, South Atlantic.**
Michael B. Usher.   *Journal Of Zoology*, vol. 200, no. 4 (August 1983), p. 549-60. bibliog.
Spiders from Beauchêne, Falkland Islands, South Atlantic.
Michael B. Usher.   *Journal Of Zoology*, vol. 200, no. 4 (August 1983), p. 571-82. map. bibliog.

Whilst conducting a two-week survey of the plant and bird life of Beauchêne Island in December 1980, R. I. Lewis-Smith and P. A. Prince, of the British Antarctic Survey, collected fifty-five spiders of seven species. The first of these two scientific papers focuses on two species previously known only in New Zealand and Central Africa, whilst the second describes all seven species. The entire collection is now deposited at the British Museum (Natural History).

150   **Spiders in the Falkland Islands.**
Michael B. Usher.   *Falkland Islands Foundation Newsletter*, no. 2 (August 1984), p. 2-3.

An alphabetical list of Falkland Islands spiders, supplying the species name, family and authority, is included in this historical review of their discovery. 'Their scientific names are used . . . because they have not yet been assigned popular English names'.

151   **Insects of the Falkland Islands: a checklist and bibliography.**
Gaden S. Robinson.   London: British Museum (Natural History), 1984. 38p.

A 'state-of-the-art' summary of Falklands insects, this paper is intended 'as a springboard for further studies on the Falklands insect fauna and as an incentive to further collecting and fieldwork'. Three interesting features emerge: 'all groups of insects appear to be very much under-collected, many species being known only from single specimens'; 'a large proportion of the species recorded here are endemic to the islands'; and 'a large number of species exhibit the classical oceanic-subantarctic adaptation of brachyptery or complete loss of wings'. The checklist, which is arranged by orders, families within orders, genera within families, and species within genera, refers to books and articles listed A-Z by author.

152   **The great Falkland Islands bug hunt.**
      C. M. St. G. Kirke.   *Falkland Islands Newsletter*, no. 33 (November
      1987), p. 8-9.

When posted to Headquarters British Forces Falkland Islands, Major Kirke, a keen
entomologist, contacted the Natural History Museum in London for a definitive list of
South Atlantic moths. The Museum's response was that no such list existed but would
he please send back specimens of moths, beetles, flies, ladybird, and other insects.
This report, first printed in the September 1987 issue of *Gunner*, the journal of the
Royal Regiment of Artillery, tells how he enlisted the help of his Army colleagues,
Stanley residents, and the Stanley Boy Scouts, to collect 2,000 specimens, including a
moth named Chater's Leaping Moth, new to science and found on New Island.

Tourism and Travel Guides

153 The Falkland Islands South America.
C. McDonald Hobley. Port Stanley: Christ Church Cathedral, 1917.
52 unnumbered pages.

Opening with a copy of the inscription engraved in lead fixed on the door of the block-house at the British settlement on Saunders Island on 20 May 1744, this pictorial guide covers: the Falkland Islands Company; kelp; Port Stanley (Catholic and Government schools, St. Mary's Church and Convent, the Tabernacle, Public Library and Museum, Government House, King Edward Memorial Hospital, Falkland Islands Volunteers Headquarters and the Town Hall); bird life; local shells; Falkland Islands sheep; the whaling industry; the local cattle industry; plant life; the Stanley hulks; stone rivers; Stanley sports; and the 1914 naval battle. It would stand reprinting if only for its historical value.

154 Guide to Christ Church Cathedral Port Stanley.
P. J. P. Helyer. Brighton, England: Southern Publishing Company, 1973. 12p.

Intended for short-stay visitors to the cathedral, this brochure provides historical detail of the building, fabric, and memorials, and also includes a list of Bishops of the Falkland Islands.

155 Backpacking in Chile & Argentina plus the Falkland Islands.
Hilary Bradt, John Pilkington. Boston; Chalfont St. Peter, England: Bradt Enterprises, 1980. 144p. maps. bibliog.

The last section of this guide (p. 122-38) is devoted to the Falkland Islands. Although now somewhat dated, its information on the 'Camp' and the weather, and its advice on what to wear when backpacking still have some value.

156 **Falklands tourism.**
Falkland Islands Newsletter, no. 28 (August 1986), p. 8-9.
Outlines United Kingdom travel services, the facilities for touring the Islands by horse
or boat, notes the possibilities for scuba divers and camp and tramp holidays and
estimates overall costs.

157 **Tourism: British tour operators visit.**
Steve Green. *Falkland Islands Newsletter*, no. 30 (February 1987),
p. 11.
During November 1986 a group of British tour operators, whose interests included
birdwatching, military history, and young adventurers expeditions, spent a week on
the Islands at the invitation of Falkland Islands Tourism. Their itinerary took in
Kidney Island, Sea Lion Islands, Port Howard, Pebble Island, Bluff Cove, and Steeple
Jason.

158 **Tourism: the battle scene – five years on.**
Heather Boulter. *Falkland Islands Newsletter*, no. 32 (August 1987),
p. 10-11.
Staying at the Upland Goose hotel in Stanley, the writer was one of the first party of
tourists to travel to the Falklands with Battlefield Tours. This short account provides a
vivid and sympathetic glimpse of Stanley and the Camp, including Pebble Island and
Goose Green.

159 **A guide to the Stanley Harbour maritime history trail.**
Graham L. Bound. Stanley: Falkland Islands Tourism, 1990. 37p.
map.
An illustrated guide to the signposted trails, running east and west of the Public Jetty,
at the north end of Philomel Street. These mark the historical maritime associations of
the Harbour, especially the nineteenth and early twentieth century hulks moored there.
The landlubber reader will appreciate the drawing which identifies the sails of a ship
rigged vessel from the flying jib to the mizzen royal.

160 **Holidays in the Falkland Islands.**
Patrick Roper. London: Falkland Islands Tourist Board, 1990. 16p.
map.
This attractive, semi-stiff, colour-illustrated brochure focuses on the Islands' natural
history and wildlife, the Islanders' way of life, the maritime heritage and battlefields,
and on fishing, walking, horse-riding, Port Stanley, and external and internal travel. It
is available from: Falkland Islands Tourist Board, Falkland House, 14 Broadway,
Westminster, London SW1H 0BH.

161 **Port Louis.**
R. N. Spafford. *Falkland Islands Newsletter*, no. 48 (August 1991),
p. 6-7; no. 49 (November 1991), p. 8-9; no. 50 (February 1992), p. 8-9.
An illustrated descriptive tour of the original French settlement now easily visited
along a newly completed road from Stanley. The features described include the first

Government House, Fort St. Louis, two old cannons and early survey marks drawn by *HMS Erebus* and *Terror*.

162 Argentina, Uruguay & Paraguay a travel survival kit.
Wayne Bernhardson, Maria Massolo. Hawthorn, Australia: Lonely Planet Publications, 1992. 606p. maps.

Replacing Alan Samalgalski's *Argentina – a travel survival kit*, this guide comprises eight national and regional chapters, of which the Falkland Islands (Islas Malvinas) (p. 441-65) is one. It incorporates information on the Islands' history, geography and climate, flora and fauna, government, economy and population, with notes on visas and customs, money and costs, when to go and what to take, tourist offices, useful organizations, business hours and holidays, cultural events, post and telecommunications, weights and measures, books and maps, media, film and photography, health, and accommodation. It also includes a map of the Islands and a street map of Stanley. Similar information is condensed in *South America on a shoestring* (Lonely Planet, 1994. 3rd ed. p. 1126-40).

163 Walks and climbs in the Falkland Islands.
Julian Fisher. Bluntisham, England: Bluntisham Books, 1992. 67p. maps.

Six short walks (less than fifty minutes in duration), two longer walks (of two hours) and a number of mountain climbs, all in the Stanley area, are described in this illustrated booklet. Also included are notes on the weather, the terrain, and suitable outdoor clothing.

164 Stanley: capital of the Falkland Islands: a guide to Stanley.
Joan Spruce. Stanley: Falkland Islands Tourist Board, 1994. 52p. map. bibliog.

Produced primarily for short-term visitors, this informative guide contains sections on: information sources; transport in and around Stanley; the emergency services; banking and money; communications and postal services; government departments; public houses; hotels and guest houses; restaurants; laundry, hairdressing, and shoe repair services; shops; religious faiths; clubs and organizations; sporting and outdoor activities; walks; and travel to and within the Islands. A two-page list of street names and their origins is of strong historical interest.

165 1995 South American handbook.
Edited by Ben Box. Bath, England: Trade & Travel Publications, 1994. 71st ed. 1504p. maps.

Based on the editor's personal travels, contributions from national tourist offices, and on reports from local correspondents, this long-established handbook has earned an enviable reputation for its reliable and up-to-date information. Its last seven pages of text are devoted to the Falklands and include general information on the Islands (location, area, 1991 population), their early history, administration and climate, with further sections on Stanley, accommodation and food, camping, the National Tourism Bureau, rentals, the economy, entry requirements, communication, cost of living, currency, and mail. It covers everything, in fact, the independent traveller needs to know.

166   **New Falklands flights on the wild side.**
   Nick Nuttall.   *The Times*, no. 65144 (22 December 1994), p. 38.
Reports on the intention of Aero Vias DAP to lease a British Aerospace 146 jet, able to carry cargo and up to 100 passengers, for a rapid air service from the Falklands to Santiago (Chile) where it would connect with scores of international flights. This service was planned to start in September 1995.

Prehistory and Archaeology

167 **Fuegian Indians in the Falkland Islands.**
  G. Hattersley-Smith. *Polar Record*, vol. 21, no. 135 (September 1983), p. 605-06. bibliog.

Discusses the likelihood of Fuegians having reached the Islands via the Falkland current flowing northeastwards from Drake Passage into the South Atlantic. Chilean scientists have suggested that Fuegians may have reached the South Shetlands in canoes. In more modern times (1856-98) Fuegians were settled on Keppel Island, West Falkland by the Patagonian Missionary Society. W. Barbrooke Grubb's 'The Yahgan Indians of the West Falkland Group', *Folk-Lore*, vol. 38, no. 1 (March 1927), p. 75-80, is an anthropological study.

168 **Falkland Island corrals.**
  Joan Spruce. *Falkland Islands Foundation Newsletter*, no. 7 (January 1988), p. 5-6. map.

Turf, turf and gorse and, later, stone corrals, came into use in the nineteenth century to provide paddocks for wild cattle and to divide areas of land. Most of the turf corrals are only visible from the air. Joan Spruce has discovered fourteen stone and numerous turf corrals, many of which are now in disrepair and urgently needing attention. A map shows the stone corrals so far located.

169 **An archaeological survey at Port Egmont, Saunders Island.**
  Rob Philpott. *Falkland Islands Journal*, vol. 6, no. 3 (1994), p. 86-105.

Commissioned by the Falkland Islands Museum and funded by the Falkland Islands Government, Falklands Conservation, and the National Museums and Galleries on Merseyside, Rob Philpott, Fieldwork Archaeologist at Liverpool Museum, and David Barker, Keeper of Archaeology at the City of Stoke-on-Trent Art Gallery and Museum, carried out twelve days of fieldwork in January 1992. The main aim of the survey was to identify and record the surviving underground and surface elements of the earliest British settlement in the Falklands.

Prehistory and Archaeology

Port Louis.
See item no. 161.

Maritime Archaeology

General

170 Falkland's other fleet.
Michael Mensun Bound. *Popular Archaeology*, vol. 4, no. 2 (August 1982), p. 11.

In putting forward a conservation list of eight American, British and Canadian derelict ships, mostly in Port Stanley harbour, Bound explains how they arrived there, provides a historical context to the ships themselves, and assesses their importance. The ships in question are *The Vicar of Bray, Snow Squall, Charles Cooper, Jhelum, Lady Elizabeth, William Shand, Actaeon*, and *Egeria*.

171 Should we restore the Falkland ships?
Michael Mensun Bound. *Popular Archaeology*, vol. 4, no. 3 (September 1982), p. 24-31.

In this wide-ranging and provocative discussion paper on what should be done with the above-water wrecks and sunken ships in Stanley Harbour and elsewhere, Bound reminds readers that the shipwright skills that built the Falklands ship have largely died out. He also points out that it is not absolutely necessary to house old ships in purpose-built museums, that underwater wrecks are often more important, and that 'the Falklands underwater wrecks are, as an assembly, of more archaeological value than similar groups of submerged wrecks elsewhere in the world'. Above all, he is adamant that 'the emphasis should be on conservation rather than restoration or reconstruction'.

172 The historic ships of the Falkland Islands.
Michael Mensun Bound. *Falkland Islands Foundation Newsletter*, no. 1 (December 1983), p. 4-5.

'Clustered round the Falklands is a unique collection of wrecks of deep-ocean ships which comprise the finest natural museum of the 19th century nautical antiquity in the world. . . They are mostly survivors of the great trade which flourished during the last century with the West coast of South America'. Featured here are historical and descriptive notes on *The Vicar of Bray, Margaret, Jhelum, Capricorn, Charles Cooper* and *Snow Squall*.

173 First steps towards stabilising the 'Jhelum' and other hulks.
Tim Parr. *Falkland Islands Foundation Newsletter*, no. 3 (January 1985), p. 4-5.

'Tim Parr, a naval architect, and expert in wooden ship restoration, spent three weeks in the Falklands in June 1984 looking at the *Jhelum* and other old hulks with a view to finding a way of minimising their deterioration at a manageable cost. He soon discovered that the problems involved in trying to preserve the remnants of these fascinating old ships are immense' (Abstract). Other vessels studied were *Snow Squall, Charles Cooper*, and *Lady Elizabeth* with fleeting visits to *Egeria, St Margaret, William Shand* and *Fleetwing*.

174 Condemned at Stanley: notes and sketches on the hulks and wrecks at Port Stanley Falkland Islands.
John Smith. Chippenham, England: Picton Publishing, 1986. 40p. map.

The history of sixteen sailing vessels and steamships which were at one time, or still remain, derelict in Stanley Harbour is briefly recounted in this attractive booklet. Arranged in order, working west to east, on both shores of the harbour, they include: *Philomel*; *Capricorn*; *Jhelum*; *Margaret*; *Charles Cooper*; *Actaeon*; *Snow Squall*; *William Shand*; *Egeria*; *Fleetwing*; *Afterglow*; *Golden Chance*; *Gentoo*; *Lady Elizabeth*; *Plym*; and *Samson*. The author was formerly Curator of Britannia House Museum in Stanley.

175 International register of historic ships.
Norman J. Brouwer. Oswestry, England: Anthony Nelson, 1987. 321p.

Published in association with the World Ship Trust, this comprehensive directory of preserved historic ships is arranged A-Z by country. The Falkland Islands section (p. 46- 50) records *Asgard, Guillemot, Charles Cooper, Egeria, Fleetwing, Garland, Jhelum, Lady Elizabeth*, and *The Vicar of Bray* whilst South Georgia (p. 177-79) lists *Bayard, Brutus, Louise* and *Petrel*. The data given includes the year the ship was built, its builders, original and present use, type of rig, hull, decks, registered length, overall length (hull), extreme breadth, maximum draught, gross and net tonnage, original and present owners, present location, condition, and history and significance.

176 Cape Horners of the Falkland Islands.
Barbara Last. *Gibbons Stamp Monthly*, vol. 19, no. 11 (April 1989), p. 31-33, 35.

Last summarizes the history of many of the American, British, French, and German windjammers that sailed round Cape Horn, pictured on an issue of definitive Falkland Islands stamps, some with illustrations and detailed drawings.

177 **News from the Falkland Islands.**
Anne Bowman. *International Journal of Nautical Archaeology*,
vol. 21, no. 2 (May 1992), p. 167-69.

Presents the latest reports of the state and condition of *Garland* (Choiseul Sound),
Concordia (between Lion Point and Rincón de los Indias, Salvador Territory, East
Falkland), *Christina* (Christina Beach, West of Cape Pembroke, East Falkland), and
Bertha (Bertha's Beach, East Falkland).

SS Great Britain

178 **The Great Britain.**
Grahame Farr. *Mariners Mirror*, vol. 36, no. 1 (January 1950),
p. 41-54.

This authoritative article covers the *Great Britain*'s engineering (its engine, propeller
shaft, piston valves, and boiler), its voyages (which included trooping to the Crimea),
and its ignominious ending as a hulk occasionally used by the Falkland Islands
Company as a coal and wool store.

179 **The saga of the Steam Ship Great Britain.**
John O'Callaghan. London: Rupert Hart-Davis, 1971. 190p. bibliog.

In recounting the long and dramatic career of the *Great Britain*, the author took full
advantage of the extensive dossier compiled by the San Francisco Maritime Museum.

180 **The Great Britain.**
K. T. Rowland. Newton Abbot, England: David & Charles, 1971.
132p. bibliog.

This popular, illustrated historical outline presents a succinct, readable account of
Great Britain's construction, fitting out, trading voyages, and of the salvage operation
which brought her back to her home port of Bristol. Among the illustrations is a
photograph of her beached in Sparrow Cove where she spent thirty-seven years.

181 **The return of the Great Britain.**
Richard Goold-Adams. London: Weidenfeld & Nicolson, 1976.
226p.

Goold-Adams, Chairman of the SS Great Britain Project, who was associated with the
salvage operation from the beginning, recounts its history from the time the hulk was
first surveyed, when on the point of disintegrating in Sparrow Cove, and its successful
refloating, to its long tow home, lashed to a pontoon, and the intricate manoeuvring
into dry dock in Bristol. See also Euan Strathcona's 'The salvage of the Great Britain',
Falkland Islands Journal, no. 5 (1971), p. 1-11, and Grahame Farr's 'The Steamship
Great Britain – homecoming and approach to restoration', *Maritime History*, vol. 1,
no. 1 (April 1971), p. 96-102.

182　**The iron ship: the story of Brunel's SS Great Britain.**
　　Ewan Corlett.　London: Conway Maritime Press, 1990. 224p. bibliog.
First published in 1975, this authoritative technical history of the *Great Britain*'s construction, launching, fitting out, and voyages, is firmly embedded in the context of nineteenth-century ship design and construction methods, especially with regard to the introduction of ships and screw propulsion. Dr Corlett was the driving force behind the restoration project and it was his letter to *The Times* in November 1967 which set it in motion. He adds the full story of the salvage operation in this superbly illustrated volume.

183　**S.S. Great Britain.**
　　Bristol, England: SS Great Britain Trading Limited, 1992. rev. ed. 32p.
First published in 1980 this official 'walk through' guide includes sections on the *Great Britain*'s concept and design, its construction and launch, its early voyages, its stranding on the beach of Dundrum Bay on the east coast of Ireland, its subsequent career on the Australia run, its recovery from Sparrow Cove in 1970, and its restoration in drydock in Bristol. All visitors to the ship are advised to obtain a copy of this inexpensive and well-illustrated guide.

Other ships

184　**The wreck of the Pacific Steam Navigation Company's vessel**
　　***Oravia* on 18 November 1912.**
　　Harry W. Townson.　*Falkland Islands Journal*, no. 12 (1978),
　　p. 11-15.
Presents the personal narrative of Harry Townson, Chief Inspector of Stock in the Falklands, who was on board the ship when the *Oravia* was wrecked.

185　**Bringin' her back home: the story of the St Mary.**
　　Falkland Islands Journal, no. 12 (1979), p. 35-41.
Launched on 20 March 1890 from Phippsburg, the *St Mary* was fitted out for San Francisco, but was involved in a collision whilst attempting to clear Cape Horn. She eventually became stuck fast on Pinnacle Rock in the Falklands, a total wreck less than five months after launching. This is an illustrated account of recovering sections of the ship and reassembling them in the Maine State Museum at Augusta. See also Michael Mensun Bound's 'The Down-Easter St Mary, her history, rescue and exhibit', *Falkland Islands Foundation Newsletter*, no. 2 (August 1984), p. 7-8. bibliog.

186 **The Snow Squall project: report on the 1986 expedition to the Falkland Islands.**
David Switzer, Fred Yalouris. *Falkland Islands Foundation Newsletter*, no. 5 (June 1986), p. 5-7.

Launched in South Portland, Maine, in 1851, the *Snow Squall* is the only surviving example of an American built clipper ship. After suffering heavy damage off Cape Horn, she put into Port Stanley in March 1864, where she was used eventually as a jetty end by the Falkland Islands Company. Under the auspices of the Peabody Museum, Harvard University, the Snow Squall Project began surveying, measuring and excavating the ship. This report of the 1986 expedition details the rescue work that was necessary before timber sections of the bow, and artifacts from inside the hull, could be transported back to Maine where they could be measured, photographed, cleaned, tagged, and chemically treated, before being reassembled and exhibited as a national historic landmark. See also Yalouris' report on the Project's 1987 expedition (*Falkland Islands Journal*, no. 22, [1988], p. 14-20) which gives further details and adds some museum notes on the wreck.

187 **Egeria: the nineteenth century Canadian built sailing ship in Port Stanley.**
Eric Lawson. *Falkland Islands Journal*, no. 20 (1986), p. 15-19.

After suffering a heavy battering whilst attempting to round Cape Horn, *Egeria* was forced to make for Stanley Harbour where she arrived on 15 September 1872. In this article, Lawson examines the circumstances of her being written off as a hulk, her various moorings, and her use by the Falkland Islands Company. He also reviews her construction and maritime history since she was built at the Kennebecasis shipyard in 1859 and reports that the New Brunswick Government is showing interest in her conservation.

188 **The Jhelum 1849-1871 – a brief history.**
M. K. Stammers. *Falkland Islands Journal*, no. 22 (1988), p. 21-33.

The *Jhelum*'s building and design, its launch in Liverpool on 24 May 1849, its owners, captains and crews, voyages and cargoes, and a chronicle of its maritime history, are featured in this authoritative paper.

189 **Condition report on *Charles Cooper*.**
Jim Forrester. *Falkland Islands Foundation Newsletter*, no. 8 (January 1989), p. 10.

Jim Forrester, of the Merseyside Maritime Museum, presents here a disturbing report on the condition of the *Charles Cooper*, which was built in 1856 and is now the last surviving North American packet ship and the oldest intact hull of any American deep-water sailing ship. Forrester's concern is echoed in Mensun Bound's 'The Charles Cooper last of the packet ships', *Warrah*, no. 3 (December 1992), p. 8-9, which reports on a programme of survey and research 'with the principal purpose of preparing technical drawings of her every detail, so that when she does collapse, which now seems inevitable, there will be an accurate record of her construction'.

190   **Report of the British barque Lady Elizabeth in Stanley Harbour,**
       Falkland Islands.
       E. Fred Yalouris, A. Fred Feyling.   *Falkland Islands Journal*, no. 20
       (1986), p. 22-36. bibliog.

The authors participated in an expedition, sponsored by the Peabody Museum of
Archaeology at Harvard University, to undertake archaeological work on *Snow Squall*
in Stanley Harbour. They also conducted a preliminary survey of the iron-hulled *Lady
Elizabeth* and report here on the state of her hull and decks, woodwork, forecastle,
deckhouse, masts and spars, rudder, anchor, and chains. Robert A. Wilson's 'Wreck of
the Lady Elizabeth', *Sea Breezes*, vol. 51, no. 446 (February 1983), p. 85-88, reports
on an earlier visit.

Falkland Islands shores.
See item no. 94.

A guide to the Stanley Harbour maritime history trail.
See item no. 159.

History

General

191 **The Falkland Islands etc. compiled from ten years investigation of the subject.**
G. T. Whitington. London: Smith Elder, 1840. 82p. map.
Whitington states 'This work gives the early history of the Falklands: it details the different contests for their sovereignty . . . it comprises the personal examination and general observations of Don Louis Vernet, and his people who resided on the Falklands from 1826 until 1833, as also of Captain J. Onslow R. N. who took possession and hoisted there the British flag in 1833 . . . embracing the soil, climate, natural productions, local advantages, fitness and facilities for Colonization, and for the establishment of a naval and commercial depot. Accompanied by tables of temperature, journal of weather, nautical notes, instructions for navigators, and accurate maps of the islands with chart of Berkeley Sound, the shores of Magellan, etc., with some account, as bearing upon their contiguity to the Falklands'.

192 **The story of the Falkland Islands: being an account of their discovery and early history 1500-1842.**
W. L. Allardyce. Letchworth, England: Garden City Press, 1909. 31p. map.
Enquires into the circumstances of the early discoveries and sightings of the Falklands and explains why, at various times, they were known as: Davis' Southern Islands; Hawkin's Maiden Land; Isles of Sebald de Weert; Nova Belgia, Falkland's Islands; Pepy's Island; Anican Islands; Iles Nouvelles; Les Malouines; and Las Islas Malvinas. Later material includes correspondence between Captain William Maltby (HM Frigate *Favourite*) and John Ignacio Madariaga, Commander of the Spanish forces on the Islands in June 1740.

193 **The Falkland Islands.**
W. J. Roper. *Colonial Journal,* vol. 7, no. 1 (July 1913), p. 15-31.

A short historical summary (which includes the statement that the Islands were finally ceded to Britain in 1833) introduces a general outline of life on the Islands, with sections on the climate, the sheep industry, education, flora and fauna, seals, and the stone rivers.

194 **The Falkland Islands.**
M. B. R. Cawkell, D. H. Maling, E. M. Cawkell. London: Macmillan, 1960. 252p. 5 maps. bibliog.

In this general history, the authors cover the discovery of the Islands, the first settlement and the French, English and Spanish occupations in the eighteenth century. They discuss the Port Louis murders, the development of sheepfarming, the Islands' administration, and the role of the Falklands in two world wars. Chapters on the geological structure of the islands, their climate, vegetation, and bird life are also included. There are full lists of the French Governors at Port Louis, the Spanish and Argentine Governors at Puerto Soledad, and the British Naval Superintendents and Governors of the Crown Colony. Based largely on new material published subsequently, Cawkell's *The Falkland story 1592-1982* (Oswestry, England: Anthony Nelson, 1983. 90p.) constitutes a concise history from the Islands' discovery to the Argentine invasion.

195 **Historia completa de Las Malvinas.** (Complete history of the Falklands.)
José Luis Muñoz Azpiri. Buenos Aires: Editorial Oriente, 1966. 3 vols. (549p.; 587p.; 513p.). maps. bibliog.

Volume one of this encyclopaedic work includes an eighteen-page chronology (1503-1966), a forty-page bibliography and an appendix consisting of the principals relating to the history and sovereignty of the Islands. Volume two consists of thirty-two articles by independent academics, whilst volume three includes 176 'pronunciamientos, testimonios, declaraciones y documentos officiales, españoles, ingleses, argentinos y norteamericanos'. 'These volumes have rarely been cited and have gone virtually unnoticed ... nevertheless, this compilation ... covering more than 1600 pages, contains a series of documents and statements which are hardly accessible otherwise. Thus, this work deserves attention even though it also reproduces a large number of documents which are legally entirely irrelevant' (Rudolf Dolzer, *The territorial status of the Falkland Islands (Malvinas),* 1993. p. 4).

196 **Una tierra Argentina: las Malvinas.** (An Argentinian territory: the Falklands.)
Ricardo R. Caillet-Bois. Buenos Aires: Academia Nacional de la Historia, 1982. 3rd ed. 455p. bibliog.

Superbly researched and documented, this scholarly history consists of twenty-six chapters: El descubrimiento; Las navegaciones francesas en los Mares del Sur a comienzos del siglo XVIII y las islas Malvinas; La tentativa inglesa para occupar las islas Malvinas en 1745 y su fracaso; Las posesiones hispanoamericanas y la rivalidad anglo-hispano-francesa; Los franceses en las Malvinas, Bougainville, Fundación de Puerto Luis; Bougainville y la negociación francoespañola; Los ingleses en Puerto

Egmont; La promesa secreta; Los ingleses regresan a Puerto Egmont (Puerto de la Cruzada o de Trinidad); El cumplimiento de la promesa secreta; El archipielago bajo la indiscutible soberania española; Las islas desde 1810 hasta 1820: las Provincias Unidas toman posesión del archipielago; El gobierno de Martín Rodríguez y el problema de la pesca. Vernet. La explotacion de la riqueza del archipielago. Creación de la Comandancia política y militar con sedo en Soledad. Vernet enarbola el pabellón argentino en Puerto Soledad; La Colonía; La cuestión de la pesca; El apresamiento de la Breakwater: el apresamiento de la Superior; Intervención del consul Slocum: la Lexington: el raid de la Lexington: la mission Baylies; La Colonia desde 1831 hasta 1833; Gestación del proyecto de ocupación británica; Palmerston ordena la ocupación de las islas: las instrucciones; Los ingleses se apoderan de Puerto Soledad; La negociación diplomática con Inglaterra; La actuación de M. Moreno en Londres; La misión Alvear a los Estados Unidos de Norte America; and La Colonia despues del atentado de 1833: asesinato de Brisbane: negociaciones entabladas por Vernet, Whitington: el incidente con los Estados Unidos de Norte America en el año 1854. An English-language edition, or its equivalent, is long overdue. In the meantime the work's twenty-seven-page bibliography provides not only a deep well of source material to future researchers but also an indication of the depth of feeling in Argentina on the Malvinas issue.

197   **Chief events and episodes in the history of the Falkland Islands and the Gibraltar parallel.**
R. B. M. Levick.   Budleigh Salterton, England: The Author, 1983. 3rd ed. 16p. bibliog.

First published in June 1982, with a second edition in December 1982, this is a tandem chronology for two colonies facing similar problems regarding sovereignty. In both instances the population preserve a staunch pro-British affiliation.

198   **Manuel de Las Malvinas desde 1501 a 1983.** (Manual of the Falklands from 1501 to 1983.)
Laurio H. Destefani.   Buenos Aires: Corregidor, 1984. 244p. bibliog.

In this fiercely controversial study a brief geographical description and an account of the Islands' discovery are followed by six historical chapters which are mainly concerned with the events of the eighteenth and early nineteenth centuries, culminating in the 'British usurpation'. Lists of Spanish governors, Argentine and English commanders and governors, and the British Order in Council promulgated on 21 December 1950 (in English and Spanish translation), are included. The four-page bibliography consists mainly of Spanish-language items.

199   **The Falkland Islands, their kinship isles, the Antarctic hemisphere, & the freedom of the 2 great oceans; discovery and diplomacy, law and war.**
Albert Norman.   Northfield, Vermont: The Author, 1986-93. vol. 1, The Argentinian invasion/the war's international politics and wellsprings (1986); vol. 2, From the 20th century's 2nd World War to just after 1982's short war/from about 1832 to World War II (1988); vol. 3, The 19th century to the end of the 20th century's First World War 1918/vital principals & interest of the United States of America and the United Kingdom in the Falklands/Antarctic regions (1989); vol. 4, The 1700s the imperial century (1993).
Reproduced from a close-packed typescript, this is a massive (2,397p.), heavily footnoted labour of scholarship by a former Professor Emeritus of History and International Relations at Norwich University, Vermont. His exhaustive study of the Islands' legal and diplomatic history, in which he invariably favours the British view of events, is marred by the absence of an index and by the lack of any chronological sequence to the narrative of events. With ruthless editing this work could become the definitive history of the Falklands.

200   **Beauchêne Island: a historical account.**
R. I. Lewis Smith.   *Falkland Islands Journal,* vol. 23 (1989), p. 14-22. map. bibliog.
Discovered by Jacques Gouin de Beauchêne in 1701, this small island (three square kilometres in size) is the most southerly of the Falklands at latitude 52° 54′ south. It is now a wildlife reserve and home to large colonies of black-browed albatrosses and rockhopper penguins. This well-researched article draws attention to its discovery, early charting, and exploitation.

201   **The history of the Falklands.**
Geoffrey Moir.   London: The Falkland Islands Association, 1993. 24p. map.
The essential facts of the Islands' history are complemented by a three-page chronology in this booklet. Much the same material is included in the author's *Falkland Islands history through philately* (Croydon, England: G. D. Moir, 1993. 51p. 2 maps. bibliog.).

Eighteenth century

202   **Some account of Falkland Islands.**
Gentleman's Magazine, vol. 40 (October 1770), p. 480. map.
Quotes Anson on the advantages of the Islands as a Royal Navy base and rendezvous to offer trade protection to British merchantmen. A *Map of Falklands Islands in the*

latitude of 51° 22' South, longitude 64° 30' west from the latest observations is included.

203   **A voyage round the world performed by order of His Most**
        Christian Majesty in the years 1766, 1767, 1768 and 1769.
        Lewis de Bougainville, translated by Johann Reinhold Forster.
        London: J. Nourse & T. Davies, 1772. 476p. 5 pull-out maps.

Translated by Johann Reinhold Forster from the original *Voyage autour du monde par le frégate du Roi la Boudeuse, et la fiute l'Etoile, en 1766-69* (Paris, 1771), this substantial quarto volume includes two chapters of Falklands interest. One relates the story of Bougainville's colony established at Port Louis in 1763, and its handing over to Spanish possession on this voyage. The other describes the island's natural history, its harbours, geographical position, tides, winds, water, soil, turf, plants, fruits, flowers, sea plants, birds, amphibious creatures, and crustaceous fish. In this English-language edition Forster inserts a note that the English were the first discoverers and possessed 'an undoubted prior claim to these barren rocks and marshes'.

204   **The history of a voyage to the Malouine (or Falkland) Islands**
        made in 1763 and 1764 under the command of M. de Bougainville,
        in order to form a settlement there.
        Antoine Joseph Pernetty.   London: William Goldsmith, 1773. 2nd ed.
        294p. 16p. of plates. map.

Translated from Antoine Joseph Pernetty's *Histoire d'un voyage aux îsles Malouines, fait en 1763 et 1764, avec des observations sur le Détroit de Magellan et sur les Patagons* (Paris, 1770. 2 vols.), this is a full and reliable account of the beginnings of Bougainville's settlement at Port Louis. A pull-out view of Fort St. Louis at Acarron Bay is included, as is a plan of Acarron Bay, situated in the east part of the Malouine Islands.

205   **Monsieur de Bougainville to the Malouines, or Falkland Islands.**
        James Burney.   In: *A chronological history of the voyages and*
        discoveries in the South Sea or Pacific Ocean: vol. 5: to the year 1764.
        London: G. & W. Nicol, 1817, p. 143-56.

Antoine Louis de Bougainville attempted to establish a French settlement in the Falklands in the aftermath of the loss of Quebec to the British. A colonizing expedition from St. Malo landed in what is now named Berkeley Sound on 3 February 1764. A second voyage a year later consolidated the settlement at Fort St. Louis but Bougainville was forced, by Bourbon family politics, to cede the colony to Spain. Burney's account deals fully with this episode in French colonial history which is also covered in Maurice Thiéry's *Bougainville soldier and sailor* (London: Grayson, 1932. 291p. 3 maps). John Dunmore's *French explorers in the Pacific: vol. 1: the eighteenth century* (Oxford: Clarendon Press, 1965. p. 57-113) is also useful.

206   **Commodore Byron: letters to Lord Egmont, and letters of the same year following up the proposed action – 1765.**
Falkland Islands Journal, no. 9 (1974), p. 14-23.
Three items of correspondence relating to Byron's first settlement at Port Egmont are reprinted here: a letter from Byron to the Earl of Egmont, dated *HMS Dolphin*, Port Famine, 24 February 1765, reporting his formally taking possession of the Islands; a letter from the Earl of Egmont to the Duke of Grafton enclosing Byron's charts and surveys for the King's perusal, together with accounts proving His Majesty's title; and a letter from Mr Secretary Conway to the Lords of the Admiralty, dated 20 July 1765, sending instructions for a settlement and garrison to be established at Port Egmont.

207   **Secret instructions to Capt. John McBride Commander of His Majesty's Ship 'Jason'.**
Falkland Islands Journal, no. 11 (1977), p. 53-56.
Copy of letter from Captain McBride to Mr Stephens from the Jason in the Downs, March 21st, 1767.
Falkland Islands Journal, no. 12 (1978), p. 32-35.
Dated 26 September 1765, McBride's sealed orders referred to Byron's 1764 voyage and the setting up of a settlement and garrison at Port Egmont, its defence, the survey of the coast and harbours, and what course of action to pursue if 'subjects of any foreign power' were encountered. The second item reports McBride's activities in the Falklands, his contacts with the French settlement at Port Louis, and its nature.

208   **Royal commands, minutes and despatches relating to the circumstances and policy which led to the despatch, by the Viceroy of Peru, of the frigate Aguila to Tahiti: being the suspected establishment by England of naval posts or armed settlements in the Spanish dominions of America, and the actual formation of a British post at Port Egmont, in the Falkland Islands.**
In: *The quest and occupation of Tahiti by emissaries of Spain during the years 1772-1776, told in despatches and other contemporary documents.* Edited by Bolton Glanvil Corney. London: Hakluyt Society, 1913-19. vol. 1. p. 21-193.
Translated and arranged by Corney from state papers preserved in the Archivo General de Indias in Seville, these documents include several which testify to the quality of Spanish and French intelligence gathering activities in London. These include: Orders to *HMS Dolphin*, lying at Deptford, to hold herself in readiness to sail to the Falkland Islands 'where she is to form a settlement on Egmont', 25 July 1766; Abstract of debates both between Ministers and in Council regarding the need for a settlement near the Strait of Mageland, since Lord Egmont became Head of the Admiralty (p. 32-35); Voyages of *Experiment, Jason* and *Carcass* (arrival at Port Egmont 24-29 February 1766 and completion of armed blockhouse) (p. 38-41); Despatch from the Spanish Ambassador in London accompanied by the log of *HMS Jason* (not printed), 14 May 1767 (p. 68-70); Enclosure to Despatch from Spanish Ambassador reporting that Commander Anson had received orders to fit out *Tamar* and *Florida* for a voyage to Port Egmont with details of their complement, stores, and cargo, 12 October 1767 (p. 90-95); and Memorandum submitted to King Carlos 9

November 1767 by the Secretary of State for the Indies outlining Spain's legal rights in the Seas of the Indies and suggesting that the Governor of Buenos Aires and the Malvinas should utilize frigates and coast defence vessels in preventing and forbidding all trade (p. 95-97). Documents also include: Items of information obtained from England through a Master's mate who had been at the new settlement, containing Captain McBride's orders, details of the harbour and its defences, and the prospects for colonial settlement (p. 102-04); Description of Port Egmont given by seven seamen from *HMS Carcass*, 11 June 1768 (p. 143-46); Statement made by George Barker (*HMS Carcass*) relating the occurances during a voyage to Port Egmont, including many particulars about Port Egmont, the Falklands in general, and about British ships there, 1 November 1768 (p. 165-66); and Two extracts from the log of Captain Anthony Hunt, HM frigate the *Tamar*, at the Falkland Islands, in 1769-70 and Copy of a letter to Secretary of the Admiralty, dated Plymouth Sound, 3 June 1760 (p. 194-99).

209 **Dispute with Spain relative to Falkland's Islands.**
Annual Register 1771 (History of Europe), p. 1-12, 41-53 and (State Papers), p. 232-40.

Chapter one of the 1771 *Annual Register* is entirely devoted to the discovery of the Islands, the French and English settlements at Port Louis and Port Egmont respectively, and the expulsion of the inferior British land and sea forces by the Governor of Buenos Aires in 1770. Parts of chapters four and five are taken up with the subsequent Spanish-English discussions and the views of events expressed in Parliament. Also included are copies of: letters exchanged between Captains George Farmer and William Maltby, and the Spanish Commodore Juan Ignacio Madariaga; of the articles of capitulation forced on the English forces; of the *Declaration* signed and delivered by Prince de Maserano; of the Earl of Rochford's acceptance of the *Declaration* on 22 January 1771; and of a translation of his Catholic Majesty's orders to his commanders on the Falklands to restore Port Egmont 'in the precise situation in which it was before it was evacuated'.

210 **Papers relative to the late negotiation with Spain, and the taking of Falkland's Islands from the English.**
London: J. Almon, 1777. pt. 1, 32p.; pt. 2, 48p.

Part one of these Papers prints the text of the diplomatic correspondence between the British envoy in Spain and Lord Weymouth in London from 23 August 1770 to 18 January 1771. It also includes the translated text of the Declaration signed and delivered by Prince de Maserano, Ambassador Extraordinary from his Catholic Majesty on 22 January 1771, which restored British property 'in the Great Malouine, at the Port called Egmont'. This restoration, it was claimed, did not 'affect the prior right of Sovereignty of the Malouine Islands, otherwise called Falkland's Islands'. Part two consists of extracts of the letters exchanged between British and Spanish forces on East Falkland, 1769-70. Also printed is a list of officers, sailors, mariners, soldiers, guns and their calibre, on board the frigates of the squadron under the command of the Commodore and Major General of the Royal forces comprising the expedition to Port Egmont. The articles of capitulation of the British land and sea forces and inventories of the stores and effects left by the British garrison at Port Egmont are also reproduced.

211 **Diaries and correspondence of James Harris, First Earl of Malmesbury, containing an account of his missions at the Court of Madrid.**
Edited by the Third Earl of Malmesbury. London: Richard Bentley, 1844. 4 vols.

In the autumn of 1768 Harris was appointed Secretary of Embassy at the Court of Madrid under Sir James Gray who, in 1770, left him as Chargé des Affaires. 'He had the good fortune to undertake, upon his own responsibility, the affair of the Falklands, which he conducted with such temper and firmness that the issue, so honourable to England, of that dispute, at once established his diplomatic reputation'. 'The Falklands' (vol. 1, p. 50-67) prints his despatches to London, between 23 August 1770 and 14 February 1771, providing first hand glimpses of the diplomatic history of a crisis in Anglo-Spanish relations which, at one point, seemed likely to lead to war.

212 **Declaration signed and delivered by Prince Maserano, Ambassador Extraordinary from his Catholick Majesty, the 22nd day of January, 1771; The acceptance by the Earl of Rochford, in His Majesty's name, the 22nd January 1771, of the Spanish Ambassador's Declaration of the same date.**
In: *A collection of all the treaties of peace, alliance, and commerce between Great Britain and other powers . . . Vol. 3 From 1750 to 1784.*
Edited by Charles Jenkinson. London: Debrett, 1785, p. 234-37.

This is the full English text. The original French-language text can be consulted in *The consolidated treaty series vol. 44 1767-1772*, edited by Clive Parry (Dobbs Ferry, New York: Oceana, 1969).

213 **Narrative of the proceedings in a high assembly on a motion for all letters and papers received by the Ministry between 12 Sept. 1769, and 12th Sept. 1770, containing any intelligence of hostilities commenced or intended to be commenced by the Court of Spain, or any of their officers, against any of his Majesty's dominions to be laid before the house.**
Gentleman's Magazine, vol. 40, no. 12 (December 1770), p. 570-75.

At the height of the war fever with Spain the Duke of Richmond moved that an address might be presented to the King, that his Majesty might give orders for laying before the House all letters and papers received by the ministry from 12 September 1769 to 12 September 1770, containing any intelligence of hostilities commenced or intended to be commenced by the Court of Spain. This also included any of their officers, against any of his Majesty's dominions and the times at which such intelligence was received. The motion was opposed by Lord Weymouth on the general grounds of impropriety when the matters in question were the subject of negotiations with the Spanish Ambassador. Lord Chatham's lengthy intervention in the debate was mostly in general emollient terms.

214 **The letters of Junius.**
London: Henry Sampson Woodfall, 1772. 2 vols.

Collected here is a trenchant series of letters on current affairs which first appeared in the *Public Advertiser*, January 1769 to January 1772, under the pen-name of Junius.

Letter no. 42, (30 January 1771) was 'a consideration of his Majesty's speech 13 November 1770 and the subsequent measures of government' concerning the Falklands crisis. Following the eviction of the British settlement at Port Egmont by a superior Spanish naval squadron in June 1770, war fever gripped Britain. But on 25 January 1771 the ministry laid before both houses of parliament the terms of a settlement whereby the King of Spain agreed to restore the settlement while reserving the matter of sovereignty. Junius reminded his readers that 'The king of Great Britain has been for some years in possession of an island, to which, as the ministry themselves have repeatedly asserted, the Spaniards had no claim of right. The importance of the place is not in question. If it were, a better judgement might be formed of it from the opinion of Lord Anson and Lord Egmont, and from the anxiety of the Spaniards, than from any fallacious insinuations thrown out by men, whose interests it is to undervalue that property which they are determined to relinquish'. He castigates the government's weak-kneed attitude: 'The King says, *the honour of my crown and the rights of my people are deeply affected.* The Spaniard, in his reply, says, *I give you back possession, but I adhere to my claim of prior right, reserving the assertion of it for a more favourable opportunity'.* It was against this letter that Dr Johnson was engaged by the Ministry to muster his formidable argumentative powers. By far the most scholarly redaction is *Letters of Junius,* edited by John Cannon (Oxford, Clarendon Press, 1978. 643p.).

215   **Thoughts on the late transactions respecting Falkland's Islands.**
      Samuel Johnson.   In: *Samuel Johnson: political writings.*   Edited by
      Donald J. Greene.   New Haven, Connecticut: Yale University Press,
      1977, p. 346-86.

Prepared as early as October 1770, Johnson's pamphlet was first published anonymously in March 1771 when war fever still raged. Johnson also included it in his *Political tracts* (1776). Recalling in detail the history of English involvement with the Islands and tracing the changing perception of their strategic value in time of war, Johnson brings his story up to date with a narrative of the Anglo-Spanish encounter at Port Egmont and the political and diplomatic embroglio which followed. His purpose was, in Boswell's words, 'to persuade the nation that it was wise and laudable to suffer the question of rights to remain undecided, rather than involve our country in another war'. Although *Thoughts* was reprinted by Thames Bank Publishing in 1948, this present volume in the celebrated Yale edition of Johnson's works provides the most accessible text, including a scholarly introduction, which describes its historical and political context.

216   **An account of the last expedition to Port Egmont in Falkland's**
      Islands in the year 1772 together with the Transactions of the
      Company of the Penguin Shallop during their stay there.
      Bernard Penrose.   London: J. Johnson, 1775. 81p.

Penrose was one of two surgeon's mates included in the crew of the *Penguin* (Lieutenant S. W. Clayton commanding) which formed the garrison of Port Egmont and was the last to be sent there (April 1773 to April 1774). He sketches their experiences during their turn of duty and describes the settlement, its defences, and the conflagration which threatened to destroy it before it burnt itself out. He also describes the Island's vegetables, scurvy grass, berries, sea-lions, wolf-foxes, and other bird and animal life. When they embarked for home the garrison left the Island to the *King George,* a New England whaling ship effecting repairs. Penrose contributed 'A short account of the last expedition to Port Egmont in Falkland's Islands' to *Universal Magazine of Knowledge and Pleasure*, vol. 56, no. 390 (April 1775), p. 181-83.

217 British imperialism in the eighteenth century.
Gerald Berkeley Hertz. London: Archibald Constable, 1908. 247p.

Chapter four, 'The winning of the Falkland Islands' (p. 110-49), is an excellent, dispassionate, well-documented study of the political differences between the Ministry and the opposition at the time of the great war scare of 1770 which occasioned Junius' letter to the *Public Advertizer*, 30 January 1711, and Samuel Johnson's riposte for the Ministry, *Thoughts on the late transactions respecting Falkland's Islands*, first published anonymously in March 1771. The resolving of the Anglo-Spanish dispute is described as 'a practical compromise saving the dignity of both nations but leaving the ultimate question undecided'.

218 Anglo-Spanish relations in America in the closing years of the Colonial era.
Vera Lee Brown. *Hispanic American Historical Review*, vol. 5, no. 3 (August 1922), p. 325-483. bibliog.

Chapter three of this scholarly, heavily footnoted, book-length study, 'The Falkland Islands', provides crucial reading for a full understanding of the Islands' history and of the sovereignty dispute which has its origins in the eighteenth century and earlier. Topics covered include: Byron at the Falklands; Captain John McBride of the *Jason*; Discovery of the French settlement and the British protest against its presence; Cession of the French settlement to Spain; Seizure of Port Egmont by order of the Spanish Governor of Buenos Aires; Formal restitution of Port Egmont; and Abandonment of the islands by England in 1774.

219 The Falkland Islands crisis of 1770; use of naval force.
Nicholas Tracy. *English Historical Review*, vol. 90, no. 354 (January 1975), p. 40-75. bibliog.

Placing the 1770 conflict with Spain in the context of maintaining the supremacy of British sea-power after the Seven Years War, the action of the Governor of Buenos Aires in ordering Spanish forces to evict the British garrison at Port Egmont is seen in this academic overview as part of a general challenge to that supremacy.

220 Fighting for the Falklands in 1770.
Peter Burley. *History Today*, vol. 32, no. 6 (June 1982), p. 49-51. map. bibliog.

The early history of the islands, the English and French settlements, and the political complications of the French and Spanish Bourbon 'family compact' are the chief topics of this short paper, along with the machinations of the Duc de Choiseul, the secretary of state for both Foreign Affairs and War. A map showing Anson's voyage with an incomplete outline of the Falklands, from *A voyage round the world* (1748), is reproduced.

Nineteenth century

221 **A narrative of the sufferings and adventures of Capt. Charles H. Barnard in a voyage round the world during the years 1812, 1813, 1814, 1815 & 1816 embracing an account of the seizure of his vessel at the Falkland Islands, by an English crew whom he had rescued from the horrors of a shipwreck; and of their abandoning him on an uninhabited island, where he resided nearly two years.**
New York: Printed for the author by J. Lindon, 1829. 296p. pull-out chart.

Apart from the final insult of having his ship declared a legitimate prize of war by the High Court of Admiralty in London, the title tells it all. It was a curious, bizarre episode in the Falklands chequered history. The volume contains a pull-out chart of the Falkland Islands as surveyed by the author. This work was reprinted as *Marooned: being a narrative of the sufferings and adventures of Captain H. Barnard, embracing an account of his vessel at the Falkland Islands etc. 1812-1816* (New York: Syracuse University Press, 1986. 263p.). Bertha S. Dodge's 'The Nanina's last voyage', *Western Pennsylvania Historical Magazine* (January 1979), p. 19-38, is a good summary of the incident.

222 **Memoirs of Joseph Holt: General of the Irish rebels in 1798 edited from his original manuscript in the possession of Sir William Betham.**
Edited by T. Crofton Coker.   London: Henry Colburn, 1838. 2 vols.

Without digressing into the chequered career of Joseph Holt, it is sufficient here to note that these memoirs contain a narrative (vol. 2, p. 321-73) of the wreck of the *Henrietta* off the Falklands, which occurred on 7 February 1813. The wreck set in train the events which ultimately culminated in the untoward adventures of Captain Charles Barnard (see previous item). Holt and his family were passengers on the *Henrietta*.

223 **American sealers, the United States Navy, and the Falklands 1830-32.**
Barry M. Gough.   *Polar Record*, vol. 28, no. 166 (July 1992), p. 219-28. 3 maps. bibliog.

As a result of the Argentine authorities impounding three American sealing ships, the United States Navy sloop, *Lexington*, destroyed Argentine installations in the Falklands. The United States informed Argentina that it had no historical or actual claim to the Islands. Great Britain acted swiftly and sent a warship to reactivate British control.

224   **The Falkland Islands dispute between the United States and Argentina.**
Paul D. Dickens.   *Hispanic American Historical Review*, vol. 9, no. 4 (November 1929), p. 471-87.

This is unquestionably the most detailed account of the events leading up to the Argentine arrest of the United States schooner *Harriet* in July 1831, and of two other United States vessels in August of that year. Detailing the subsequent retaliatory destruction of Argentine ordnance at Puerto Soledad by the *USS Lexington*, this study also covers the Argentine efforts to secure compensation. Chapter eight of Harold F. Peterson's *Argentina and the United States 1810-1960* (New York: State University of New York, 1964) is also useful.

225   **Great Britain and Buenos Ayres.**
Annual Register (1833), p. 371-75.

Reprints correspondence relating to the occupation of the Malvinas by Great Britain published by the Government of Buenos Aires. The text includes a letter to the House of Representatives, dated 24 January 1833, referring to the events of 15th January, plus a copy of the letter from the Commander of HM Sloop *Clio* to the Commander of the Argentine forces on East Falkland. The Argentine note to the British Chargé d'Affaires in Buenos Aires and his acknowledgement of receipt are also included.

226   **Buenos Ayres and the United States.**
Compiled by the Librarian and Keeper of the Papers, Foreign Office. In: *British and Foreign State Papers 1832-1833*.   London: James Ridgway, 1836, p. 311-411.

A 'Message of the government to the legislative body of the province of Buenos Ayres, transmitting correspondence relative to the misunderstanding with the United States, with respect to the right of fishery, *etc.*, on the coasts of the Malvinas or Falkland Islands', dated 18 September 1832, reports 'the unpleasant occurrence' which had taken place on the island of La Soledad (West Falkland). The importance of this correspondence and the accompanying documents, between the American Chargé d'Affaires and the Buenos Aires Ministry, cannot be overestimated, not only because of its research value as original source material regarding the American sacking of Puerto Soledad (Port Louis) in 1831, but because the United States Government dismissed the claim of the Argentine Republic to sovereignty and jurisdiction by virtue of having succeeded to the sovereign rights of Spain. Among the enclosures is a report by the political and military commandant of the Malvinas (Louis Vernet) detailing events from an Argentine viewpoint. In addition, there is an account of the 1760s Anglo-Spanish dispute, and an assertion of Argentine sovereignty dependent on Spain's prior discovery, first and exclusive permanent occupation, and on continued and repeated Acts of Sovereignty.

227   **Falkland facts – 1820 to 1833.**
M. B. R. Cawkwell.   *Falkland Islands Journal*, no. 19 (1985), p. 4-5.

This short article was written to make nonsense of the concept of Argentina inheriting sovereignty of the Falkland Islands from the Spanish Governor of Buenos Aires, as expressed in the Argentine statement to the United Nations in 1964. Cawkwell pours scorn on the notion that 'under the threat of its guns the British fleet evicted a peaceful

and active Argentine population that was exercising the legitimate right that the
Argentine Republic possessed as heir to Spain'.

228 Charles Darwin and the voyage of the Beagle.

Edited by Nora Barlow. London: Pilot Press, 1945. 279p. folded
map.

Edited by Lady Barlow, a granddaughter of Darwin, this collection of previously
unpublished letters and notebooks contains items of Falklands interest. A letter dated
Berkeley Sound, 30 March 1833, tells of the *Beagle*'s arrival in the Falklands. 'We
found to our great surprise the English flag hoisted . . . we hear all the southern part of
America is in a ferment . . . by the aweful language of Buenos Ayres, one would
suppose this great Republic meant to declare war against England'.

229 Massacre at the Falkland Islands.

Nautical Magazine, vol. 3, no. 28 (June 1834), p. 376-77.

Reproduces a letter from Henry Rea RN, to Rear Admiral Sir M. Seymour,
Commanding Officer of the South American Station, dated Johnson's Harbour, East
Falkland Island, 18 November 1833. The letter reports the murders of Matthew
Brisbane, William Dixon, D. Ventura, Antonio Vehingar, and Juan Simon, and
describes the flight of the other inhabitants of the settlement to Hog Island, at the head
of Berkeley Sound. Rea states: 'I feel convinced that if an English ship of war does
not arrive here soon, more murders will take place'. See also 'Further particulars of
the late murders, by one of the survivors', *Nautical Magazine*, p. 436-38.

230 The murders at Port Louis 1833.

R. S. Boumphrey. In: *Studia centenalia in honorem memoriae
Benedikt S. Thorarinsson 1861-1961.* Edited by B. S. Benedikz.
Reykjavik: Isafddarprentsmidya, 1961, p. 115-33.

Based primarily on 'Rough notes relative to the murders at Port Lewis, Berkeley
Sound, East Falkland, 26 August 1833', this account was taken from the manuscript
diary (28 August 1833-17 February 1834) of Thomas Helsby, a Port Louis resident
who narrowly escaped death himself. This is by far the most complete account of the
murders of six residents by a gang of eight transported convicts from Argentina.
Helsby vividly narrates the hardships and privations endured by the survivors who
escaped the gang's attention, until effective relief arrived in the shape on *HMS
Challenger*. On board was Lieutenant Henry Smith, first Lieutenant-Governor of the
Falklands, who eventually captured the gang. Helsby's diary was also reprinted in
Falkland Islands Journal, no. 2 (1968), p. 15-26.

231 The British reoccupation and colonization of the Falkland Islands, or Malvinas, 1832-1843.

Barry M. Gough. *Albion*, vol. 22, no. 2 (Summer 1990), p. 261-87.

This study, which is based on the reports from the Royal Navy Commanders-in-Chief
of South American Station to the Lords Commissioners of the Admiralty, examines
the motives for the British seizure of the Islands in 1833. According to Gough's
sources, the British Government was principally concerned at the constant
infringement by Argentine and American traders and sealers in territory and territorial
waters traditionally claimed but not effectively occupied by the United Kingdom. As

time passed the advantages of the Falklands as a naval base and port of call also became apparent. Gough sees this as an example of the British overall oceanic policy to occupy strategic off-shore islands to secure British trading enterprises. The Falklands were regarded as superior to Patagonia or Tierra del Fuego for the protection of maritime traffic from the eastern coasts of South America and from the Australasian colonies.

232 **Lieutenant Lowcay & H. M. Ketch 'Sparrow', 1837.**
Falkland Islands Journal, no. 11 (1977), p. 9-20.
Reproduces a despatch of 29 November 1837 to Vice Admiral Sir George Hammond, extracted from the archives held by the Hydrographic Department of the Royal Navy in Taunton. Lowcay reported on the climate and soil of the Islands; the current settler population (twelve men, three women, three children); and the need for future settlers to become established. He also recommended that five vessels should be on station to protect the wild cattle, seal rookeries, and fisheries.

233 **Ross in the Antarctic: the voyages of James Clark Ross in Her Majesty's Ships *Erebus* and *Terror* 1839-1843.**
M. J. Ross.   Whitby, England: Caedmon, 1982. 276p. 8 maps. bibliog.
It was pointed out at the eighth meeting of the British Association for the Advancement of Science in 1838 that the greatest deficiency in the knowledge of terrestrial magnetism was in the high latitudes of the southern hemisphere. James Clark Ross was given command of an exploratory and scientific expedition to obtain data in many branches of science, notably meteorology, oceanography, zoology, botany, geology, and terrestrial magnetism. After extensive storm damage Ross' ships put into Port Louis on 5 April 1842. In a reversal of the usual situation Ross was able to supply the Islanders with bread and flour and, in turn, was given permission to hunt wild cattle for the fresh meat his crews badly needed. 'Falkland Islands and Hermite Island', chapter fourteen of this account, which was written by Ross' great-grandson, tells of the shooting parties that went ashore, the erection of astronomical, meteorological, and magnetic observatories, the construction of a pier from boulders and turves, the visit of *HMS Carrysfort* bringing badly needed provisions, and the survey of Port Louis and Port William to assess their relative merits to become the colony's chief settlement.

234 **The governor's year: Moody at Port Louis.**
David Tatham.   Stanley: Government Printing Office, 1994. 38p.
Based on official archives and on Governor Moody's own papers, this booklet by the present Governor tells the story of Lieutenant Moody's first year on the new colony in 1842. The author intends to publish a more detailed assessment of Moody's term as Governor.

235 **Copies or extracts of any correspondence, relative to the Falkland Islands; since the last papers laid before the House, upon the 27th day of August 1841.**
House of Commons Accounts And Papers, vol. 33 (1843), p. 1-89.
3 maps.

Invaluable as source material for the history of the early days of the colony, these thirty-six papers contain official letters and documents relating to the colony's establishment, its development and progress, and colonization. These consist principally of correspondence between Lieutenant-Governor Moody and Lord John Russell and Lord Stanley, dated 23 August 1841-25 March 1843. The documents include the Commission appointing Moody, along with general instructions as to the exercise of his powers; correspondence on the selection of a port 'for the resort of Her Majesty's Ships' with a recommendation that Port William is more convenient than Berkeley Sound; a general report on the Falklands which is chiefly concerned with the prospects they offer to British subjects desirous of emigrating; proposals relative to rendering the Islands a self-supporting naval station; and a submission for establishing a Court of Judicature and the appointment of a chaplain and surgeon, etc. Three first-class folding maps are added: a chart of the Islands surveyed by Robert Fitzroy; plans of the settlement at Port Louis; and a sketch by Captain R. K. Dawson of the Royal Engineers.

236 **Remarks on the Government etc. of the Falkland Islands.**
G. T. Whitington. *Fisher's Colonial Magazine*, new series, vol. 1, no. 10 (1844), p. 608-16.
The British Government and the Falkland Islands.
G. T. Whitington. *Fisher's Colonial Magazine*, new series. vol. 2, no. 14 (March 1845), p. 148-56; no. 15 (April 1845), p. 205-10; no. 16 (May 1845), p. 305-09; no. 17 (June 1845), p. 363-72.

Constituting one long diatribe against the iniquities of Governor Moody's administration, and the refusal of the Colonial Office to take notice of any criticism or protest, this series of articles condemns Moody's choice of Port William as the site for the new chief settlement, his land policy, his interference in the private business of the settlers, and the arbitrary nature of his rule. Whitington calls for the publication of all papers and correspondence which passed between the Admiralty, the Treasury and the Foreign and Colonial departments, bearing on the subject and affairs of the Falkland Islands from 1700 to 1845.

237 **Annual reports on the state of the colonies 1846-48.**
In: *British parliamentary papers: colonies general 4.* Shannon, Ireland: Irish Universities Press, 1970, p. 407-10.

A copy of a despatch from Governor Moody to Earl Grey, dated 9 March 1847, in which he dilates on the reasons why Her Majesty's Government should maintain an establishment in the Islands: 'the advantage of shipping in these seas in their passage to and from the countries and Cape Horn, the British Possessions in Australia, and the Southern Ocean. There can be no doubt, also, that due weight has been given to the consideration of the advantages the possession of the islands would afford in the possible case of any future war'. Moody also outlines the civil, judicial, and ecclesiastical establishment, consisting of the Governor, chief clerk, surveyor, colonial surgeon, harbourmaster, a stipendiary magistrate, and a colonial chaplain. *Annual Report 1846* was first published by HMSO in 1847.

Falkland Islands centenary 1833-1933.
See item no. 13.

Falklands: 150 years.
See item no. 518.

The history of the Falklands.
See item no. 533.

Battle of The Falklands 1914

238 **Despatches received by the Admiralty from Vice-Admiral Sir F. C. Doveton-Sturdee reporting the action off the Falkland Islands on Tuesday December 8th 1914.**
F. C. Doveton-Sturdee. *Annual Register* (Public Documents) (1915), p. 41-45.

Sturdee arranged his report in four sections: the preliminary movements of the fleet leading up to battle; engagements with the German armoured cruisers; and those with light cruisers; and the capture of their supply ships.

239 **Coronel and the Falkland Islands.**
A. Neville Hilditch. Oxford: Oxford University Press, 1915. 37p. map. bibliog. (Oxford Pamphlets 1914-1915).

After a discussion of the British and German naval strategy in Pacific and South Atlantic waters, this well-written pamphlet concentrates on events as seen from the Falklands. These include the mobilization of the 120-strong Volunteer Rifle Company and its two nine-pounder field guns, when threatened by Von Spee's battlecruisers. The two battles are vividly depicted.

240 **The log of HMS Bristol: commission 13th May 1914, till December 1915, in Mexican waters, 4th Cruiser Squadron, and detached.**
William Buchan. London: Westminster Press, 1916. 2nd ed. 147p. (The Log Series).

Alternating between the Caribbean and South American stations on the outbreak of the First World War, *HMS Bristol* sailed from Rio de Janeiro with Vice-Admiral Sturdee's battle-cruiser squadron and took part in the Battle of the Falklands and the hunt for the *Dresden*. The author was Leading Signalman on the *HMS Bristol*.

241 The battle of the Falkland Islands: before and after.
H. Spencer-Cooper. London: Cassell, 1919. 224p. 10 maps.

Completed in 1916 but withheld from publication because of deletions by the naval censor, this expert narrative links the Falklands battle with the events which led up to it. A list of officers who participated in the engagement, a list of British casualties, and the resulting honours and awards are included.

242 Operations leading up to the Battle of the Falklands and The Battle of the Falklands.
Sir Julian S. Corbett. In: *History of the Great War: naval operations: vol. 1: to the Battle of the Falklands December 1914.* London: Longmans Green, 1920, p. 400-36.

This is a magisterial summary, based on official documents, by a vastly experienced naval historian.

243 Coronel and the Falklands.
John Irving. London: A. M. Philpot, 1927. 247p. map. bibliog.

In this masterly naval study an analysis of ocean warfare, and especially of the deployment of Allied and German warships in 1914, develops into a close examination of Von Spee's, Cradock's and Sturdee's squadrons in the events leading up to the two great battles in Southern waters. The bibliography includes a good selection of German sources.

244 A 'famous victory'.
Humphrey Pakington. *Listener*, vol. 52, no. 1346 (16 December 1954), p. 1059-60.

In 1914 Commander Pakington was a young flag lieutenant on the cruiser *Carnarvon*. He recounts here how the German battle squadron steamed towards the Islands whilst the British squadron was loading up with coal in Stanley Harbour. It was first seen by an old lady living up in the hills who sent her servant on horseback to give the alarm. Later the Admiralty presented her with a tea service.

245 Coronel and Falkland.
Barrie Pitt. London: Cassell, 1960. 184p. 5 maps. bibliog.

What distinguishes Pitt's narrative from earlier accounts of these two naval battles is his reconstruction of events during the two 'missing periods', that is the momentous hours when Cradock decided to hurl his inferior force against von Spee's battlecruisers, and when the German admiral hazarded his own ships at the Falklands on the basis of unreliable information and dubious rumours. An appendix prints all communications between Naval Staff Headquarters in Berlin, von Spee's squadron, and German agents in Africa and the Americas from 1 November to 8 December 1914. A paperback edition was also published under the title *Revenge at sea* (London: Tandem Books, 1965).

246 **Coronel and The Falklands.**
Geoffrey Bennett. London: Batsford, 1962. 192p. 3 maps. bibliog.

This was commended as the first comprehensive study of the two engagements to make full use of both British and German official documents, and of the many eye-witness accounts. Bennett's expert narrative ends with a descriptive list of the ships engaged (ship, type, year of completion, displacement, guns, speed, primary armour, commander, and complement) and a note on the difficulty of communication with naval headquarters at a time when wireless telegraphy was in its infancy. Bennett also devoted three chapters to Coronel and the Falklands in his *Naval battles of the First World War* (Batsford, 1968).

247 **Sailor at sea.**
Harold Hickling. London: William Kimber, 1965. 224p. maps on endpapers.

Vice Admiral Hickling began his career in the Royal Navy as a cadet at Osborne in 1905. In 1914 he was Lieutenant on the cruiser *Glasgow* which took part in the Battles of Coronel and The Falklands. The first part of these reminiscences (p. 14-108) provides a first-hand account not only of the two battles but of the events that led up to them.

248 **Defeat at the Falklands: Germany's East Asia Squadron 1914.**
Edwin P. Hoyt. London: Robert Hale, 1981. 240p. 5 maps. bibliog.

Hoyt's narrative follows the movements of the German East Asia Squadron, based in Tsingtao, China, from the outbreak of war in August 1914 to its victory off Coronel and its destruction at the Falklands in December of the same year. Richard Hough's *The pursuit of Admiral von Spee* (London: Allen & Unwin, 1969. 180p. maps on endpapers. bibliog.) covers much the same ground.

249 **The enemy fought splendidly: being the 1914-1915 diary of the Battle of the Falklands & its aftermath by Surgeon T. B. Dixon RNVR of HMS Kent.**
Poole, England: Blandford Press, 1983. 96p.

Reproduced here is Dixon's diary of 22 October 1914-22 May 1915, which covers not only the Falkland's battle (8 December 1914) but also *Kent's* search for the German cruiser *Dresden*. The ship eluded the pursuing British cruisers in December and was not sent to the bottom until three months later. A report from Dixon, who in peacetime was a doctor at the Bristol Dispensary, was first published in the *Western Daily Press* on 23 January 1915 and is reprinted here as an appendix.

Sovereignty

250 **Argentine dictator: Juan Manuel De Rosas 1829-1852.**
John Lynch. Oxford: Clarendon Press, 1981. 414p. bibliog.

This work is included here because of the light it throws on a little-known episode in Argentine-British relations. Among Manuel Moreno's instructions, when he returned to London in December 1838 as Argentine minister, was an order to explore the possibility of ceding Argentine 'rights' over the Falklands in return for the cancellation of the debt remaining from an 1824 Baring Brothers loan. This was rejected on the grounds that the loan was a matter for the bank and, in any case, why should Britain buy what it already rightfully possessed?

251 **The struggle for the Falkland Islands.**
Julius Goebel. New Haven, Connecticut: Yale University Press, 1927. Reprinted, 1982. 482p.

Probably the most frequently cited authority in the English language for the legitimacy of Argentine claims to the Falklands, this legalistic and erudite study, based on manuscript sources in France, Spain and Britain, discusses the implications of the various transfers of sovereignty between 1764 and 1833. Writing at a time when any vestige of European colonialism was regarded with deep suspicion in the isolationist period of United States history, Goebel delves into the complexities of international law as it emerged from the Middle Ages. He makes special reference to the Treaty of Tordesillas (1494), which gave exclusive rights of sovereignty over newly discovered lands to the Catholic kingdoms of Spain and Portugal, and to the public law of Europe in the seventeenth and eighteenth centuries. A. P. Herbert's critical review in *Law Quarterly Review*, vol. 44, no. 175 (July 1928), p. 388-89, ended: 'The relations of the two governments have been for a long time of the most friendly character, and will not be disturbed by Dr Goebel's learned researches'. The book was re-issued in 1982 with an introduction by J. C. J. Metford which presented an alternative interpretation of these historical concepts and events.

252 **Geopolitics in the Foreign Office: British representations of Argentina 1945-1961.**
Klaus-John Dodds. *Transactions of the Institute of British Geographers*, new series, vol. 19, no. 3 (1994), p. 273-90. map. bibliog.

Dodds delves deep into government records to explore how a long-standing commercial relationship was replaced by increasingly soured relations because of geopolitical conflict and confrontation in the Antarctic and South Atlantic. Generally speaking, an anti-British bias is evident, exemplified by the use of phrases like 'imperial fantasies' and 'British intransigence'. In the light of later events an extract from a letter from Vice Admiral Sir William Tennent to the First Sea Lord, dated 5 May 1948, is significant: 'I would hold onto the Falklands and South Georgia at all costs, even to the extent of going to war'.

253 **La cuestión de las Malvinas: contribución al estudio de las relaciones hispano-inglesas en el siglo XVIII.** (The Falklands question: contribution to the study of Anglo-Spanish relations in the 18th century.)
Manuel Hidalgo Nieto. Madrid: Aguirre, 1947. 762p. maps.

Based on original documents in the archives of Seville and Madrid, many of which are reproduced, this study accords the Dutch mariners, Jacob Mahu and Simon de Cordes, full credit for the discovery of unknown islands in latitude 50° 40' south, which Sebald de Weert named the Seebald Islands on 22 January 1600. The author gives short shrift to claims of prior discovery by Spanish or English navigators. From a detailed examination of diplomatic correspondence, and of the principles of international law relating to discovery and occupation, he concludes that the Spanish rather than the English could legitimately claim sovereignty. There is a full account of the events of 1770 and 1771.

254 **In defence of colonies: British colonial territories in international affairs.**
Sir Alan Burns. London: Allen & Unwin, 1957. 338p.

Together, chapter fourteen, 'The Falkland Islands and Argentina', and chapter fifteen, 'The Falkland Islands Dependencies, Argentina and Chile', form a comprehensive survey of the sovereignty issue. Topics covered include the diplomatic history of the dispute, the refusal of the Argentine and Chilean governments to take the Dependencies question to the International Court of Justice, and Argentina's *de facto* and *de jure* claims.

255 **Falklands or Malvinas? The background to the dispute.**
J. C. J. Metford. *International Affairs*, vol. 44, no. 3 (Summer 1968), p. 463-81.

Reprinted as an introduction to a reissue of Julius Goebel's *The struggle for the Falkland Islands* (1982) (item no. 251) and intended as a contribution to Anglo-Argentine understanding, this article closely examines the events of the period 1764-1833 to establish the merits of the rival claims to sovereignty over the Islands. Metford's conclusion is that Argentina's claim is 'founded on emotion and recurrent irredentist fever' whilst Britain 'would like to dispossess itself of the last remnants of an imperial past . . . but she has an inescapable moral commitment to the Falkland Islanders who have no wish to be other than British'.

256   The Falkland Islands.
Richard Luce.   *World Today*, vol. 28, no. 3 (March 1972), p. 98-101.

Luce outlines the background to the talks which were about to take place in Stanley between British and Argentine government officials and the Falkland Islands Government reviewing progress since the Buenos Aires Joint Statement on Communications in 1971. Richard Luce attended these talks and, as a junior Foreign Minister, was a member of the British team engaged in talks in New York at the end of February 1982. He resigned from the government three days after the Argentine invasion.

257   Falkland Islands – continuation of UK-Argentina dispute over sovereignty – The Shackleton Report – visit of British team for negotiations.
Keesing's Contemporary Archives, vol. 23 (24 June 1977), p. 28405-07.

This is a progress report relating to the reassertion of Argentine sovereignty in 1973-75; the Shackleton mission 'to carry out an economic and fiscal survey of the Islands at the request of the Falkland Islands Executive Council'; the withdrawal of ambassadors in Buenos Aires and London; the Shackleton Report; the 1976 UN General Assembly Resolution; the visit of the Minister of State at the Foreign & Commonwealth Office to the Falklands and to Argentina; and an offer by Argentine businessmen to buy out the Falkland Islands Company.

258   Mandarin: the diaries of an ambassador 1969-1982.
Nicholas Henderson.   London: Weidenfeld & Nicolson, 1994. 517p.

The author of these diaries was British Ambassador to the United States at the time of the Argentine invasion. Apart from the invaluable first-hand insight into the British diplomatic effort to secure United States backing and support, their most notable feature is an account of the visit of a senior Foreign Office diplomat who, acting without Government authorization, flew to Buenos Aires in 1979 to encourage Argentina to seize the Falklands. Michael Binyon's 'British official flew to Argentina to urge Falklands takeover', and Peter Jay's review, 'A sort of treason', both printed in *The Times*, no. 64964, 26 May 1994, investigate this sensational story.

259   Cooperative confrontation in the Falkland Islands dispute: the Anglo-Argentine search for a way forward 1968-1981.
Peter J. Beck.   *Journal of Interamerican Studies and World Affairs*, vol. 24, no. 1 (February 1982), p. 37-58. bibliog.

If ever a paper was overtaken by events this is it. Beck argues that in recent years both governments had 'an appreciation of their economic interdependence' which dissuaded them from pressing their dispute to actual conflict. His analysis of events is sound and his perception of the British Government's policy to achieve a solution 'which would be acceptable to all parties', and which would in particular 'preserve

British administration, law, way of life for the islands while releasing the potential of the islands' economy and of their maritime resources', is sharp and acute.

260 The Falklands and the law.
J. E. S. Fawcett. *World Today*, vol. 38, no. 6 (June 1982), p. 203-06.

'Answers to questions about the status and future of the Falkland Islands and Dependencies will vary with who is asked – lawyers, ministers, parliamentarians, or the public – though answers may sometimes coincide'. In this article Fawcett is satisfied that the International Court of Justice would find 'that the taking of the Islands in 1833 was not contrary to the law applicable at the time; but that, in any case, their continuing and undisturbed occupation and administration by Britain for a century and a half established a valid title'. This paper specifically examines the relevance of Article 51 of the United Nations charter; the High Seas Convention in 1962; the Territorial Seas Convention of 1964; and the Continental Shelf Convention in 1964.

261 The Falkland Islands: the facts.
London: HMSO, 1982. 12p. 2 maps.

Produced for the Foreign and Commonwealth Office by the Central Office of Information in May 1982, this pamphlet was the government's initial response to the invasion of the Falklands by the armed forces of the Republic of Argentina in April 1982. Topics discussed include the incident on South Georgia; the question of British sovereignty; the peaceful settlement of international disputes; decolonization and self-determination; the Falkland Islands constitution; British interests in the Falklands; negotiations with Argentina; and Britain's right of self-defence.

262 The disputed islands: the Falkland crisis: a history and background.
London: HMSO, 1982. 36p. map.

The topics treated in this short outline are the Islands' geography (including geology and landforms, climate and vegetation); their history; their government (including the economy, social welfare, communications and services); the Falkland Island Dependencies; the dispute with Argentina; and Britain's view of the Argentine occupation.

263 The Falklands crisis: the rights and the wrongs.
Peter Calvert. London: Francis Pinter, 1982. 183p. 2 maps.

In this well-researched study, Calvert covers the nature and history of the Falklands crisis of 1982, the legal basis for the competing claims for sovereignty and the political background and events in Argentina and Britain that led up to the crisis. He also discusses the progress of the war and the attempts to effect a diplomatic solution, and considers the political, diplomatic, and military aspects of the outcome of the war. There is no bibliography but the extensive chapter notes carry numerous references to contemporary newspaper reports and articles.

264 **The Malvinas, the South Georgias and the South Sandwich Islands, the conflict with Britain.**
Rear Admiral Laurio H. Destefani.   Buenos Aires: Edipress, 1982.
143p. 3 maps. bibliog.

This important study was printed in six languages for world distribution 'to fulfil a need to clarify the Argentine truth and make it known everywhere' so that 'it may be possible for people who do not have access to more material on the subject of our Malvinas, and especially in the case of those abroad, to better understand how substantial our rights are'. It contains sections on the Argentine interpretation of British imperialism; eight English invasions of Argentina; a brief description of the Malvinas; the islands' discovery and history up to 1763; Spanish rule of the islands; the Argentine presence there; 150 years of British appropriation; the South Georgia and Aurora Islands; and the South Sandwich Islands. Lists of the Spanish governors and of the Argentine and British authorities are produced in appendices. There is a good bibliography of Argentine source material. Destefani is also the author of *Las Malvinas en la época hispaña 1600-1811* (The Falklands in the Spanish period 1600-1811) (Buenos Aires: Corregidor, 1981).

265 **The Falkland Islands/Islas Malvinas conflict: a question of zones.**
R. P. Barston, P. W. Birnie.   *Marine Policy*, vol. 7, no. 1 (January 1983), p. 14-24.

The principal theme of this important article is the legal aspect of the Total Exclusion Zone and the Maritime Protection Zone around the Falklands. These were imposed by the British Government during and after the South Atlantic War, in the context of the evolution of coastal state jurisdiction.

266 **The Falkland Islands: origins of the British involvement.**
F. S. Northedge.   *International Relations* (November 1982), p. 2167-89.

Northedge conducts a detailed investigation of the legitimacy of Britain's claim to sovereignty, scrutinizing in particular the Anglo-Spanish agreement of 1771. He dismisses the notion that the British unofficially pledged to relinquish their claims in return for a short-term restitution of its Port Egmont settlement, and argues that Argentina would be better served 'to criticise the British claim to sovereign rights *before* 1771 than to make the spurious allegation that these rights were abandoned *in* 1771'.

267 **Research problems in studying Britain's Latin American past: the case of the Falklands dispute 1920-1950.**
Peter J. Beck.   *Bulletin of Latin American Research*, vol. 2, no. 2 (1983), p. 3-15. bibliog.

'In this article, the intention is to concentrate upon the researcher's position during the period 1920-1950 particularly in the light of the fact that in theory all of the British government files on the Falklands for the period should be available. However, in practice, the position is very different, because many files and documents within the files are interpreted as being "extremely sensitive", and hence are candidates for external closure: thus certain papers have been placed under a fifty-year rule, while there are instances of seventy-five and even hundred-year closures'. Beck asks whether the British Government has something to hide, points out the futility of extended closures, and discusses the effects of the Franks Report (item no. 307).

268 **Sovereignty and decolonization of the Malvinas (Falkland) Islands.**
Adrian F. J. Hope. *Boston College International and Comparative Law Review*, vol. 6, no. 2 (1983), p. 392-446.

'In any rational analysis of this controversy, a resolution of the issue of sovereignty must necessarily precede any discussion regarding the rights of the islanders because it calls into question the legitimacy of the British presence . . . in this connection the Islanders, as British subjects, are strictly speaking, the chief visible representatives of that presence and occupation'. In that context Hope attempts to show that the Argentine claim to the Islands is firmly based on international law and on the fact that the United Nations regards the issue as a colonial situation within the terms of Resolution 1514, 14 December 1960. This article was later issued as an offprint.

269 **Millennium.**
Oxford: Martin Robinson, special issue, vol. 12, no. 1 (Spring 1983), 96p.

The Spring 1983 issue of this international law journal was designed 'to look at some issues which were ignored, or simply subordinated to the day-to-day accounts and instant histories which followed the crisis in the South Atlantic'. Relevant papers are 'The Anglo-Argentine dispute over title to the Falkland Islands: changing British perceptions on sovereignty since 1910' (Peter J. Beck); 'Title to the Falkland-Malvinas under international law' (Jeffrey D. Myhre); and 'Argentine claims to the Malvinas under international law' (Alfredo Bruno Bologna).

270 **Sovereignty and the Falklands crisis.**
Peter Calvert. *International Affairs*, vol. 59, no. 3 (Summer 1983), p. 405-13.

First dealing with the sovereignty issue in three sections (before 1833; the emergence of rival claims; and the anachronistic nature of the Argentine claim), Calvert then concludes 'the claims on both sides are based on historical facts that are by turns vague, confused and disputed, and if there is to be any resolution of the question a great deal of homework will have to be done first by both parties'. The article was later reprinted in the *Falkland Islands Journal*, no. 21 (1987), p. 4-14, when the editor described the paper as an 'accurate description of the full historical story of these Islands, which thoroughly exposes the false foundation of the claims of Argentina'. However, see M. B. R. Cawkell's 'Notes on Professor Calvert's recent article', *Falkland Islands Journal*, no. 22 (1988), p. 4-6, in which she remarks 'The picture Professor Calvert gives of the historical record is interesting but not strictly accurate'.

271 **Self-determination and the Falklands.**
Denzil Dunnett. *International Affairs*, vol. 59, no. 3 (Summer 1983), p. 416-28.

This abstract essay on the principle of self-determination focuses on five points with regard to the Falklands: Self-determination is universally accepted as an imperative, not least in many solemn documents and declarations of the United Nations; Self-determination means let the people decide their own destiny; The people means the inhabitants; The inhabitants of the Falkland Islands have declared their firm wish to remain under British sovereignty; and therefore the world, and in particular the United Nations must approve the maintenance of British sovereignty over the islands.

272   **The Falkland Islands dispute in international law and politics: a documentary source book.**
Raphael Perl.   New York: Oceana, 1983. 722p. 2 maps. bibliog.
This massive reference work reproduces the texts of fifty-two documents, in their original language, concerned with sovereignty over the Falklands. These range from the Papal Bull of Alexander VI, dated 4 May 1493 and relating to the overseas discoveries of Spain and Portugal, to various United Nations papers of 1982. They are arranged in thirteen sections: Introduction; Geography and terminology; History; Modes of acquisition and loss of territorial sovereignty under customary international law; United States policy on sovereignty over the Falklands; Argentine position; British position; Analysis of sovereignty rights; Recent historical precedents; Conclusion; Historical chronology (by Everette E. Larson); Documents; and Bibliography (Larson). Most documents are printed without commentary although the first ten sections present an introductory text incorporating quotations and citations to the relevant authorities.

273   **The case of Antonio Rivero and sovereignty over the Falkland Islands.**
Richard Ware.   *Historical Journal*, vol. 27, no. 4 (1984), p. 961-67.
Reflexions on 'The case of Antonio Rivero and sovereignty over the Falkland Islands'.
John Mufty.   *Historical Journal*, vol. 29, no. 2 (1986), p. 427-32.
Reply to reflexions on 'The case of Antonio Rivero and sovereignty over the Falkland Islands'.
Richard Ware.   *Historical Journal*, vol. 30, no. 3 (1987), p. 735-36.
The purpose of Ware's original article was to demonstrate that 'when Britain was asserting its sovereignty over the Falkland Islands against the claims of the United Provinces of the River Plate (soon to be known as Argentina) there was no clear consensus with the British Government as to the grounds on which sovereignty was claimed'. Advice from the King's Advocate General, Sir Herbert Jenner, was that the Spanish claim, from which the United Provinces' claim derived, had never been recognized by Britain. The United Provinces' claim could only be sustained if it were believed that the British evacuation of Port Louis in 1774 amounted to an abandonment of the right acquired 'by original discovery and subsequent occupation . . . the symbols of property and possession which had been left on the Islands sufficiently denoted the intention of the British Government to retain their rights which they had previously acquired'. Continuing government doubts as to the legitimacy of Britain's claim to sovereignty again surfaced when the right of a British court to try Antonio Rivero, the ringleader of the gang of cutthroats responsible for the Port Louis murders in 1833, was questioned. Using the same documentary sources as Ware, Mufty argues that far from harbouring doubts, the government memorandum 'Case respecting certain prisoners lately brought from the Falkland Islands charged with murder. For the opinion of the King's Advocate, the Attorney and Solicitor', was in fact a carefully constructed official statement of Britain's sovereignty claims. Ware's 'Reply' repeats his concern to show that there was no clear consensus in

Britain about sovereignty in 1829 and that, contrary to received opinion, Antonio Rivero had not stood trial in a British court but had been shipped to Montevideo where he was released.

274 The future of the Falkland Islands.
C. D. Townsend. *Contemporary Review*, vol. 245, no. 1427 (December 1984), p. 289-93.

The author of this article was Chairman of the South Atlantic Council which was formed in December 1983 'to carry through many of the ideas set out in the report on the Select Committee on Foreign Affairs in the last Parliament'. The aims of the Council were 'to secure long-term, peaceful solutions to the problems of the South Atlantic, to establish good relations between the British Government and the new democratic government in the Argentine, and to safeguard the security and British way of life of the Islanders'. To this end an all-party parliamentary delegation was sent to Buenos Aires, between 25th June and 1 July 1983, where it held a long session with Argentine senators and deputies. Townsend, a member of the delegation, reports that among the possibilities discussed were United Nations trusteeship for the Falklands; joint sovereignty; the Islands to become an autonomous region within Argentina; and leaseback (that is, Argentine sovereignty and British administration).

275 Sovereignty in dispute: the Falklands/Malvinas 1493-1982.
Fritz L. Hoffman, Olga Minto Hoffman. Boulder, Colorado: Westview Press, 1984. 194p. 10 maps. bibliog.

Based mainly on official documents and on contemporary periodicals and newspapers, many of which were collected during extended stays in Argentina, this history investigates the history of the Falklands dispute, the United States involvement, and the impact of the 1982 war on inter-American relations. Although analytical in their approach, the authors steadfastly refuse to recognize any merit in the British claim to lawful sovereignty; they totally accept the notion that Spanish sovereignty was either transferred to, or inherited by Argentina.

276 An annotated legal chronology of the Malvinas (Falkland) Islands controversy: cronologia legal anotada sobre la cuestión Malvinas (resumen).
Enrique Ferrer Vieyra. Cordoba, Argentina: Marcos Lerner, 1985. 173p. bibliog.

Solely concerned with the study of Argentine and British territorial claims to the Islands, this chronology prints extracts from those treaties, letters, inscriptions, official instructions, proclamations and memoranda deemed to be crucial in determining the legal basis for sovereignty over the Falklands between 1648 and 1983.

277 Errors and inaccuracies in the statement presented by Argentina to the Decolonisation Committee of the United Nations in September 1964.
M. B. R. Cawkell. *Falkland Islands Journal*, no. 20 (1986), p. 4-9.

Cawkell indignantly catalogues the errors, misleading discrepancies, omissions and distortions contained in the Argentine statement. 'It is a long, rambling repetitious document which makes no attempt to define the Argentine claim . . . it is long on generalities, short on particulars, especially historical particulars. Misrepresentation is endemic throughout'.

278 The way forward: Falkland-British-Argentine relations.
London: Falkland Islands Association, [1987]. 36p.

An excellent publication of its type, this staunchly pro-British pictorial booklet 'sets out briefly and clearly the facts on which our claim is based'. The Foreword is written by Sir Rex Hunt.

279 The Falkland Islands as an international problem.
Peter Beck.   London: Routledge, 1988. 211p. 4 maps. bibliog.

Furnished with detailed chapter notes and references, this study looks in turn at modern aspects of the Falklands problem, at British and Argentine versions of history, at the development of the dispute from 1833 to 1985, and at the War and subsequent events. 'Although an attempt has been made to offer balanced coverage of divergent attitudes, it does tend nevertheless to represent a British interpretation' (Preface). However, Thomas G. Reid in *Falkland Islands Journal* (1990, p. 34) disagrees entirely: 'Beck pinpoints every weakness in the British claim to the sovereignty of the Falkland Islands and tends to be less critical of Argentine ones. Obviously disdainful of the Falkland Islanders, the Falklands lobby in Britain, and any British politician supporting British sovereignty and the islanders' "wishes" (not "interests")'.

280 The sovereignty dispute over the Falkland (Malvinas) Islands.
Lowell S. Gustafson.   New York: Oxford University Press, 1988.
268p. bibliog.

In this academic treatise Gustafson evaluates each country's argument for sovereignty. He discusses Argentina's contention that international law makes their historical right to the Islands more than a political aspiration, and considers Britain's claim that length of occupation and the principle of self-determination legalizes *de facto* control. He also examines the concept of legal sovereignty and, in particular, addresses three questions: When did which nation exercise sovereignty?; To what degree do historical rights affect contemporary claims?; and How is the principle of self-determination to be applied in this instance? A very useful twenty-two-page bibliography is divided into books, government publications, current journals and newspapers, recent articles, interviews, and United Nations and League of Nations documents.

281 Whose island story?
Peter Beck.   *History Today*, vol. 39, no. 2 (February 1989), p. 8-11.

Despite Argentina's 'dogmatic and myopic attitude towards sovereignty' which qualifies its ability to conduct useful negotiations, Beck is encouraged by a series of articles by Carlos Escudé, in the *Buenos Aires Herald* in November 1985, exposing the faulty history and reasoning transmitted by successive Argentine governments. He quotes: 'I will not argue that Argentina has no rights, nor that her claim is weaker than the British one, but only that her rights are relative, stem from a highly complex analysis with many arguments and counter-arguments, that in the final instance it is very difficult to say objectively whose rights are better, and that it is therefore a case in which fanaticism is by no means warranted and much less so the recourse to force'.

282 **National interest/national honor: the diplomacy of the Falklands crisis.**
Douglas Kinney. New York: Praeger, 1989. 372p.

Published in co-operation with the Institute for the Study of Diplomacy, Georgetown University, this well-documented book provides a remarkably competent, rational, and even-handed study of the historical context of the Falklands crisis. Kinney also offers a comprehensive account of the diplomatic efforts made to effect a cease-fire, to reach agreement on an interim administration, and to resolve the sovereignty dispute. He distinguishes five major stages in the diplomacy of the crisis: conflicting claims since the European discovery of the New World; United Nations consideration of decolonization; seventeen years of bilateral negotiations accompanied by Argentine threats and use of force; attempts at preventive diplomacy by the United Nations and United States; and the Haig shuttle, the Peruvian proposals, and the United Nations Secretary-General's intervention. Chapter notes, a forty-page chronology, and an extensive bibliography add to the usefulness of this authoritative and scholarly work.

283 **British-Argentine relations: a joint report compiled by Royal Institute of International Affairs Chatham House London; Centro de Investigaciones Europeo-Latinoamericanas.**
Buenos Aires: EURAL, 1991. 114p.

Following links between the Royal Institute of International Affairs and EURAL (Europeo-Latinoamericanas), and two Anglo-Argentine conferences held in April 1988 and November 1990, which concentrated on political, economic and social issues to identify points of agreement rather than divisions, this paper sums up the Argentine and British points of view. Clearly, a solution to the dispute will require compromise: 'For the Argentines the compromise requires recognition that their full, unfettered sovereignty over the Islands is not a realistic goal; for the British, it requires recognition that the status quo cannot represent a permanent or stable solution; and, finally, the Islanders need to accept that their wishes cannot forever constitute a veto over the actions of the British government' (Foreword).

284 **Towards resolution? The Falklands/Malvinas dispute.**
Edited by Wayne S. Smith. Boulder, Colorado: Lynne Rienner, 1991. 159p.

In this work ten Argentine, American and British academics explore the reasons why the sovereignty dispute over the Falklands must be solved. They consider how the two sides should reduce the tension and eventually work out a solution acceptable to both London and Buenos Aires as well as to the Islanders. The text of the joint statement issued by the British and Argentine delegations to the Madrid Conference in February 1990 is printed in an appendix. Copious chapter notes underline the scholarly nature of this study.

285 **Britain's dependent territories: a fistful of islands.**
George Drower. Aldershot, England: Dartmouth, 1992. 276p.
7 maps. bibliog.

Part one of this book attempts to analyse the reasons why Britain wished to decolonize her dependent territories and bring the imperial era to an end. Part two includes four well-documented case-studies on territories subject to irredentist disputes. The

Falklands example (on p. 91-102) is particularly useful for its résumé of Anglo-Argentine diplomatic relations, 1952-88.

286 **The Falkland Islands/Malvinas: the contest for Empire in the South Atlantic.**
Barry Gough. London: Athlone Press, 1992. 212p. 2 maps. bibliog.

Based on primary source material in the Admiralty files, Foreign Office papers, and Colonial Office correspondence, this 'five-sided study of Spanish, French, British, American and Argentine aspirations and enterprises in regards to the Falklands Islands or Las Islas Malvinas' is an exceptionally well-researched and documented study. It closely examines the British reoccupation of the Islands in 1832-33, British naval activity in southern seas, and Britain's attempts to colonize and defend the Islands in the nineteenth century.

287 **The territorial status of the Falkland Islands (Malvinas) past and present.**
Rudolf Dolzer. New York: Oceana, 1993. 454p. bibliog.

The first half of this substantial treatise is concerned with a detailed chronological narrative of the development of the territorial status of the Falklands, beginning with the pre-1764 period, and ending with the legal implications subsequent to the British annexation of 1832-33. The author also includes a discussion of the application of the right to self-determination, and the current status of the Islands. The second part of the work comprises fifty-one annexes, in which the original texts are reproduced of such documents as official memoranda, declarations, treaties, international conventions and United Nations statements. Many of these can be consulted elsewhere, but they are most conveniently assembled *en bloc* in these pages. There is also a valuable twelve-page bibliography.

288 **War stories: British elite narratives of the 1982 Falklands/ Malvinas War.**
K. J. Dodds. *Environment and Planning D: Society and Space*, vol. 11, no. 6 (1993), p. 619-40. bibliog.

Dodds introduces his paper by identifying five different categories of study which apply to the South Atlantic War: in the context of Britain's imperial decline; investigations of inconsistencies in the official attempts to cover the war in moral justification; how the Foreign Office ignored evidence of imminent Argentine aggression until it was too late; examinations of the diplomatic, legal and military implications of the war; and investigations of how British élites discursively fought the campaign in the South Atlantic. In this analysis Dodds concentrates on international geopolitics and the official account of the war in the context of the Second World War, and the Suez Crisis, and considers how dissident views and opinions were marginalized. As is explained in the introduction to this bibliography, items referring to political motives and discussion in Britain relating to events in the South Atlantic are generally excluded. However, researchers requiring such material can turn with confidence to this authoritative paper which ends with an extensive bibliography.

289 **Looking at the Falkland Islands from Antarctica: the broader regional perspective.**
Peter J. Beck. *Polar Record*, vol. 30, no. 174 (July 1994), p. 167-80.
3 maps. bibliog.

This paper is an updated version of one presented at the Airlie House Colloquium on the Falklands/Malvinas conflict, organized by the Institute of Conflict Analysis and Resolution, George Mason University, in May 1992. Beck uses as his starting point the progress that has been achieved across a broad range of topics (such as air transport, cultural exchanges, drug trafficking, the conservation of fish stocks and the abolition of visas) since the resumption of diplomatic relations between Britain and Argentina in 1990. Through a geographical, legal, political, economic, scientific and environmental comparison between Antarctica and the Falklands, he then poses a number of questions: Does the Antarctica model offer a way of either resolving or accommodating the Anglo-Argentine differences about sovereignty over the Falklands?; Can sovereignty become a constructive rather than a destructive force?; Do the Falklands have a 'gateway role', most notably in Antarctic tourism and science?; and, lastly, does the evolution of the Antarctic Treaty System provide guidelines on environmental management in the Falklands?

290 **Argentine constitutional claim.**
P. J. Pepper. *Falkland Islands Newsletter*, no. 60 (September 1994), p. 11.

Pepper reports the adoption of a new clause in Argentina's constitution which became law on 24 August 1994. The clause states that 'the Argentine nation ratifies its legitimate and everlasting sovereignty over the Falkland, South Georgia and South Sandwich Islands and their corresponding island and maritime areas, as integral parts of the territory of the nation. The recovery of the said territories and the full exercise of sovereignty, respecting the way of life of the inhabitants, and in conformity with international law, constitutes a permanent and unrenounceable objective of the Argentine people'. Another clause asserted the right to self-determination but a rider made it clear that this did not apply to the Falklands.

291 **Falkland islanders offered $1.5m each.**
Helen Johnstone. *The Times*, no. 65099 (31 October 1994), p. 13.

Johnstone reports that President Menem of Argentina would be willing to pay $1.5 million to Falklanders for their support in bringing British rule to an end. This story is continued and extended in: Nick Nuttall's 'Islanders at odds over cash and wildlife' (*The Times*, 3 November, p. 11), Eve-Ann Prentice's 'Falklands alarmed by Britain's closer ties with Argentina' (p. 11), 'No price on sovereignty', a *Times* leader (p. 19), urging Menem not to risk diplomatic gains by electoral ploys and Alan Walter's 'Falklands' sovereignty for sale?' (*The Times*, 25 July 1995, p. 14). Prentice's 'Falklands retain deep hostility to Argentina' and Nuttall's 'Bewilderment over the "missing question" in opinion poll' (*The Times*, 4 November, p. 14) discuss the results of a wide-ranging MORI poll on the future of the Falklands of more than 200 islanders. Seventy-six per cent of those polled expressed no confidence in Argentina keeping its promises about the islands if there was some kind of compromise over the sovereignty issue. See also Michael Binyon's 'Britain rejects latest claim on Falklands' (*The Times*, 10 June 1995, p. 14) which reports President Menem floating the possibility of Argentina and Britain sharing administration and flying both flags over the Falklands.

Sovereignty

Whose flag over the Falklands?
See item no. 22.

Geography of the Falkland Islands.
See item no. 60.

Early charts of the Falkland Islands.
See item no. 85.

Maps on postage stamps as propaganda.
See item no. 96.

Una tierra Argentina: las Malvinas. (An Argentinian territory: The Falklands.)
See item no. 196.

Argentine's claim to the Falkland Islands.
See item no. 507.

The 1933 centenary issue of the Falkland Islands.
See item no. 514.

Argentina's philatelic annexation of the Falklands.
See item no. 519.

War In The South Atlantic 1982

292 **Falkland Islands – Anglo-Argentine talks in London – 'Symbolic' invasion of the Falklands by Argentine extremist group – Anti-British demonstrations in Argentina – 'Invaders' taken back by Argentine Government.**
Keesing's Contemporary Archives, vol. 15 (29 October-November 1966), p. 21693.

This is a remarkably detailed account of the curious episode of 28 September 1966, when a self-styled, eighteen-strong 'commando' group, members of an extreme right-wing nationalist organization, Movimiento Nueva Argentina, mounted *Operation Condor*. An internal Argentine flight to the Patagonian port of Rio Gallegos was hijacked and re-routed to Stanley Airport. There the 'commando' group formed an armed cordon round the aircraft, ran up the Argentine flag, and proclaimed that the Islanders were now Argentine citizens. The Argentine Government's response and the return of the 'commando' group to Argentina are also chronicled.

293 **Britain and the Falklands crisis: a documentary record.**
London: HMSO for the Central Office of Information, 1982. 95p.
2 maps.

Designed to show the British view of the diplomatic and military crisis, this official government account of events is supported by the texts of thirty-one relevant documents. These begin with the British-Argentine communiqué issued following talks in New York, on 26-27 February 1982, and end with extracts from the United Nations Charter.

294   Falkland Islands: invasions by Argentina – Background to crisis –
       Dispatch of British Task Force to South Atlantic – British and
       European Community sanctions against Argentina – Haig peace
       initiative – Military developments in South Atlantic – Repossession
       of South Georgia by British forces.
       Keesing's Contemporary Archives, vol. 28, no. 23 (11 June 1982),
       p. 31525-39. 2 maps.

Provides a straightforward factual narrative of events, encompassing the historical
background to the dispute. Also covered are the February 1980 round of negotiations
and the Argentine warning on its future attitude to the negotiations; the landing of
Argentine scrap merchants on South Georgia, British and Argentine naval movements,
and the meeting of the UN Security Council; the invasion of South Georgia and the
Falkland Islands; the military operations; the installation of a military governor;
further Security Council meetings and the adoption of Resolution 502; the immediate
United States and European Community response; emergency debates in the House of
Commons; the United Kingdom and European Community import ban on Argentine
goods; the enforcement of the British maritime exclusion zone around the Falklands;
Latin American attitudes; the United States peace initiative; the Argentine request for
a special meeting of the Organisation of American States; and the British repossession
of South Georgia.

295   Falkland Islands: British military campaign to recapture Islands –
       Argentinian surrender – Accompanying military developments –
       Political aftermath of military conflict.
       Keesing's Contemporary Archives, vol. 28, no. 38 (24 September
       1982), p. 31709-18. 2 maps.

Continues the narrative of events in the Falklands covered by previous issues,
including the failure of the United States peace initiative; the meeting of Organisation
of American States Foreign Ministers and their recognition of Argentine sovereignty;
the commencement of British attacks on military targets; the sinking of the *Belgrano*
and the destruction of *HMS Sheffield*; further diplomatic efforts; the extension of the
Exclusion Zone; British commando landings on Pebble Island; landings at Port San
Carlos; the recapture of Darwin and Goose Green; the British advance on Port
Stanley; Bluff Cove and Fitzroy landings; the Argentine surrender; the end to
hostilities and the return of prisoners of war; the political aftermath and the
establishment of a Board of Inquiry; and the Latin American resubmission of the
Falklands issue to the United Nations General Assembly.

296   Despatch by Admiral Sir John Fieldhouse GCB, GBE, Commander
       of the Task Force operations in the South Atlantic: April to June
       1982.
       Supplement to *London Gazette*, no. 49194 (13 December 1982),
       p. 16109-29.

This straightforward account is organized under headed paragraphs which cover
various aspects of the conflict: background; aim; command and control; military and
logistic considerations; Ascension Island; medical support; the Maritime Exclusion
Zone; repossession of South Georgia; the extension of the exclusion zone; the
intensification of operations; land forces; the selection of beachhead; landing;

consolidation; breakout; the advance on Port Stanley; the final battle; and recapture of South Thule. A list of all armed forces units engaged and of Ships Taken Up From Trade (STUFT) is appended.

297 **The Falklands War.**
   Paul Eddy, Magnus Linklater, Peter Gillman.   London: Deutsch,
   1982. 274p. map.

'We have gone back to the sources and contacts we established during the war and tried, through their diaries and recollections, to piece together the full story... In addition we have managed to talk to many who were unable, unwilling, or simply unavailable to discuss the affair while its outcome was still in doubt. The result is an account which traces decisions taken in the corridors of Whitehall right through to the marine advancing in darkness through an Argentinian minefield'. This remarkably thorough and expeditious account was produced by the *Sunday Times* Insight Team.

298 **Eyewitness Falklands: a personal account of the Falklands campaign.**
   Robert Fox.   London: Methuen, 1982. 337p. 3 maps.

As the BBC correspondent covering the land campaign, the author sailed on board the *Canberra*, accompanied the first troops ashore at San Carlos, was present at the Battle of Goose Green, yomped across the Island with the Royal Marines, and was in Port Stanley within minutes of the Argentine surrender. This eye-witness account constitutes 'a view from the field, of what was happening there and of what the men thought was happening both to them in the Falklands and in London, at the United Nations and in Argentina'.

299 **'I counted them all out and I counted them all back': the battle for the Falklands.**
   Brian Hanrahan, Robert Fox.   London: British Broadcasting
   Corporation, 1982. 139p. map.

Millions of listeners relied on Hanrahan and Fox's despatches on BBC radio and television for authentic detail of the Falklands campaign. These despatches are printed *verbatim* here, along with Fox's 'The rat-pack war' (*Listener*, 8 July 1982), 'Winter warriors' (15 July 1982), and 'Welcome home, and after' (22 July 1982). The title is taken from Hanrahan's celebrated remark when reporting the first attacks by the Royal Navy's Sea Harriers on 1 May 1982: 'I'm not allowed to say how many planes joined the raid, but I counted them all out, and I counted them all back'.

300 **The great white whale goes to war.**
   J. L. Muxworthy.   London: The Peninsular and Oriental Steam
   Navigation Company, 1982. 191p. 7 maps.

One of the strangest sights of the 1982 war was the improbable vision of *Canberra* and *Queen Elizabeth 2* anchored in Cumberland East Bay, South Georgia. This glossy pictorial publication tells 'the unique story of a cruise liner that went to war after three days preparation, and served her country with distinction in numerous roles in excess of 15 weeks. It is a record of all the activities engaged in during *Canberra*'s deployment when she became effectively known as the 'Great White Whale' serving as a sort of mother to the Falkland Islands Task Force' (Foreword). Besides

Canberra's log (1 April-11 July 1982), there are illustrated features on the Royal Marine band, 40 and 42 Commando, 3 Para, the gentlemen of the press on board, and a list of Royal Navy and Royal Marine personnel who served on board throughout the conflict. Steven Rabson's *P & O in the Falklands: a pictorial record 5 April-25 September 1982* (London: Peninsular and Oriental Steam Navigation Company, 1982. 86p.) outlines the war story of all of the P&O ships taken for the naval task force: *Canberra; Elk; Uganda; Anco Charger;* and *Strathewe*.

301 **75 days of conflict: from invasion to surrender: the Falkland Islands.**
Rear-Admiral Martin La Touche Wemyss.   London: Confex (Sales) Ltd., 1982. 32p. 2 maps.
Published for the Trustees of the South Atlantic Fund, Ministry of Defence, this pictorial brochure graphically portrays the course of the war from its beginning to end. It reproduces the typed surrender document signed by General Mario Menendez, Commander of the Argentine forces, and Major General Jeremy Moore.

302 **The long-distance war.**
Bob Elliot.   *Geographical Magazine*, vol. 55, no. 1 (January 1983), p. 35-37. map.
Major Robert Elliott, Information Officer at the Institute of Strategic Studies, outlines the factors that influenced the campaign in the South Atlantic: the logistics of the operation; the distance involved; the operational control of the Task Force; the need for air superiority; tactical dispositions; the terrain; and the effect of the winter conditions on the British and Argentine land forces.

303 **The Falklands crisis in the United Nations 31 March-14 June 1982.**
Anthony Parsons.   *International Affairs*, vol. 59, no. 2 (Spring 1983), p. 169-78.
Related here in detail are the relevant proceedings at the United Nations from the day the Argentine Permanent Representative informed the President of the Security Council that his government was contemplating bringing the question of South Georgia to its attention, to the final Argentine surrender in Port Stanley. Parsons, who was the United Kingdom Permanent Representative from 1979 to 1982, claims that Britain's reputation in the United Nations was greatly enhanced by its handling of the crisis. For the Argentine view of the diplomatic history of the war see Nicanor Costa Méndez: *Malvinas: ésta es la historia* (Falklands: this is the story) (Buenos Aires: Editorial Sudamericana, 1993. 335p.).

304 **Miscalculation in the South Atlantic: the origins of the Falklands War.**
Richard Ned Lebow.   *Journal of Strategic Studies*, vol. 6, no. 1 (March 1983), p. 5-35.
Written under the aegis of the Frankfurt Peace Research Institute, this well-documented paper (there are no less than seventy-two footnotes) constitutes an analytical study of the two serious and mutually reinforcing misjudgements that contributed in no small part to the outbreak of armed conflict: 'the belief in London that Argentina would not invade the Falkland Islands and the expectation in Buenos Aires that Britain would accommodate itself to a military takeover of the Islands'.

305   **The British army in the Falklands 1992.**
London: HMSO, 1983. 32p.

Distributed to all ranks in the army, this illustrated booklet narrates the exploits of all regimental or corps units in the Falklands campaign. The citations for the war's two Victoria Crosses are printed and there is a description and illustration of the South Atlantic Medal.

306   **Falklands War: the day by day record from invasion to victory.**
Edited by Peter Way.   London: Marshall Cavendish, 2 April-26 June 1983. 14 weekly parts.

Weapon profiles, unit and regimental histories, battle narratives, personal reminiscences, naval and mercantile marine ships, and weekly progress reports of the war, all feature in this colourfully illustrated publication which many libraries have preserved in a specially prepared binder from the publishers. Volume fourteen ends with a full roll of honour; a two-page map, 'The theatre of war' on a scale of 1:643,000; a list of units involved in Operation Corporate, which includes illustrations of ships' badges, and other military insignia; and a six-page index.

307   **Falkland Islands review: report of a committee of privy counsellors.**
Lord Franks, Chairman.   London: HMSO, 1983. 106p. map. (Cmnd. 8787).

On 6 July 1982 the Prime Minister announced in the House of Commons that the Government had decided to appoint a committee of Privy Councillors 'to review the way in which the responsibilities of government in relation to the Falkland Islands and their Dependencies were discharged in the period leading up to the Argentine invasion of the Falkland Islands on 2 April 1982, taking account of all such factors in previous years as are relevant; and to report'. The first three chapters of the Committee's printed report (*The Franks Report*) attempted an analysis of the background to the conflict, from 1965 to April 1982. This included United Nations involvement, an assessment of the Argentine threat, uneasy diplomatic relations, government ministers' visits to Argentina and the Falklands, and military contingency plans. The fourth chapter presented the Committee's conclusions via a series of questions: How did the dispute become critical?; How did the present Government handle the dispute?; and Could the present Government have prevented the invasion of 2 April 1982? 'Taking account . . . of all the evidence we have received, we conclude that we would not be justified in attaching any criticism or blame to the present government for the Argentine Junta's decision to commit its act of unprovoked aggression'. For a considered opinion on the *Report*, see William Wallace's 'How frank was Frank?', *International Affairs*, vol. 59, no. 3, (Summer 1983), p. 453-58.

308   **Air war South Atlantic.**
Jeffrey Ethell, Alfred Price.   London: Sidgwick & Jackson, 1983. 260p. 6 maps.

Between them, the two authors – Ethell in Argentina and Price in Britain – interviewed over a hundred Argentine and British fliers to produce a detailed study of the air war including the movements of the aircraft carrier *25 de Mayo*, immediately prior to the sinking of the *Belgrano*, the successful and unsuccessful Exocet missile attacks by the Argentine Super Étendards, and the story of the RAF Vulcan which landed in Brazil. A series of appendices provides factual information on the combat units, losses, and ships damaged or sunk on both sides. Another brief but still valuable summary of RAF operations is 'Corporate success', prepared by the Air Historical Branch in conjunction with the Directorate of Public Relations of the RAF and printed in *Royal Air Force Yearbook 1983* (p. 15-17, 19-21, 23, 25). A separate feature, 'The RAF's year 1982' consists of an illustrated chronology of significant events (p. 56-58).

309 2 Para Falklands.
John Frost.   London: Buchan & Enright, 1983. 192p. 6 maps.

Major-General Frost was at first Adjutant, and then Commanding Officer of the 2nd Battalion of the Parachute Regiment, during the Second World War, and subsequently in Palestine. Here, he follows the Battalion's Falklands' War, from Aldershot to Stanley, via the heavy fighting at San Carlos, Goose Green, Bluff Cove, and Wireless Ridge.

310 Harrier: ski-jump to victory.
Edited by John Godden.   Oxford: Brassey's Defence Publishers, 1983. 132p.

'Without the Sea Harrier', remarked Admiral Sir Henry Leach, First Sea Lord, and Chief of Naval Staff, 'there could have been no Task Force'. Combining the personal narratives of operational air-crew with specialist chapters on the design history of Vertical/Short Take Off and Landing (V/STOL) aircraft, this authoritative account drives home the fact that no conventional fixed-wing aircraft could possibly have operated in the heavy seas of the South Atlantic with adequate safety. J. D. R. Rawlings' 'RAF Harriers in the Falklands', *Air Pictorial*, vol. 44, no. 11 (November 1982), p. 416-17 is also of value.

311 The battle for the Falklands.
Max Hastings, Simon Jenkins.   London: Michael Joseph, 1983. 390p. 7 maps. bibliog.

Concerned neither with the sovereignty issue, nor with the problems of the islanders, this narrative is 'primarily an account of British political decision-making and of naval and military operations' (Foreword). Hastings, the war correspondent for the *Evening Standard* and *Daily Express*, who sailed with the Task Force and entered Stanley ahead of the British vanguard, reports the war from the British side, whilst Jenkins, the then political editor of *The Economist*, traces political and diplomatic events in London, Washington, and Buenos Aires. A chronology of military and political events between 2 April and 14 June 1982, a military equipment glossary, the Task Force and British land forces orders of battle, and lists of the principal combat aircraft engaged in the South Atlantic are appended.

312 HMS Endurance 1981-82 deployment: a season of conflict.
Edited by Andrew Lockett, Neil Munro, David Wells.   Gosport, England: Andrew Lockett, 1983. 149p. 40 plates. 3 maps.

In the form of a tribute to *Endurance*, to her commanding officer, officers and crew, a number of luminaries and scientific workers record their experiences of voyages in southern seas. In 1981-82 *Endurance* totalled 41,466 miles in 311 days at sea, including a crucial role in the recapture of South Georgia. A list of the ship's company and a detailed itinerary complete an affectionate chronicle.

313   Falklands commando.

Hugh McManners.   London: William Kimber, 1984. 235p.

Working alongside the SAS and Special Boat Squadron, Captain McManners of the Royal Artillery, the first combatant soldier to land on the Falklands, led five men on a hazardous undercover mission to direct the naval bombardment of Argentine positions throughout the land campaign. He describes that mission in this account.

314   Operation Corporate: the Falklands War, 1982.

Martin Middlebrook.   London: Viking, 1985. 430p. 13 maps. bibliog.

Operation Corporate was the code-name given to the British military actions to recover the Falkland Islands and South Georgia. Based on 200 interviews, including a visit to the Islands to hear first-hand accounts from the Islanders, and on thorough documentary research, this is one of the more readable and comprehensive accounts of the war. It was reissued as a Penguin paperback under the title *Task Force* in 1987.

315   74 days: an Islander's diary of the Falklands occupation.

John Smith.   London: Century Publishing, 1984. 255p. map.

Graphic, but curiously matter-of-fact, descriptions of seeing foreign troops in the streets, encountering scared and hungry Argentine soldiers, living in a hastily constructed bunker underneath the porch floor for protection against British bombing and shelling, and listening to BBC broadcasts from London to find out what was happening around Stanley, are features of Smith's diary, which runs from 1 April to 15 June 1982. He includes extracts from the *Argentine Gazette*, the journal distributed by the Argentine High Command to its forces on the Islands to boost their morale and urge them to fulfil their patriotic duties.

316   Merchant ships at war: the Falklands experience.

Roger Villar.   London: Conway Maritime Press and Lloyd's of London Press, 1984. 192p.

The full story of the merchant ships taken up from trade – inevitably and irresistibly known as STUFT – which played such an important part in the Falklands Task Force, is told in this comprehensive illustrated record. Merchant ships were not only used as troop transports but also as assault ships, minesweepers, dispatch vessels, fleet and support tankers, aircraft ferries, ammunition and storeships, and repair ships. Further details of STUFT can be found in: Russell Plummer's 'Ferries to the Falklands', *Ships Monthly*, vol. 17, no. 7 (July 1982), p. 28-29, 'Heroines of the South Atlantic', no. 8 (August 1982), p. 22-23, and 'Merchant ships return from active service in the South Atlantic', no. 9 (September 1982), p. 22; Chris Clarke's 'Ferry to the Falklands', no. 10 (October 1982), p. 12-14; and in Plummer's 'Norland returns from Falklands Task Force service', vol. 18, no. 4 (April 1983), and 'Shadow Fleet for the Task Force', *Sea Breezes*, vol. 56, no. 438 (June 1982), p. 370-77.

317 **Above all, courage: first hand accounts from the Falklands front line.**
Max Arthur. London: Sidgwick & Jackson, 1985. 463p. map.

These thirty interviews, which were selected from 250 carried out with service men and women of all ranks, relate eye-witness accounts of the principal engagements of the war: the invasion of the Falkland Islands; the bomb attack on *HMS Ardent*; sea, air, and ground support; the sinking of *Sir Galahad*; the battle of Darwin and Goose Green; the attacks on Mt. Longdon and Mt. Harriet; the assaults on Two Sisters and Tumbledown Mountain; and the command at sea. A glossary of service terms and equipment helps the uninitiated.

318 **Bibliography on the 1982 Falklands War.**
Marilyn B. Yokota. Santa Monica, California: Rand Corporation, 1985. 19p.

About 260 unannotated references to books and articles are entered in this bibliography which is perhaps of most use in locating material in specialist United States defence journals.

319 **Falklands the air war.**
Rodney A. Burden, et al. London: Arms & Armour Press, 1986. 480p. maps on endpapers.

Compiled by the British Aviation Research Group, this encyclopaedic work is organized in the form of a step-by-step reconstruction of all movements, deployments, and actions by British and Argentine aircraft and shipping during the Falklands conflict. Aircraft types engaged are listed under the military arm (Commando Aviación Naval y Prefectura; Commando de Aviación del Ejército; Fuerza Aerea Argentina; Royal Navy Fleet Air Arm; Army Air Corps and Royal Marines; and Royal Air Force) and 'presented in a style which provides a balanced summary of the activities of every flying unit and which records their achievements against a common measure' (Introduction). A further section outlines aviation in the islands and lists aircraft war losses. There is a glossary of abbreviations and acronyms.

320 **March to the South Atlantic: 42 Commando, Royal Marines, in the Falklands War.**
Nick Vaux. London: Buchan & Enright, 1986. 261p. 5 maps.

'To the South Atlantic – Quick March' was Nick Vaux's final order to 42 Commando when it paraded at Bickleigh Barracks in Devon in the Spring of 1982. This first-hand narrative by a serving Commanding Officer vividly relates the fighting exploits of 42 Commando on South Georgia, in the defence of Mount Challenger ridge, and its daring night attack on Mount Harriet. A series of appendices lists 42 Commando's casualties in the Falklands campaign and its honours, awards and unit citation. The work was also published in the United States as *Take that hill! Royal Marines in the Falklands War* (McLean, Virginia: Brassey's US, 1986).

321   **The Royal Navy and the Falklands War.**
       David Brown.   London: Leo Cooper, 1987. 384p. 5 maps. bibliog.
This splendidly illustrated volume tells in detail the full story of how the Naval Task
Force was assembled. It describes how the merchant ships, varying in size from the
mighty *Canberra* and *Queen Elizabeth II* to more humble cargo carriers, were 'Taken
Up From Trade', at miraculously short notice and how thousands of tons of stores and
equipment needed by the invasion force were carried 7,000 miles to the battlezone.
The way the Navy participated in and guarded the landings in San Carlos Bay, and the
terrible price it paid is also discussed. Full lists of Royal Navy ships, Royal Fleet
Auxiliaries, merchant ships, and also of Argentine warships and auxiliaries, are
appended. In addition, a very useful select list of American, Argentine, British and
Spanish defence journals appears in the bibliography. David Brown was formerly
Head of the Naval Historical Branch at the Ministry of Defence.

322   **The fight for the 'Malvinas': the Argentine forces in the Falklands
       War.**
       Martin Middlebrook.   London: Viking, 1989. 321p. 12 maps. bibliog.
Based on interviews with Argentine servicemen and senior officers in all three
services, this was the first full-length English-language account of operations from the
Argentine side. Middlebrook eschews all political judgements and presents a neutral
approach to the sovereignty issue.

323   **The history of the South Atlantic conflict: the war for the
       Malvinas.**
       Reubén O. Moro.   New York: Praeger, 1989. 360p. 8 maps. bibliog.
Translated by Michael Valeur from the original Spanish title, *La guerra inaudita*, this
account of the war by an Argentine Air Force Officer attempts to blend military and
diplomatic history into a single narrative. It succeeds well enough but there are
inevitable discrepancies with most English-language accounts. A strong resentment at
United States support for Britain is evident.

324   **The Falklands military machine.**
       Derek Oakley.   Tunbridge Wells, England: Spellmount, 1989. 192p.
       10 maps. bibliog.
Oakley presents a brief but informed study of the effect of the volatile nature of post-
1945 Argentine politics on diplomatic relations with Britain over the Falklands
sovereignty issue in this lucid illustrated history of the campaign. He follows this with
well-organized separate sections on British naval, air and land forces, the supporting
arms, strategy and tactics, and the course of the war. There are also lists of major
honours and awards, and casualties, and a chronology of events. Captain Oakley
served in the Royal Marines for over forty years, the last eighteen as editor of the
regimental journal *Globe & Laurel*.

325 **Signals of war: the Falklands conflict of 1982.**
Lawrence Freedman, Virginia Gamba-Stonehouse. London: Faber,
1990. 476p. 6 maps. bibliog.

A collaboration by two leading military historians – one Argentine, one British – this comprehensive and bilateral account is undoubtedly one of the most authoritative studies of the events leading up to the Argentine occupation, the course of the war, and the diplomatic attempts to bring the fighting to an end. The authors agreed not to arrive at a definitive conclusion as to the rightful ownership of the Islands but did not restrain themselves from confronting 'the many controversial questions of historical interpretation' which surround this intractable international problem.

326 **Goose Green: a battle is fought to be won.**
Mark Adkin. London: Leo Cooper, 1992. 305p. 30 maps. bibliog.

The Second Battalion Parachute Regiment's struggle for the tiny settlements of Darwin and Goose Green – the longest land battle of the war – is told in all its graphic detail in this account. Appendices provide the British and Argentine orders of battle, the artillery support available, the British surrender ultimatum, the Regiment's roll of honour, and its honours and awards.

327 **Sea Harrier over the Falklands: a maverick at war.**
N. D. Ward. London: Leo Cooper, 1992. 299p. map.

As Commanding Officer of 801 Naval Air Squadron on *HMS Invincible* during the South Atlantic War, the author acted as principal Sea Harrier adviser on tactics and the progress of the air war. He took part in sixty sorties and claimed three Argentine aircraft in air-to-air kills. This first-hand account of the Royal Navy's air war also takes time to examine inter-service rivalry, bureaucratic interference, and the sometimes ambivalent attitudes towards the correct use of air-power by senior commanders. George Baldwin's 'Sea Harrier operations in the Falklands', *Air Pictorial*, vol. 44, no. 12 (December 1982), p. 472-78 is an authoritative overview.

328 **The Falklands War: background, conflict, aftermath: an annotated bibliography.**
Andrew Orgill. London: Mansell, 1993. 132p.

A sound and well-organized bibliographical essay on the literature of the war introduces this bibliography of 822 books, document collections, and journal articles, published up to December 1991. The bibliography is arranged in five broad sub-divided subject areas: bibliographies; the sovereignty dispute; the 1982 crisis; the war; and the aftermath. Most refer to English- and Spanish-language publications although French, German, Russian, Italian and Portuguese material is also included. It is especially useful for articles which appeared in British and Argentine armed forces journals and other military periodicals.

329 **The Falklands war.**
Denys Blakeway. London: Sidgwick & Jackson in association with
Channel Four Television Company, 1992. 168p. 3 maps. bibliog.

Published to accompany a major Channel Four television series, this profusely illustrated account has the benefit of ten years' hindsight over the many similar publications which poured from the press immediately after the war. Blakeway takes full advantage of the readiness of participants in the conflict, politicians, senior military officers, and troops on the ground, to speak freely of their experiences.

330 The Falkland/Malvinas campaign: a bibliography.

Eugene L. Rasor.   Westport, Connecticut: Greenwood Press, 1992.
196p. (Bibliographies of Battles and Leaders, no. 6).

The objective of this bibliography is 'to incorporate all published books, monographs, oral histories, official histories and other governmental publications, dissertations, bibliographies, pertinent journal and periodical articles, anthologies, conference papers etc'. It is divided into two main parts: A narrative and historiographical survey (consisting of a number of mini-bibliographical essays to make the campaign more understandable, ending with a chronology of events 1494-1982, and a glossary of important names); and an annotated bibliography of 554 entries arranged A-Z by author.

331 One hundred days: the memoirs of the Falklands Battle Group Commander.

Admiral Sandy Woodward with Patrick Robinson.   London: Harper
Collins, 1992. 360p. 2 maps.

'My story swings inevitably through the sagas of the weather, the sea conditions and sudden, intense, short-lived action'. Based on his diary, and personal correspondence, these memoirs of the senior British commander of the Falklands operation dramatically underline how narrow the margin between victory and defeat was. Margaret Thatcher contributes a foreword.

332 Reasons in writing: a Commando's view of the Falklands War.

Ewen Southby-Tailyour.   London: Leo Cooper, 1993. 383p. 7 maps.
bibliog.

The author commanded the Royal Marine detachment on the Islands in 1977-79 during which time he made an exhaustive study of the coastline, including a detailed survey of the beaches. He later commanded all the major amphibious landings in the Falklands War. Of particular value is his account of garrison life before Fortress Falklands came into existence.

333 Falkland Islands: Madrid talks – Formal ending of hostilities.

Keesing's Record Of World Events, vol. 35, no. 10 (October 1989),
p. 36973.

Reports on the three days of talks, from October 17 to October 19 1989, between the United Kingdom's permanent representative at the United Nations, and the special envoy of the President of Argentina, after which both countries declared the formal ending of hostilities existing since the Falklands War of 1982. The question of sovereignty was left aside. 'Argentina-UK restoration of diplomatic relations', *Keesing's*, vol. 36, no. 2 (February 1990), p. 37245, relates how further talks in Madrid, on 14-15 February 1990, ended in an agreement to restore full diplomatic relations. See also 'Main points from the Joint Statement by the British and Argentine delegations at Madrid, 19 October 1989', *Falkland Islands Newsletter*, no. 41 (December 1989), p. 8, and 'Main points from the Joint Statement by the British and

Argentine delegations at Madrid, 15 February 1990', *Falkland Islands Newsletter*, no. 42 (March 1990), p. 8-9.

The Falklands Task Force: a postal history.
See item no. 517.

The Falklands War: postal history and stamps of the Argentine occupation.
See item no. 520.

Forces postal history of the Falklands & the Task Force.
See item no. 521.

War in the Falklands.
See item no. 522.

The Posties went to war.
See item no. 530.

Reconstruction and Rehabilitation

334 **Patching up the Falklands.**
John Madson. *New Civil Engineer*, no. 505 (19/26 August 1982),
p. 22-24, 27-29, 34-35.

Written by the first technical journalist to visit the Islands after the war, this composite feature includes 'Engineering the Islands' recovery' (warning that if the Shackleton recommendations are unadventurous, or if the British Government fails to take positive action to build up the Islands' infrastructure then the Falklands will be a serious embarrassment within ten years); 'Prospects for the future' (an interview with the Civil Commissioner who sets down his expectations and fears); 'Islanders press for action' (demanding more action from the Civil Commissioner); 'Stanley airstrip' (the stopgap plan to repair the airport and extend the runway); 'Road plans wrecked by mines' (recent roadbuilding); and 'The battle for water' (restoring utilities, a new filtration plant, new road network high on priority list, and the overloaded sewerage and drainage system).

335 **Falkland Islands: passing on a lifestyle.**
Ian Strange. *Geographical Magazine*, vol. 55, no. 1 (January 1983),
p. 30-35. map.

Disappointment and regret rather than triumph is evident in Strange's thoughts on the invasion, island life and relations with Argentina. He says: 'Even with the wide gap that separated the two cultures, my own feelings were that one day a harmonious link would probably be found and that the dispute over sovereignty might yet be resolved. The signs had been there for an amicable relationship: trade, communications, and exchanges between the two countries had started to demonstrate that the average person, from both nations, wanted nothing but a friendly co-existence'. Strange underlines the effect on the Islanders' way of life of both the Argentine invasion and the British reoccupation, stressing that the previous growth of trade, communications, and goodwill, had been destroyed in a few hours by rash military and political decisions in Buenos Aires.

336 **Falklands: PWD struggles with day to day repairs.**
John Brodrick. *New Civil Engineer*, no. 531 (10 March 1983),
p. 34-35.

The Public Works Department was severely stretched in the restoration of essential municipal services in Stanley in the immediate aftermath of the war. Initial assistance from the Royal Engineers lapsed when they had to commit all their resources to vital defence projects. John Brodrick was the senior Falkland Islands government officer responsible for the restoration of the public utilities.

337 **Stanley Airport – airfield damage repair.**
D. I. Reid. *Royal Engineers Journal*, vol. 97, no. 1 (March 1983),
p. 6-14.

Major Reid, who was responsible for the repair and development of Stanley Airport, outlines both the war damage to the airfield, and the repairs effected by the Royal Engineers in the immediate post-war period. 'Within ten days of the cessation of hostilities and three days of the last Prisoner of War leaving the airfield, a C130 Hercules aircraft landed'.

338 **The Falklands 1982 – July to December – the beginning of rehabilitation.**
Royal Engineers Journal, vol. 97, no. 2 (June 1983), p. 73-114 and
Army Quarterly & Defence Journal, vol. 113, no. 3 (July 1983),
p. 266-88.

Five expert papers relate the progress made by the Royal Engineers who were given the responsibility of securing the Islands' defences and rehabilitating the working life of the Islanders. This involved clearing the minefields, restoring public utilities, securing fuel supplies, and repairing essential roads, jetties, and moorings, in the initial two months after the end of the war. The papers include 'The background' (Col. D. Brownson); 'The airfield' (Lieut.-Col. P. R. Ievers); 'Accommodation' (Lieut.-Col. J. W. R. Mizen); 'Battle area clearance' (Lieut.-Col. A. Howgate); and 'Human behaviour: the key to leadership' (Brig. H. F. Everard). Lieut.-Col. F. A. F. Daniell and Major W. B. Cobb's '37 Engineer Regiment', *Royal Engineers Journal*, vol. 99, no. 3 (September 1985), p. 141-52, continues the story to March 1985.

339 **The price of Fortress Falklands: sooner or later the Treasury will slam the till shut.**
Christopher Wain. *Listener* (2 February 1984), p. 2-4.

Christopher Wain, the BBC Defence Correspondent, accompanied the then Defence Minister, Michael Heseltine, on a visit to the Falklands. He reports on the changes visible since the Argentine surrender, and expresses the Islanders' continuing worries and fears, especially their anxiety that Britain should establish a 200-mile fishing zone around the Islands. For his part Wain doubts whether Argentina would recognize such a zone and feels the country might be prepared to issue licences of its own. He also examines the relations between the military garrison and the Islanders and the possible effect of British construction workers on the Islands' way of life.

340   **The Falklands now.**
Anthony Holden. *Sunday Express Magazine* (29 February 1984),
p. 14-17, 20, 22-29, 31.

Reporting on the mixed feelings among the 'kelpers', now easily outnumbered by the
military garrison, advisers of all descriptions, and by entrepreneurs, Holden presents a
grim and not very encouraging picture of the Falklands two years after the Argentine
occupation came to an abrupt end. The inequality of wealth, the shabbiness of poverty,
the ubiquitous Argentine minefields, and harassment by 'drunken squaddies', are some
of the troubles commented on.

341   **Pipelines in the Falklands and on Ascension Island.**
R. Meston, C. J. Penn.   *Pipes and Pipelines International*, vol. 29
(November-December 1984), p. 16-26.

The main interest of this paper contributed by two serving officers lies in its outline of
the work of the Corps of Royal Engineers in the two years following the Argentine
surrender in June 1982. Top priority was given to an improved water supply system at
Stanley to meet the increased demands of the civil and military population, whilst
other work included the construction of garrison accommodation at Navy Point and
Lookout Camp; a military logistical complex, incorporating a covered storage area; an
electrical engineering workshop; improved postal, provost, and welfare facilities; a
floating-port system for Stanley Harbour; and runway repairs and a fuel installation
system at Stanley airport.

342   **The Falklands: the aftermath.**
London: Marshall Cavendish, 1984. 144p. 2 maps.

Concerned with events in the Falklands during the first twelve months after the 1982
war, and related matters, this splendidly illustrated book looks at the military and
naval lessons to be drawn from the war. It considers the new airbridge to the Islands,
and the building of a strategic air base on East Falkland and discusses the political
decisions made, life after the war (such as clearing the mines and other battle
clearance by the Royal Engineers, garrisoning the Islands, new civil and military
housing, and economic prospects), and post-war Argentina. A final section identifies
individual Islanders (the owner of *Penguin News*, farmers, the manager of the
philatelic bureau, and the fish-and-chip van owner) and listens to their memories of
the war and what effect it had on their future.

343   **The Falkland Islands: trouble looms in the clear air of the South
Atlantic.**
Christopher Wain.   *Listener*, vol. 113, no. 2910 (23 May 1985), p. 2-4.

Undoubtedly the most urgent of the points raised in this wide-ranging article is the
desperate need for more settlers, craftsmen-like builders, plumbers, carpenters, and
other self-reliant types, but not the 'after-shave brigade in sandals and beards', do-
gooders and advisers. Other topics touched upon include the mixed feelings of the
Islanders regarding the airport, a symbol of the British Government's commitment to
defend the Islands, and a big stride for the tourist industry, and of their feeling that
forthcoming changes would not always be for the better.

344 **South Atlantic opportunities.**
Sir John Biggs-Davison. *Contemporary Review*, vol. 248, no. 1442 (March 1986), p. 124-26.

In this diffuse overview the author considers the improbability of a further Argentine attack, the Falkland Islands Development Corporation, the prospects for tourism, and the fishing industry. He ends with a plea for reconciliation and co-operation, and for a South Atlantic Treaty Organization, a southern hemisphere security system with its headquarters and main base on the Falklands.

345 **The Falkland Islands: life after the war.**
Bryan Hodgson. *National Geographic*, vol. 173, no. 3 (March 1988), p. 390-411.

'I came to the islands not to study war, but because they had suddenly become the center of one of the world's richest fisheries. Britain had just declared a 150-nautical-mile-radius conservation zone around these islands where hundreds of vessels from Asia and Europe were catching squid worth 500 million dollars a year', states Hodgson in this article. However, he doesn't concentrate all his attention on the Falkland fisheries and the Falkland Islands Fisheries Protection Service; he also visits farms and settlements, woollen mills, and trout fisheries all over the Islands, travelling mainly on Falkland Island Government Air Service flights. A portfolio of colour photographs of Falkland Islands wildlife follows on pages 412-22.

346 **The Falklands aftermath: picking up the pieces.**
Edward Fursdon. London: Leo Cooper, 1988. 205p. 7 maps.

Although Major-General Fursdon was Defence and Military Correspondent of the *Daily Telegraph* between 1980 and 1986, this book is not another study of the Falklands campaign. Rather, it is an examination of the problems confronting the British Armed Forces once the fighting had stopped, and a description of the effect of the war on the Islands' inhabitants, livestock, and wildlife. An epilogue traces the progress and developments that have been made since the cessation of hostilities, notably the construction of a new international airfield, linking Britain and the Falklands directly, with a refuelling stop at Ascension Island, at a cost of over £350 million, and the inaugural meeting of the Falkland Islands Development Corporation in July 1984.

347 **Falkland Islands.**
Clive Nichols. *Traveller*, vol. 20, no. 2 (Summer 1990), p. 40-44.

Wildlife, the fishing industry, the scars of war, the new Mt. Pleasant airport, agriculture, and the Islanders' 'commitment and determination to make the islands an economic and political force with some power over its own destiny', are all featured in this illustrated article.

Biographies and Autobiographies

348 Who's who: an annual biographical dictionary.

London: A & C Black, 1849- . annual.

Career outlines of surviving Governors of the Falkland Islands, and of senior officers of the armed forces, who held positions of command in the South Atlantic War of 1982, are to be found in this authoritative dictionary of contemporary biography. Entries for deceased Governors have been transferred to the decennial volumes of *Who was who*. Immediate access to the appropriate volume is provided by *Who was who: a cumulated index 1897-1990* (1991).

349 The story of Commander Allen Gardiner, R. N. with sketches of missionary work in South America.

John W. Marsh, Waite H. Stirling. London: Nisbet, 1857. 172p. folded map.

Intertwined here with a short biography of Allen Gardiner is the story of the missionary schooner named after him, the transfer of Fuegian Indians to the Patagonian Missionary Society's school on Keppel Island, and the arrival there of the Reverend G. Pakenham Despard and his family.

350 The dictionary of national biography.

Oxford: Oxford University Press, 1917- .

Founded in 1882 'to supply full, accurate, and concise biographies of all noteworthy inhabitants of the British Isles and the Colonies (exclusive of living persons) from the earliest historical period to the present time', this massive collective biography is of surprisingly limited use for our present purposes. It is manifest that most Governors and Commanders in Chief of the Falkland Islands were not considered noteworthy enough for inclusion. However, there are interesting entries for: George Farmer (1732-79), Captain of *HM Sloop Swift* who surrendered Port Egmont to the Spaniards in March 1770 (vol. 6, p. 1074-75); John McBride (died 1800), Captain of *HMS Jason*, who sailed to the Falklands to establish the settlement and garrison at Port Egmont in 1766 (vol. 12, p. 427-28); George Rennie (1802-60), second Governor and

Commander in Chief (1848-55) (vol. 13, p. 903-04); Robert Fitzroy (1805-65), Commander of *HMS Beagle* (vol. 7, p. 207-09); Sir Woodvine Parish (1796-1882), the British Chargé d'Affaires in Buenos Aires in 1833 who 'brought the importance of the Falkland Islands under the notice of his majesty's government, and in consequence was instructed to lay claim to them as a British possession' (vol. 15, p. 213-14); Richard Clement Moody (1813-87), the first Governor of the Colony (1842-48) (vol. 13, p. 779-80); Sir Bartholomew James Sullivan (1810-90) who, as a young Lieutenant, surveyed Stanley Harbour in 1838 and continued his survey of the Islands in *HM Brig Philomel* in 1842 (vol. 19, p. 156-57); and Sir Frederick Charles Doveton-Sturdee (1859-1925), the victorious Admiral of the British battle-cruiser squadron at the Battle of the Falklands in 1914 (*DNB 1922-1930*, p. 820-21).

351 **The bird man: an autobiography.**
Ian Strange. London: Gordon & Cremonesi, 1976. 182p. maps on endpapers.

The author first settled in the Falklands in 1959, since when books and articles about the Islands have flowed from his pen. A renowned painter and photographer, he has tirelessly involved himself in the recording, protection, and conservation of Falkland wildlife. Here he skilfully interweaves his personal and professional life.

352 **My Falkland days.**
Rex Hunt. Newton Abbot, England: David & Charles, 1992. 488p. map.

Although the dispute with Argentina naturally dominates this autobiography it does not wholly preoccupy it. The Islands' former Governor is obviously a gregarious person and he lost little time on his arrival in getting out and about, visiting remote sheepfarms on barely inhabited islands, South Georgia on board the *Endurance*, and elsewhere. His own role in the conflict, his return to the Falklands after the war was over, and the effect of the war on the day-to-day life of the islånders, is cogently and sensibly narrated.

Falkland Islands cartographers.
See item no. 88.

Bishop Stirling of the Falklands.
See item no. 355.

Colonel George Abbas Kooli D'Arcy.
See item no. 395.

Profile William Lamond Allardyce.
See item no. 491.

Religion

353 **Patagonian Missionary Society – Keppel Island 1855-1911.**
Sydney Miller. *Falkland Islands Journal*, no. 9 (1975), p. 8-13.
It was the Reverend George Pakenham Despard who formed the Patagonian
Missionary Society's settlement on Keppel Island. His ambition was for it to be 'a
durable centre of operations, a place of rendez-vous for the Missionaries, a safe depot
for stores, a model community for the natives, and produce a considerable revenue'.
All of these objectives were to some degree realized. J. H. McAdam's 'The great fire
on Keppel Island 1855' *Falkland Islands Journal*, no. 23 (1989), p. 23-28, presents a
vivid account of the grass fire which rapidly got out of control on the very first day of
the settlement.

354 **A brief account of the Falkland Islands and Tierra del Fuego with
an appeal for funds on behalf of Christ-Church Stanley.**
Bishop Stirling. Buenos Aires: Kidd, 1891. 28p.
This item has essentially been included for its curiosity value although it does record
the early strivings for a new church in Stanley and the consequent need for funds due
to high rates of wages, heavy freight charges, and the cost of skilled labour from
England. The account includes details of liberalities from the Falkland Islands
Company (£1,000), from the Society for the Propagation of Christian Knowledge
(£800), and from Queen Victoria (£30), and ends with a list of stalls and their
presiding ladies at a fund-raising bazaar in Buenos Aires. It was reprinted in 1969 in
connection with the centenary celebrations of Bishop Stirling's consecration in
Westminster Abbey on 21 December 1869 (Stanley: Christ Church Cathedral, 1969.
20p.).

355   **Bishop Stirling of the Falklands: the adventurous life of a soldier of the Cross whose humility hid the daring spirit of a hero & an inflexible will to face great risks.**
Frederick C. Macdonald.   London: Seeley Service, 1929. 255p. map.
This biography of Waite Hockin Stirling (1829-1923), the first Bishop of the Falklands, devotes almost 100 pages to his episcopate. The constitution of the English Episcopal Church in the Falkland Islands is printed in full and there is a detailed account of the construction of Christ Church Cathedral. P. J. Millam's *Centenary of the consecration of Waite Hockin Stirling as the first Bishop of the Falkland Islands* (Stanley: Government Printing Office, 1969. 32p.) is a souvenir booklet.

356   **Faith under fire.**
Harry Bagnall, David Porter.   Basingstoke, England: Marshalls, 1983. 159p.
A personal record of the Anglican chaplain to the Falklands who chose to remain throughout the Argentine occupation.

357   **Keppel Island: its current state and importance in the early history of the Falkland Islands.**
Jim McAdam.   *Falkland Islands Foundation Newsletter*, no. 8 (January 1989), p. 2-6. map. bibliog.
In 1855 the Patagonian Missionary Society established a mission station on Pebble Island to serve as a training centre to educate the Patagonian Indians in Tierra del Fuego. Here McAdam narrates the history of the Society's origins and describes its objectives, the establishment of the mission station and the serious fire on the day of the first landing on the Island. He also discusses the mission's progress and the prominent figures associated with the mission, including the Reverend Waite Stirling, who was destined to become the first Bishop of the Falklands as well as the final years of the station, its subsequent years as a farm, and the current need for urgent restoration. Peter J. Millam's 'The South American Missionary Society celebrates 150 years', *Falkland Islands Newsletter*, no. 36 (September 1988), p. 10-11, covers some of the same ground.

358   **Christ Church Cathedral The Falkland Islands: its life and times 1892 to 1992.**
Gervase Murphy.   Stanley: Lance Bidwell on behalf of Christ Church Cathedral Council, 1991. 32p.
Published to mark the Cathedral's centenary, this illustrated booklet contrives to cram in an extraordinary amount of information concerning the history of Christian worship in the Falklands from the 1840s onwards: the Patagonian Missionary Society's station on Keppel Island; the previous Holy Trinity church on the cathedral site; the campaign for a new church after it was demolished by a peat slide; the inception of the Bishopric of the Falklands; the repairs and restoration in the 1980s; and the prominent figures involved. There is a complete chronological list of Bishops, Colonial Chaplains, Deans, Senior Chaplains, and Rectors of the Cathedral.

359 **To the uttermost part of the world.**
Falkland Islands Newsletter, no. 48 (August 1991), p. 14-15.

Provides an outline sketch of the Anglican Bishopric and Diocese of the Falkland Islands from its origins in the work of the Patagonian Missionary Society (renamed the South American Missionary Society in 1868). Beginning with a description of the consecration of the Reverend W. H. Stirling as the first Bishop of the Falkland Islands on 21 December 1869, in Westminster Abbey, when all the consular chaplaincies in South America were placed under his jurisdiction, this article then recounts the history of Holy Trinity Church (originally a corn exchange), its destruction by fire in 1886, and the building of Christ Church Cathedral on the same site, restored at a cost of £600,000 in 1992 as part of its centenary celebrations.

360 **Argentina and the Falklands (Malvinas): the Irish connection.**
Dermot Keogh. In: *The land that England lost: Argentina and Britain, a special relationship.* Edited by Alistair Hennessy, John King. London: British Academic Press, 1992, p. 123-41.

Relates the nineteenth-century concern for the spiritual well-being of the Irish Roman Catholic community on the Islands.

361 **A short history of the Catholic Church.**
Monsignor Spraggon. *Falkland Islands Journal*, no. 10 (1976), p. 34-38.

Source material for the history of the Catholic Church in the Falklands is both sketchy and scarce but it is known that land was granted in letters patent under the seal of Queen Victoria in 1858 for a church building. Great changes occurred in the status of the church in 1952 when a Papal Bull created an Apostolic Prefecture of the Falkland Islands. 'The Falkland Islands is said to be the largest Prefecture Apostolic in the Catholic Church with the least number of people'.

362 **The Catholic Church on the Falkland Islands.**
Monsignor A. Agreiter. *Falkland Islands Journal*, vol. 6, no. 1 (1992), p. 6-9. bibliog.

Principally an organizational history, this short survey covers the French period (1764-67); the Spanish period (1767-1810); the years of confusion (1810-33); the British possession (1833); the Irish chaplains (1856-87); the Salesian Fathers (1888-1952); and the Mill Hill Missionaries (1952-   ). It was also printed in *Falkland Islands Newsletter*, no. 51 (May 1992), p. 8-9, and no. 52 (August 1992), p. 8-9. bibliog.

363 **The history of the Non-Conformist Church in the Falkland Islands.**
Gerry Hoppé, Reverend John Fraser. *Falkland Islands Journal*, vol. 6, no. 1 (1992), p. 17-25. bibliog.

The early history of the Tabernacle United Free Church of the Falkland Islands, the ministry of Forrest McWhan and the work of the Church since the 1982 conflict, are just some of the topics covered in this article. An appendix lists the ministers and others who have served the church in the Falklands.

364 **Churches of the South Atlantic Islands 1502-1991.**
Edward Cannan.   Oswestry, England: Anthony Nelson, 1992. 315p.
5 maps. bibliog.

This scholarly history is organized in four sections dealing respectively with St. Helena, Ascension Island, Tristan da Cunha, and the Falklands (p. 237-57). Lists of Anglican Bishops, Colonial Chaplains, Deans and Senior Chaplains, Roman Catholic clergy, Mill Hill missionaries, and Free Church Ministers are appended. The author served as Anglican Bishop of St. Helena in 1979-85.

Guide to Christ Church Cathedral Port Stanley.
See item no. 154.

The story of Commander Allen Gardiner.
See item no. 349.

Education

365 **Annual reports on the state of the colonies 1857-60.**

In: *British parliamentary papers: colonies general 9.* Shannon,
Ireland: Irish Universities Press, 1970, p. 928.

A 'despatch from Governor Moore to Sir Edward Bulwer Lytton', dated 6 February
1859, reports his intention to submit a plan for the employment of a schoolmistress.
'At present there are 32 boys and 30 girls, who are all in charge of an old pensioner of
the marines; but I apprehend that great advantage would be gained if the girls were
placed under the charge of a respectable woman, who might teach needlework and the
duties of a household in addition to reading and writing'. He notes that there are no
religious objections to a general school. This was originally published as *Annual
Report 1858* by HMSO in 1860.

366 **Annual report on the state of the colonies 1873-74.**

In: *British parliamentary papers: colonies general 15.* Shannon,
Ireland: Irish Universities Press, 1970, p. 448-54.

A despatch from Governor G. D'Arcy to the Earl of Kimberley, dated 27 February
1872, this includes a copy of the Annual Report of the Inspectors of Government
Schools (23 December 1871). The report notes that ninety-nine children are currently
on the school roll, that attendance is improving although not without conspicuous
blemishes, and that a decreasing number of children in the camp are still without any
prospect of instruction. *Annual Report 1871* was first published by HMSO in 1873.

367 **Annual reports on the state of the colonies 1876.**

In: *British parliamentary papers: colonies general 17.* Shannon,
Ireland: Irish Universities Press, 1970, p. 52-54.

Included in Governor G. D'Arcy's 14 March 1876 despatch to the Earl of Carnarvon
was an extensive report from John Wright Collins, the Government Schoolmaster. In a
wide-ranging document he included remarks 'on the present condition and prospects
of education in the Falkland Islands generally', providing a valuable insight into the
methods of instruction – such as mixed classes and a monitorial system – and also into

the current three-stage educational system which comprised an infant department and an upper school of two divisions. Collins outlined the crucial handicap under which the system laboured: 'the progress of education here is necessarily slow and irregular, chiefly on account of the labour of the children being so valuable at home that constant attendance at school is uncertain and apparently impossible'. *Annual Report 1875* was first published by HMSO in 1876.

368 **Annual reports on the state of the colonies 1894-95.**
In: *British parliamentary papers: colonies general 33.*   Shannon,
Ireland: Irish Universities Press, 1970, p. 559-70.

The total numbers of boys and girls on the rolls of four schools in Stanley, and one in Darwin, are included in the Education section of Governor Roger T. Goldsworthy's report to the Marquis of Ripon, dated 21 June 1895. The schools in question were: The Government School (seventy-two boys and seventy-nine girls); The Roman Catholic School (twenty boys and twelve girls); The Baptist School (thirty boys and twenty-three girls); a Private School (twenty boys and twelve girls); and a Falkland Islands Company School at Darwin (thirty-seven pupils). The *Annual Report 1894* was first published by HMSO in 1895.

369 **Education in the Falkland Islands.**
A. R. Hoare.   *Oversea Education*, vol. 2, no. 3 (April 1931),
p. 129-33.

In this account the Superintendent of Education for the Falkland Islands reported that the Government School in Stanley was generously equipped with furniture and materials, and was staffed by four United Kingdom certificated teachers and three local assistants. He provided details of the curriculum and of special events in the school year and ended by discussing the perennial difficulties in the education of Camp children, notably the inadequacy of the travelling teachers system, the lack of support for a Government hostel for Camp children to attend the school in Stanley, and the absence of parental interest in supporting tuition by correspondence.

370 **Antarctic schoolchildren: problems of the Falklands.**
Times Educational Supplement, no. 1889 (13 July 1951), p. 565.

Discusses the situation in the Falkland Islands at the end of 1950, when there were 350 children of school age in a colony made up of one small town and remote settlements, with no roads, and only horses and a few tracked vehicles as the means of transport. School provision amounted to an infant school in Stanley and ten settlement schools staffed by certificated teachers from the United Kingdom and local recruits. Two government scholarships were available to the British School at Montevideo. Over fifty per cent of Camp children relied on travelling teachers. A Colonial Development and Welfare grant of £12,000 in 1950 was intended to recruit more qualified teachers from the United Kingdom to improve Camp education and to train local teachers.

371 **Education in the Falkland Islands.**

E. M. Cawkell. *Oversea Education*, vol. 26, no. 4 (January 1955), p. 132-34.

Although concerned with only 400 children at the time of writing, all of whom were English speaking, the Islands' education service, of which the author of this paper was Director, was faced with some apparently intractable problems: a scattered, sometimes remote, population; a poor internal road system; a low standard of education and apathy of many parents (the legacy of a century of inadequate teaching services); the distance from England, affecting the supply of teachers and materials; and the difficulties of recruiting locally. Settlement schools, which usually involved boarding for three days a week, and a travelling teacher system were only partially successful remedies.

372 **Falkland town and 'camp': link with Dorset.**

Times Educational Supplement, no. 2491 (15 February 1963), p. 296.

In reporting the arrival of two children from the Falklands to attend a Dorset grammar school on scholarships, the opportunity is taken to elaborate on the overall problems of education in the Islands. Only in Stanley is a day-school education really practicable although there is a small day-school at Port Howard, and a Falkland Islands Company boarding school at Darwin. In other settlements tiny school rooms, each attended by handfuls of children, are served by travelling teachers for a fortnight at a time. A general reluctance by parents to send their children to boarding schools is also noted.

373 **What lies in store for the Falklands.**

C. H. Wilson. *Times Educational Supplement*, no. 2809 (21 March 1969), p. 915.

The Argentine educational system, to which Falkland Islanders would be compelled to conform should sovereignty over the Islands be transferred, is described here as rigid and unpalatable, notably for its parrot-like teaching and blinkered nationalism.

374 **Islands' teachers defy Argentine invasion force.**

Philip Venning. *Times Educational Supplement*, no. 3435 (30 April 1982), p. 1.

Based on an interview with the returning Headmaster of Stanley Junior School (130 pupils) and his wife, who is also a teacher, Venning reports that teachers in Stanley had unanimously ignored an order to open their schools, refused to accept Argentine salaries, and taught pupils in their own homes as a mark of protest. An Argentine naval officer had been put in charge of the education service and had warned that 100 bilingual Argentine teachers could replace recalcitrant English teachers.

375 **Memories of a schoolie 1964-1968.**

Charles R. Wood. *Falkland Islands Newsletter*, no. 42 (March 1990), p. 8-9.

Relates the author's memories and experience of Camp teaching, of sharing family life, of classes in front rooms, and of Christmas holidays, at a time when what education existed away from Stanley relied on itinerant teachers.

376 **Church, state and schooling in the Falkland Islands.**
David B. Smith. *Journal Of Educational Administration and History*,
vol. 22, no. 2 (July 1990), p. 1-7. bibliog.

In part derived from Smith's Hull University PhD thesis, 'Schooling in the Falkland Islands: an analysis of educational change in a small country', presented in 1988, this paper examines the none too harmonious relationship that existed between the various denominational church schools in Stanley, and the conflict between the Governor and the church authorities over religious instruction from 1869, when the Colonial Chaplain first requested a school, to the 1950s. At that time members of the clergy held classes for children of their own denomination once a week. Attendance was voluntary and dependent on their parents' wishes.

377 **Changes in education in the Falklands in the last ten years.**
Phyllis Rendell. *Falkland Islands Newsletter*, no. 57 (November 1993), p. 10-11.

The Director of Education, and a native Islander, Phyllis Rendell outlines the radical changes that have taken place in the Islands' educational system since 1982. Previously some teachers were unqualified and older children were forced to go to Argentina or Uruguay for their higher education. Now every child on the Islands, no matter how remote, has access to effective schooling whether it is at farm settlement schools, by radio lessons or visiting teachers, or in a boarding school in Stanley. A new secondary school/community centre built in 1992 is the most modern in the southern hemisphere. Government grants provide free college and university education in Britain.

378 **Schooling in the South Atlantic Islands 1661-1991.**
Dorothy Evans. Oswestry, England: Anthony Nelson, 1994. 414p.
bibliog.

Additionally concerned with Ascension Island, St. Helena, and Tristan Da Cunha, part four of this important history of education in the British colonies in the South Atlantic is devoted to the Falkland Islands. It consists of just two chapters: 'The Scattered Islands: education at schools and at home 1843-1969'; and 'The Falklands on the world map 1970-92'. An appendix lists leading Falklands educationalists.

Colonization, Immigration and Population

379   **The Falkland Islands, 1833-1876: the establishment of a colony.**
Stephen A. Royle.   *Geographical Journal*, vol. 151, no. 2 (July 1985),
p. 204-14. 2 maps. bibliog.

Based on information buried in parliamentary papers – a very useful list of these is
included in the list of references – Royle examines 'the crucial decades after 1833
when the Islands progressed from a resident population of nine, fed by naval rations,
to one of over 1,100, supported by extensive ship repair and provisioning business
and, increasingly, by wool production'. He is particularly informative on population
problems, the lack of single women, the high turnover as many of the early settlers
declined to make a long-term commitment to the Islands, the possibilities of
indentured labour and of a penal colony, voluntary emigration from Britain (the
Falklands faced competition from the United States and New Zealand), the arrival of
thirty Chelsea Pensioners and their families in 1849, and a garrison of married Royal
Marines in 1858. The article was reprinted in *Falkland Islands Journal*, vol. 21
(1987), p. 15-22.

380   **Some account of the Falkland Islands from a six months' residence
in 1838 and 1839.**
Lauchlan Bellingham Mackinnon.   London: A. H. Baily, 1840. 79p.
maps.

Mackinnon was first mate of the cutter *Arrow*, sent by the Admiralty to survey the
Islands. His account ranks either as an elementary economic survey, an emigration
prospectus, or as a strategic assessment. He reports on the Islands' peat beds, cattle,
wildlife, and fisheries, on the lack of timber and domesticated horses for new settlers,
and the advantages of a permanent settlement, including a small naval depot: 'Port
Louis, Berkeley Sound would be the most desirable spot as the seat of government . . .
it is much the easiest and best port to make; there is good and safe anchorage for
vessels of all sizes, and it is the only port so clear and free from danger, that a strange
vessel might enter with perfect safety, without a previous knowledge of the harbour'.

381 **Colonization of the Falkland Islands by convicts: importance as a naval station, and the Malta of the Pacific.**
Colonial Magazine, vol. 2, no. 7 (July 1840), p. 304-12.

The main thrust of this closely argued paper is the belief that the Falklands should be made the Gibraltar or Malta of the south, since it is 'a naval depot of such magnitude as, in the event of war, should afford not only a harbour of refuge for our mercantile marine, but a rendez-vous and port of equipment and repair for men-of-war'. Convicts are seen as appropriate labour to build the dockyards since the Islands are 'solitary cells created by nature', with abundant rations of food and 'a salubrious but not paradisiacal climate'.

382 **The Port Louis settlement, 1842.**
Anthony B. Dickinson. *Falkland Islands Journal*, no. 22 (1988), p. 34-41. bibliog.

The settlement at Port Louis was formally established on 15 January 1842 with Richard Moody as its first Governor. Taken from his report, which is now in the Public Record Office, this account surveys the current population of the settlement, living conditions and the establishment of Government House and other private houses. The settlement was moved to Point William in August 1843 primarily because it offered a much improved maritime access and in July 1845 Port Stanley officially came into existence. The article contains tables of Port Louis residents in January 1842 (name, age, origin, present occupation/status, former occupation, arrival date and religion); buildings and residences; and numbers of livestock.

383 **Some account of the Falkland Islands, with an abstract of the plan about to be pursued by Government in disposing of land there.**
Colonial Magazine, vol. 7, no. 28 (April 1842), p. 430-39.

With reason to believe that land in the Falklands would shortly be offered for sale by the Colonial Land and Emigration Commissioners, and that a port for the refit and refreshment of the Royal Navy ships on the South American Station was contemplated, this paper reports on the agricultural and pastoral potential of the Islands. 'With such internal resources as the Falklands even now possess, it is clear that a body of emigrants settling upon them would not have to endure the great evil of most new colonies – a want of food during the first years of their settlement'. The population of the west coast of Scotland, the Hebrides, and the Orkneys, 'pining in want and misery', was regarded as admirably suited 'for the exercise and industry of a half-farmer and half-fisher population' in the Falklands.

384 **Reasons for the formation of a convict establishment at the Falkland Islands.**
[G. T. Whitington]. London: Printed by Cuthbert & Southey, 1845. 4p.

Published anonymously, but known to be written by Whitington, this pamphlet was no doubt inspired by his eagerness to find a convenient source of labour for the operations of a still unformed Falkland Islands Company. A wide trawl for facts elicited the information that the Spanish used the islands as a place of transportation for felons and political offenders; similarly, the Buenos Aires Government introduced 'refractory characters which the disorganizing spirit of revolution had raised among their population'. In addition, there were no forests or woods for concealment, no great military or civil guard would be required, 'every grade of convict may be placed in disconnexion with another', convicts of the lowest class could be employed in the construction of the naval dockyard, whilst a better class could build the gaol and a church and engage in horsebreeding, curing beef, in making salt, and in shepherding. Transporting convicts to the Falklands would halve the cost of transporting them to Australia.

385   The Falkland Islands.
Bartholomew James Sullivan.   *New Monthly Magazine*, vol. 86, no. 341 (May 1849), p. 17-20.

Sullivan argued that the Falklands offered 'numerous advantages to the nation at large, and to settlers in particular', in the form of: a convenient stopping place for ships engaged in trade; a place of refuge for ships damaged sailing round Cape Horn; a profuse supply of wild cattle, fish, rabbits, and wildfowl; a large extent of pasture; no trees to be felled; an abundance of peat for fuel; and only half the distance compared to Australia. He states 'Another year will serve more fully to develop the capabilities of the Falkland Islands. On their productiveness much depends whether they become thickly populated, and serve as a field towards which British emigration may be taught to flow; but, at all events, their very position makes them valuable, and they must ultimately prove an important entrepot for the commerce of the southern world'.

386   Annual reports on the state of the colonies 1861-63.
In: *British parliamentary papers: colonies general 10.*   Shannon, Ireland: Irish Universities Press, 1970, p. 315.

A 'despatch from Governor Moore to the Duke of Newcastle', dated 28 January 1860, remarks that: 'The population of the colony is now about 540. This does not, however, include the many men now engaged in coasting and sailing vessels, who are continually leaving ships in the harbour, and after a stay of 2 or 3 months or longer, reshipping. As regards the interests of the Colony, it is important to remark that the population includes 64 families almost all of whom have acquired a personal interest in the islands, besides 34 families of soldiers of the garrison, making a total of 98 families'. *Annual Report 1859* was printed by HMSO in 1861.

387   The cruise of Her Majesty's Ship 'Bacchante' 1879-1882.
Compiled from the private journals, letters, and note-books of Prince Albert Victor and Prince George of Wales.   London: Macmillan, 1886. 2 vols. maps.

At the end of *Bacchante*'s voyage the diaries and journals of the two royal princes, serving on board as midshipmen, were entrusted to the acting chaplain, John Neale Dalton, for him to prepare for publication. The passage relating to the Falklands (volume one, p. 305-08) remarks: 'what little importance they ever presented for Imperial purposes has now almost gone. By far the best thing for England to do with the Falklands would be to exchange them with France for New Caledonia. . . The small sum that might be claimed as compensation to the few settlers here would be a cheap price to pay for the riddance once and for all of our Australian fellow-countrymen from a perpetuated and increasing menace to their peaceful prosperity'.

388   **Annual reports on the state of the colonies 1884-85.**
      In: *British parliamentary papers: colonies general 23.*   Shannon,
      Ireland: Irish Universities Press, 1970, p. 294-304.

Enclosed with Governor T. Kerr's despatch to the Earl of Derby, dated 19 February 1884, was a report on the census conducted on 3 April 1881. The total population at that date was 1,553 (976 males and 577 females) of whom 534 were under the age of fifteen. Six pages of tables were attached to the despatch, detailing: area, houses and population; the civil condition of the population (i.e. marital status); religion; relative ages; occupations; places of birth; and the population in the districts occupied for pastoral purposes. *Annual Report 1881* was first published by HMSO in 1884.

389   **Falkland Islands: report of 1972 census.**
      Stanley: Government Printing Office, 1973. 12p.

This report of the census taken on 3 December 1972 provides statistical information on the distribution of population by age and sex; marital status; births and deaths in 1962-72; population by nationality and sex; distribution of the population by occupation; religion; and housing accommodation.

390   **Immigration: Islanders opinion.**
      Falkland Islands Newsletter, no. 36 (September 1988), p. 1, 9.

Alarmed by reports that a public meeting in Stanley had recommended that immigration be limited to forty persons (not families) a year, when other sources suggested 5,000 over ten years, the Falkland Islands Association canvassed the views of a number of prominent islanders. Their response voiced the need for a reinvigorated housing programme, the need not to overcrowd Stanley, and fears that the islanders would no longer have an effective say in the running of their own country.

391   **An odd society battles on.**
      David White.   *Financial Times* (27 March 1993), p. 4.

White reports that the Colony's 2,200 inhabitants, almost all of whom are of British descent, scarcely outnumber the 2,000 United Kingdom service personnel defending them. He is also concerned that 'since the UK-Argentine conflict over the islands, an influx of new blood has reversed the population decline. But numbers have never been much greater than today and as a surge of prosperity based on squid fishery peters out, nothing short of an oil bonanza is likely to change that'.

Constitution, Law and Administration

392 An Act to enable Her Majesty to provide for the government of Her Settlements on the coast of Africa and the Falkland Islands.
In: *The statutes of the United Kingdom of Great Britain and Ireland: vol. 16 containing the Acts of 5 & 6 Victoria (1842) and 6 & 7 (1843).* London: Eyre & Spottiswoode, 1843, p. 604.

'Whereas divers of Her Majesty's Subjects have resorted to and taken up their Abode and may hereafter resort to and take up their Abode at divers places on . . . the Falkland Islands: And whereas it is necessary that Her Majesty should be enabled to make further and better provision for the Civil Government of the said Settlements: Be it . . . lawful for Her Majesty . . . to establish all such Laws, Institutions, and Ordinances . . . as may be necessary for the Peace, Order, and good Government of Her Majesty's Subjects and others within the said present or future Settlements . . .' (Cap. XIII). This legality demonstrated that the United Kingdom intended to exercise suzerainty over the Islands.

393 Governor Moore 1855-1862.
A. G. E. Jones. *Falkland Islands Journal*, no. 11 (1977), p. 37-40.

Jones first outlines Governor Moore's Royal Navy career, which included participation in the search for the missing North-west Passage explorer, Sir John Franklin, and an Antarctic magnetic survey expedition. He then narrates the difficulties confronting him on arrival in the Falklands, where drunkenness was rife and the Islanders were 'little better than savages'.

394 The murder of John Rudd in 1864.
W. M. Dean. *Falkland Islands Journal*, no. 12 (1978), p. 16-19.

Reproduces the despatch of James Lane, the Falkland Islands Company manager in Stanley, which reported the murder of John Rudd, the Company's Camp Manager, by a half-breed Indian named Gill, on 15 October 1864. Lane gives a graphic account of the murder, the hunt for the murderer, his capture, and his hanging on 15 November.

395 **Colonel George Abbas Kooli D'Arcy: Governor of the Falkland Islands 1870-1876.**
R. N. Spafford. *Falkland Islands Newsletter*, no. 53 (November 1992), p. 8-9.

After briefly outlining D'Arcy's military career, and his term as Governor of the Gambia Dependency, this biographical sketch concentrates on his tour in the Falklands, where he immediately championed the cause of the farmers who were facing bankruptcy. By the time he left the Colony was on a much improved financial footing. During his governorship D'Arcy introduced a postal service between Stanley and West Falkland, two new roads were completed, street lighting was brought in in Stanley, and a bonded warehouse, a new reservoir, and a quarantine station were built in the town. The article was reprinted in *Falkland Islands Journal*, vol. 6, no. 2 (1993), p. 53-56.

396 **The laws of the colony of the Falkland Islands and its dependencies containing the ordinances and subsidiary legislation and a selection from the imperial legislation in force on the 31st day of December 1950.**
R. W. S. Winter, Sir Henry Webb. Stanley: Falkland Islands Government, 1951. 2 vols.

Volume one, *Ordinances*, reproduces the text of all such measures enacted to the end of 1950 arranged A-Z by title, from 'Administration of Estates' to 'Workmens Compensation'. This is complemented by a thirty-page chronological table of ordinances. Volume two, *Imperial legislation*, similarly reproduces Letters Patent, Royal Instructions, and a selection of Orders in Council relevant to the Falklands. This volume also includes subsidiary legislation, such as rules, regulations and orders, made under the authority of various ordinances.

397 **Justice and police force.**
Ian J. Strange. *Falkland Islands Journal*, no. 7 (1973), p. 15-20.

Strange traces the progress of law enforcement in the Falklands from the time the first stipendiary magistrate arrived in the colony on 3 March 1845, when policing was the responsibility of the Royal Navy and the Royal Marines. He chronicles the appearance of the first constables, the early decision to form the Supreme Court from the Islands' Executive Council (it was impossible otherwise to obtain sufficient numbers to sit on a jury) and ends with the 1970s Falklands Police Force establishment of an Inspector, a Sergeant, four Constables, and six Special Constables as required.

398 **The constitution of the Falkland Islands.**
L. G. Blake. *The Parliamentarian*, vol. 65, no. 4 (January 1984), p. 43-47.

Written by the Chairman of the Select Committee on the Constitution of the Falkland Islands, this article outlines the programme of constitutional reform, beginning with the 1948 Legislative Order in Council introducing elected members to the Islands' government. Blake follows in detail the progress made, up to and including the proposals of the 1981 Commission.

399   **Falkland Islands general election.**
      Falkland Islands Newsletter, no. 25 (November 1985), p. 8-9.
Reports on the October 1985 general election, which was the first held since the 1982
war, and the first under the new constitution , and details the number of seats, the
nomination of candidates, and the election results.

400   **The Falklands election: absentee ownership issue heats up politics.**
      Gerald Robson.   *The Parliamentarian*, vol. 71, no. 2 (April 1990),
      p. 112-13.
Robson follows the political debate in the Legislative Council over the Appropriation
Bill, presented by the Financial Secretary, which included measures to make more
money available for agricultural grants. Strong opposition to such grants being made
to absentee landlords, thus increasing their profits, and quickening the flow of capital
from the Islands, was registered. At the October 1989 general election the previous
political apathy of the Islanders was not in evidence, with an eighty-two per cent and
ninety-four per cent turnout of the electorate for the Stanley and Camp seats
respectively. All the successful candidates were first-time Council members.

401   **Freedom of choice in the South Atlantic.**
      Andrew Imlach.   *The Parliamentarian*, vol. 73, no. 4 (October 1992),
      p. 255-57. 2p. of illustrations.
Reporting that the Falkland Islanders were putting the events of 1982 behind them,
Imlach notes the progress towards a democratic parliamentary government, and also
looks at the Islands' continuing economic development.

Falkland Islands Gazette.
See item no. 537.

Armed Forces and Defence

402   Annual reports on the state of the colonies 1857-60.

In: *British parliamentary papers: colonies general 9.*   Shannon,
Ireland: Irish Universities Press, 1970, p. 927.

A 'despatch from Governor Moore to Sir Edward Bulwer Lytton', dated 6 February
1859, reports that: 'The arrival of the small garrison in January relieved the
government from the inconvenience of having no force wherewith (if necessary) to
compel obedience to law on the part of unruly crews of merchant vessels, and the
possibly serious consequences which might at any moment have flowed from such a
state of things. Nor was this a danger purely imaginary. Within eight months after the
arrival of the garrison, a British ship put in here with her whole crew in a state of open
and pertinacious mutiny, followed by a riot on shore when the law was put in force.
Nothing but the hopelessness of resistance to the power of the government reduced the
men to submission'. *Annual Report 1858* was published by HMSO in 1860.

403   Falklands notes August to December 1914.

Sir William Allardyce.   *Falkland Islands Journal*, no. 11 (1977),
p. 21-36.

Rescued from papers deposited at the Scott Polar Research Institute in Cambridge,
these personal reminiscences of the first five months of the First World War illustrate
how the title of Commander-In-Chief held by the Islands' Governor was no empty
one. Acting with great determination Allardyce prepared to defend the Islands, and its
vitally important radio station, with 120 rifles (not all of them serviceable), and two
ancient muzzle-loading guns, against the might of Graf von Spee's German East Asia
Battle-Cruiser Squadron.

404   The Falklands honour the Royal Engineers.

Falkland Islands Newsletter, no. 29 (November 1986), p. 13.

This article celebrates the long-established links the Royal Engineers have enjoyed
with the Falklands. Indeed, the first colonial Governor was an officer of the Royal
Engineers who arrived in 1842 with a detachment of Royal Sappers and Miners. In

addition, RE personnel landed with Task Force 122 in 1942 to prepare defences against a possible Japanese invasion, whilst their work in restoring utilities and communications after the Argentine surrender in 1982 was crucially important.

405 The history of the Falkland Islands Defence Force.

Sydney Miller. Unpublished typescript, [1982]. 64p.

Unpublished typescripts are not usually entered in World Bibliographical Series volumes but this particular title is given a thirty-line entry in Roger Perkins' *Regiments: regiments and corps of the British Empire and Commonwealth 1758-1993: a critical bibliography of their published histories* (Newton Abbot, England: Roger Perkins, 1994. 806p.). He writes 'Completed only a few weeks before the Argentine invasion, this is an excellent summary of part-time soldiering on the Falkland Islands from the mid-19th century. Sydney Miller, a leading local resident, drew upon many official and unofficial sources and his account is clear, concise and liberally seeded with the names of those who served'. Clearly it warrants publication.

406 R. A. F. Stanley.

Richard Gardner. *Air Pictorial*, vol. 45, no. 4 (April 1983), p. 131-35.

Since, at the time of writing, Argentina had refused to renounce the use of force in the pursuit of its claim to sovereignty, the refurbished and extended airport at Stanley, 'almost certainly the most heavily defended RAF base anywhere', played an essential role in the defence of the Islands. This fully-illustrated article describes its accommodation, facilities, and the aircraft based there.

407 Military engineering in the Falkland Islands 1982-83.

G. B. Sinclair, F. G. Barton, L. J. Kennedy. *Proceedings of the Institution of Civil Engineers Pt.1.,* vol. 76 (February 1984), p. 269-77.

This detailed paper, contributed by three senior officers, describes the involvement of the Corps of Royal Engineers from the beginning of the Argentine invasion to February 1983. The account of the war concentrates on the planning to make Stanley Airport a feasible base for RAF requirements once it had been recaptured and repaired; the work of the bomb disposal units; defensive positions at San Carlos; the construction of a Harrier forward base, including fuel installations; and on mine clearing operations during the advance on Stanley. Once the war was over the Royal Engineers played a vital role in the restoration of public utilities, notably water and electricity supplies, the construction of a land base for the RAF, and in the building of garrison accommodation, including a floating hotel, or 'Coastel' as it was named.

408 Mount Pleasant Airport construction.

H. M. Hoey. *Royal Engineers Journal*, vol. 100, no. 2 (June 1986), p. 91-100. map.

This is an illustrated account of the project to construct the Mount Pleasant complex, thirty miles from Stanley, to serve as an airport for wide-bodied jets, and as a garrison headquarters for British Forces in the Falklands. Major Hoey was attached to the Public Services Agency site control at Mt. Pleasant in March 1985.

409 **A brief history of the Falkland Islands Defence Force.**
Sydney Miller, Brian Summers. *Falkland Islands Journal*, vol. 6,
no. 1 (1992), p. 1-5.

The Falkland Islands Volunteers were formed in 1892 when 200 fully-armed soldiers arrived in a Chilean steamer en route to the civil war then raging in that country. This history traces the early activities of the Volunteers, the part they played in the First World War when German battle cruisers approached the Islands, the 1919 reconstitution into the Falkland Islands Defence Force and the close relationship with the West Yorkshire Regiment during the Second World War. It also discusses the Argentine declaration of 1982 that it was an illegal organization, and its reformation in June 1983. See also 'Falkland Islands Defence Force celebrates 100th anniversary 1992', *Falkland Islands Newsletter*, no. 53 (November 1992), p. 13.

410 **Falklands: flying fortress.**
Eric Beech. *Flight International*, vol. 131, no. 4059 (25 April 1987),
p. 30-34.

Beech describes the front-line operational base at Mt. Pleasant, the aircraft deployed there and the operations carried out, and discusses the future of the airbridge, the restriction of the airfield at Stanley to mainly civil aircraft, and the curtailment of its runway to prevent Argentine special forces landing to establish a base. 'Central to the Fortress Falklands policy was the construction of an air and military base which, in an emergency, would permit the Islands to be reinforced quickly by widebodied jet'.

Economy

General

411 Annual reports on the state of the colonies 1846-48.
In: *British parliamentary papers: colonies general 4.*   Shannon,
Ireland: Irish Universities Press, 1970, p. 725-27.

An 'extract of a despatch from Governor Moody to Earl Grey', dated 30 September
1847, is mainly concerned with economic affairs. 'With respect to the colony being
able at any time to maintain itself, it appears to me there is nothing in the character
either of its climate or soil, to prevent its not only providing the requisite supplies for
the maintenance of its inhabitants, but also for the accumulation of wealth, through the
ordinary operations of trade, and partly also by means of agriculture'. Moody states
that capital investment is needed for the export of wool; hides, tallow and beef; fish
oil; and salt fish. *Annual Report 1847* was first published by HMSO in 1848.

412 The economic activities of the Falkland Islands.
Clarence F. Jones.   *Geographical Review*, vol. 14, no. 3 (July 1924),
p. 394-403. map.

The sheep industry, the export trade, and the whaling industry; the import trade (coal,
groceries, hardware, machinery and structural timber); Stanley; and the future of the
colony, are the principal features of this brief study. The sheep industry and the ship
repair industry were not capable of drastic improvement but agriculture, dairy
products, and the fishing industry could experience rapid development.

413 The Falkland Islands: memorandum on potential minor industries.
Stanley: Government Printing Office, 1939. 23p.

Despairing of sufficient information in obscure Bluebooks, gazettes, reports, and the
like, ever catching the eye of potential entrepreneurs, the Governor, Sir Herbert
Henniker-Heaton, instigated the publication of this booklet to attract investment. Peat,
vegetables, kelp (for the manufacture of iodine and potash), guano, and fish, were
marked out for profitable exploitation.

414 **Overseas Development Administration reports.**
London: Foreign Office. Overseas Development Administration,
1971-79.

A number of extremely useful, but now dated, economic reports on the Falklands were issued in the 1970s. They included G. A. Armstrong, *Report on the economy of the Falkland Islands* (1973); J. E. Combon, H. Waller, *Public Finance of the Falkland Islands*; T. H. D. Davies, *Sheep and cattle industries of the Falkland Islands* (1971); I. C. Griggs, *Technical survey of the Falkland Islands* (1972); L. Stewart, *Fisheries of the Falklands* (1973); T. W. D. Theophilus, *Economics of wool production in the Falkland Islands* (1972); and White Fish Authority, *Fishing opportunities in the South West Atlantic* (1979).

415 **Economic survey of the Falkland Islands.**
Lord Shackleton, Chairman. London: The Economist Intelligence
Unit, 1976. vol. 1, 344p.; vol. 2, 110p. 4 maps. bibliog.

In the light of the colony's weakening economy, and the decline in its population the Shackleton Committee was asked: (1) To examine the resources of the colony and the dependencies and the prospects for economic development with particular reference to agriculture, the wool industry, the need for diversification and possible developments in oil, minerals, fisheries, and alginates and to make recommendations; (2) In this context to examine the present fiscal structure and the provision of government services in the colony and dependencies in the light of the present uncertain economic climate and to make recommendations. To advise on priorities for capital expenditure over the next five years with particular reference to the need for improved infrastructure and to programmes for public utility development and housing; and (3) To assess the financial, manpower and social obligations of any recommended economic strategy, with particular reference to the encouragement of small scale enterprise and scope for local investment, and the extent to which all these needs can be met from local resources and to the degree which recourse to all potential external resources may be necessary. The Committee's *Report* was issued in two volumes: *Resources and development potential* contains an analysis of the Falklands' overall economy, a description of the Islands' resources including its surrounding waters, and an assessment of their development potential; whilst *Strategy, recommendations & implementation* summarizes volume one, proposes a development strategy, and presents recommendations for a policy and a programme of economic development with their financial implications. For Shackleton's own account of his survey see 'Prospect of the Falkland Islands', *Geographical Journal*, vol. 143, no. 1 (March 1977), p. 1-13.

416 **Prospects for the Falkland Islands.**
London: The Falkland Islands Research and Development Association,
1982. 12p. map.

The purpose of this A4 brochure-type publication was to demonstrate that the colony's well-being did not depend on Argentine goodwill. It was in no way intended to be a complete blueprint for economic development but to illustrate that, provided their security was guaranteed, the Islanders could look forward to a prosperous future. Sheep farming, the fisheries, alginates, oil, and tourism, were all expected to secure substantial income.

417   **Falkland Islands economic study 1982.**
Lord Shackleton, Chairman.   London: HMSO, 1982. 137p. 3 pull-out
maps. (Cmnd. 8653).
At the end of May 1982, when it was apparent that the British Task Force would very
shortly repossess the Islands for the Crown, Lord Shackleton was asked to update his
1976 Report (see item no. 415). Five out of six of the original team who had produced
the earlier report were given the task 'to revise as necessary, examining social as well
as economic aspects, the conclusions and recommendations made in the original
study; and to report to the Prime Minister as soon as possible'. They should carry on
their deliberations in the light of the changed circumstances arising from the
Argentine invasion and occupation and the changed world economic environment. The
revision should also encompass South Georgia and the South Sandwich Islands. The
topics discussed included: the existing economy and its prospects; population, social
aspects and immigration; the impact of the military garrison; agriculture; fisheries;
tourism; wool and skin processing; alginates; hydrocarbons; transport, infrastructure,
energy supplies and planning; and conservation. Among its recommendations was the
creation of a Falkland Islands Development Agency, the transfer of ownership of
absentee-owned farms, and the strengthening of the Government structure. The
financial implications also received due attention.

418   **Options for a Falklands future.**
Lord Shackleton. *Geographical Magazine*, vol. 55, no. 1 (January
1983), p. 35-37. map.
Halfway through the 1982 campaign Lord Shackleton was asked to update his original
report. Here he summarizes his findings and explains the thinking behind his
revisions. He finds that the Islands' economy is still almost entirely dependent on
wool production and export and reiterates the importance of establishing small owner-
occupier farms and the setting up of a Falkland Islands Development Agency which
would take over all absentee-owner farms. He also examines the prospects for salmon
ranching, krill harvesting, hydrocarbons, tourism, and the knitwear industry.

419   **On Fortress Falklands: two billion on defence; £50 million on the
Falkland Islanders.**
Robert Fox. *Listener*, vol. 3, no. 2854 (19 April 1984), p. 2-4.
Fox is concerned that comparatively little is being spent on the development of the
Islands' economy, although improvements in fishery and farming are visible with
large estates being broken down into smaller holdings. Nevertheless, the government
bureaucracy is still moving very slowly and little assistance is given to the new farm
owners in drawing up accounts, assessing cash flow, and the need for working capital.
Fox reports on a new wool mill at Fox Bay East (West Falkland), new enterprises in
Stanley, including a less than profitable mini-brewery, and notes the Islanders' desires
for new housing, new schools, and better public utilities.

420   **A big economic boost in Fortress Falklands.**
Harold Briley. *Listener*, vol. 117, no. 3016 (18 June 1987), p. 8-9.
Briley argues that the colony appears to be on the edge of an economic and social
development unparalleled in its history. He instances the £3,000 million spent on the
new Mount Pleasant airport, and its associated Mare Harbour, as particularly good
value for money, not simply as a base for swift military reinforcement, but of

immense civil and economic potential. He also remarks on thirty couples sinking their life-savings into the purchase of their farms; inshore fishery projects; the 150-mile fishing zone round the Islands, coming into force as from February 1987 to regulate and conserve stocks of fish; and the blossoming tourist industry.

421 The Prynn Report – a personal view.
David Taylor. *Falkland Islands Newsletter*, no. 34 (March 1988), p. 4-6.

At the end of November 1987 Environmental Resources Ltd. presented its Falkland Islands Long Term Economic Development Strategy Interim Report to the Falkland Islands Development Corporation. Its author was Peter Prynn, Director of Environmental Resources Ltd., who summed up in the final paragraph: 'we must emphasise that the responsibility for choice of priorities for the future rests with the Falkland Islanders. The aim of this study is to interpret their needs and develop a reasonable programme for the implementation of a plan – not to impose a series of externally held views'. David Taylor, Chief Executive of the Falkland Islands Government, 1982-87, examines the complex background to fishing control and its effect on the Falkland way of life. He perceives three options: exploit the maximum fisheries resource involving long-term investment in shore based fisheries activities under the control of the Falkland Islands Development Corporation and the fishing companies; increase licensing fees for the Falkland Islands Government to invest through the Development Corporation or a development bank in a more broadly based range of economic activities; or invest a considerable proportion of the fisheries income of £10 million a year in the markets as a long-term saving. The first two options would involve a population increase of 1500 to 3000 in ten years, the third 750 to 2700 in the same period.

422 Keeping a stiff upper lip.
Ann Hills. *Geographical Magazine*, vol. 63, no. 6 (June 1991), p. 22-24.

The year 1992 marked the last of the £31 million development grant allocated to the colony by the British Government at the end of the 1982 war in order to achieve a measure of economic self-sufficiency. Great strides were taken principally in education, the development of the staple wool industry, and in the introduction of fishing licences (£25 million income in 1991). However, the slump in the world price of wool threatens to undermine the Islands' economic prosperity.

423 Changes in the Falkland Islands since the conflict of 1982.
Stephen A. Royle. *Geography*, vol. 79, no. 2 (April 1994), p. 172-76. 3 maps.

This expert article compares the declining economy of the Falklands at the end of the 1970s with the transformation brought about by the 1982 war. In the late 1970s the Islands were suffering from a falling population; an economy dependent on wool production from thirty-six large sheep farms, twenty-three of which were owned by foreign companies; and the political prospect of being handed over to Argentina. Since the war there has been an enormous injection of financial aid; a substantial rise in government income from fishery licences; a diversified economy encouraged by the Falkland Islands Development Corporation; a marked increase in productivity on smaller, family-owned sheep farms, a nine per cent jump in the population figures;

and, to cap it all, tangible evidence of continuing British support in the shape of the massive Mt. Pleasant airport and military complex. Royle ends by noting the social costs of the transformation which include less employment on the farms; worries about employment in Stanley; complaints about the number of tourists; the sheer pace of development; and fears about the effects of a potential oil industry.

Oil industry

424   Oil riches in the Falklands still only speculation.
Petroleum Review, no. 36 (May 1982), p. 7.
Reprinted from the 12 April 1982 issue of *Petroleum Information International* (published in Houston, Texas), this report assesses the prospects of finding commercial quantities of offshore oil in the Falklands region. In 1975 the United States Geological Survey suggested that the potential yield could be up to 200 billion barrels but subsequent exploration by Esso and Shell proved disappointing.

425   What future for the Falklands?
Colin Phipps.   London: Faber, 1983. 16p.
The main section of this pamphlet is given over to the prospects for hydrocarbon development. Himself a petroleum geologist, and Head of a firm of international petroleum consultants, who visited the Islands in November 1975, as a member of a Commonwealth Parliamentary Association Delegation, Phipps uses his expertise to good effect to discuss the prospects of offshore oil, the facilities required to exploit it, the time-scale involved, the social and environmental issues, and the political and economic dimensions.

426   Oil.
Peter J. Pepper.   *Falkland Islands Newsletter*, no. 46 (February 1991), p. 12.
'There isn't really any doubt that there are oil resources in Falklands waters' writes Pepper. 'The Patagonian continental shelf is the biggest in the world, and contains huge thicknesses of the carbonaceous sediments from which oil derives'. This report investigates how much oil is there, what it would be worth, and what it could offer the Islands' economy. Cheap fuel and electricity, asphalt for roads, and fuel for airlines to fly the South Polar route to New Zealand, are some of the possibilities.

427   Off shore oil prospects.
E. W. H. Christie.   *Falkland Islands Newsletter*, no. 53 (November 1992), p. 1.
Reporting that oil exploration commenced in November 1992, Christie states 'If reserves of hydrocarbons are identified and drilling for oil proves to be commercially viable, then the Islands will be set for a great future'. Christie is of the opinion that if a substantial oil field is discovered it will offset the dwindling resources of the North

Sea and would therefore be of immense consequence for the United Kingdom and for Europe.

428 **Will the offshore Falkland Islands be a major oil province?**
   Philip Richards.   *Falkland Islands Newsletter*, no. 57 (November
   1993), p. 4-7. 3 maps.
A member of the British Geological Survey's Petroleum Group, Dr Richards relates how the Group is using its expertise to help the Falkland Islands Government to initiate serious exploration of Falkland Islands waters. It is also enlightening those oil companies who are unaware of the Falklands' offshore potential. He concludes that 'the potential for high reward should be sufficient to encourage oil companies to commit the requisite funds to start the serious search for hydrocarbons in the area'.

Falkland Islands Development Corporation.
See item no. 549.

Falkland Islands Company

429 **Some account of the Falkland Islands to which is added a preliminary sketch for the formation of a chartered company to be called the Falkland Islands Company, 1851.**
2nd ed. 26p. map.

This prospectus reports that 'it is proposed to form a Select Association, for turning to profitable account the privileges of a highly beneficial contract entered into with the British Government, and thereby developing the varied, extensive and hitherto much neglected resources of the Falkland Islands, and particularly of a portion of East Falkland'. These are calculated to comprise hides, tallow, horns, bones, beef of superior quality, fresh and salt provisions (for ships rounding the Horn), an ample supply of salt, the richest seal rookeries in the world, and fertile soil. The aim was to raise £50,000 by a charter of incorporation, limiting the liability of shareholders to the amount of their subscriptions. A pull-out map shows the Islands as surveyed by Captains Fitzroy, Robinson and Sullivan up to 1848. The account was reprinted as 'The Royal Falkland land, cattle, seal and whale fishery company', *Falkland Islands Journal*, no. 4 (1970), p. 1-9.

430 **Speech by Mr. F. E. Cobb, Chairman of the Falkland Islands Co., at a general meeting 12 June 1917.**
Falkland Islands Journal, no. 9 (1975), p. 24-30.

Constitutes an extremely informative review of the Company's operations during the first fifty years of its existence. Its business essentially consisted of 'providing settlers with stores and cash, collecting, shipping, and selling their produce on commission and transacting necessary business in Stanley'. In addition the Company engaged in local coasting by schooner and held a monopoly of shipping repairs.

431 **The Falkland Islands Company Ltd. 1851-1951.**
London: Harvey Publishing, 1951. 34p.

Printed privately for the Company to mark its centenary, this official history first charts its beginnings, including a note on the preliminary prospectus of the Royal

Falkland Land, Cattle, Sea and Whale Fishery Company, its initial financial difficulties, and its eventual success. This is followed by separate sections on the Company's headquarters at Stanley; the competition of J. M. Dean who proved a formidable rival; the personality of F. A. Cobb, perhaps the most capable of all the Company's colonial managers; the development of the Company's shipping services, including the ship repair service and, for a time, the mail service; the Company's Farm and the extension of its flock from thirty to 200,000 sheep; and the Company's organization at the end of its first century. There are lists of the Company's chairmen, managing directors, London secretaries, and colonial and camp managers. A two-page map of the Falklands shows the areas owned by the Company.

432 **Falkland Islands Company.**
Rudolph Robert. In: *Chartered companies and their role in the development of overseas trade.* London: G. Bell, 1969, p. 166–73. bibliog.

Chapter thirteen tells the Falkland Islands Company story in brief, from the early cattle trading activities of Samuel Fisher Lafone and his brother Alexander Ross Lafone, the formation of the Company in 1851 and its floating on the Stock Exchange in 1968, to the looming shadow of Argentine expansion. Robert highlights the career of the Company's Colonial Manager, F. E. Cobb, who lived and worked in the Islands for twenty-three years, and who was Managing Director in England for another thirty-one. The sheep industry, the store in Stanley, the Company's mail contract, and its educational, medical and religious responsibilities also come under scrutiny.

433 **The beginnings of The Falkland Islands Company, 1850-51: an account of the developments that led to the creation of the Falkland Islands Company, incorporated under a Royal Charter as from 1 January 1851, and some of the Company's initial history: from the late W. M. Dean's unpublished history of the Company.**
Sydney Miller. *Falkland Islands Journal*, no. 12 (1979), p. 8-21; no. 13 (1980), p. 10-19; no. 14 (1981), p. 37-44; no. 15 (1982), p. 32-44; no. 16 (1983), p. 37-42; no. 17 (1984), p. 43-50; no. 18 (1985), p. 50-57; no. 19 (1986), p. 37-44; no. 20 (1987), p. 32-35; no. 21 (1988), p. 42-46.

Without doubt one of the most protracted company histories ever printed, this chronicle of the Falkland Islands Company's successive managers, its sheepfarming and shipping activities, its modernization and reorganization, is not really suitable for the general reader. To economic and imperial historians, however, it presents a wealth of detailed and authoritative information.

434 **The Falkland Islands Company Limited.**
Falkland Islands Foundation Newsletter, no. 2 (August 1984), p. 10-11; no. 3 (January 1985), p. 7.

Formed to purchase the cattle and sheepfarming interests of the Lafone Brothers, who had become heavily indebted to a London firm of merchants, the Falkland Islands Company was granted a royal charter on 1 January 1852. Today its activities encompass sheepfarming (for wool), general wholesaling and retailing, shipping and agency services for the internationally owned fishing vessels in Falklands waters.

Reasons for the formation of a convict establishment at the Falkland Islands.
See item no. 384.

Transport and Communications

435 Camp transport before the machine age.
Sydney Miller. *Falkland Islands Journal*, no. 12 (1978), p. 20-25.

This is a nostalgic account of the transport used for mail and materials on the Falklands sheep stations in the days of horses. Because their livelihood depended on horses 'the large majority of hands in those days were first-rate horsemen, and of course they had never heard of eight-hour days'.

436 The railways of the Falkland Islands and South Georgia.
R. A. Smith. *Falkland Islands Journal*, no. 19 (1985), p. 29-37.

Focusing on the construction of the single-line, twenty-four-inch-gauge Camber Railway, which ran for three and a half miles in the period from 1916 to the late 1920s carrying naval stores, this article also looks at the industrial railways of the South Georgia whaling stations which needed huge quantities of coal to drive the steam saws and boilers used for cutting and processing.

437 Remember the Darwin.
Charles R. Wood. *Falkland Islands Newsletter*, no. 44 (September 1990), p. 10-11.

Purpose-built for the Falkland Islands Company by Goole Ship Building and Repair Company, and launched on 18 February 1957, the *RMS Darwin* had a service speed of nineteen knots, accommodation for thirty-six passengers, and specially designed holds for carrying drummed and bulk oil. It offered regular services between Montevideo and Stanley on a monthly basis, and also provided an inter-island service, collecting the wool clip and delivering stores, before it was withdrawn from service in 1972. These recollections of a passage on board also include a plan of the ship.

438 **Wasn't it fun! The early days of the Falkland Islands Government Air Service.**
John Huckle. *Falkland Islands Newsletter*, no. 39 (June 1989), p. 8-9.
Among the topics and incidents touched upon in this affectionate look back to 'the bad old days' of FIGAS, before strict regulations were enforced, are the first mail drop, and the occasion when a report that the Argentine navy had mutinied and was steaming towards Stanley, caused a reconnaissance flight over the Islands' western approaches. John Huckle was Harbour Master and Director of Civil Aviation in the Falklands between 1951 and 1957. Sir Miles Clifford's 'FIGAS: the birth of an air service', *Falkland Islands Journal*, no. 5 (1971), p. 29-31, describes the efforts to start an air service within the Islands with two RAF Austers in 1948. Although the Governor met with initial opposition, their use for urgent medical cases soon won approval. Radio transmitters were set up at every farm on the islands so that flights could be directed to meet emergencies.

439 **FIGAS at forty.**
Eric Beech. *Flight International*, vol. 133, no. 4095 (2/9 January 1988), p. 30-31.
Since the 1982 war FIGAS (the Falkland Islands Government Air Service) has expanded its route network to forty-one airstrips and added more aircraft to its fleet to meet whatever challenges the future might bring. In this article Beech examines its role as a flying doctor service, the types of aircraft employed, and the supply of spares. He also includes a chronology of FIGAS' forty-year history.

440 **The history of the Falkland Island Government Air Service (FIGAS).**
Douglas A. Rough. *Falkland Islands Journal*, vol. 5, no. 5 (1991), p. 27-44. map.
Civil aviation in the Falklands began in November 1948 with the arrival of two partially dismantled Auster aircraft on board the Falkland Islands Dependencies Survey ship *John Biscoe*. This was the result of an initiative by the Governor, Sir Miles Clifford, who realized that a widely-scattered and isolated population in remote settlements badly needed a rapid means of transport in case of serious illness or injury. The Colony's limited finances could not sustain an extensive roadmaking programme and to him an air ambulance service was the obvious answer. This history covers the fishery patrol and current domestic services. It also includes a table of FIGAS aircraft between 1948 and 1991 (registration, type and previous identity) and a map showing the destinations, mostly settlements, served by FIGAS.

441 **Falkland Islands – Anglo-Argentine agreement on Falkland Islands communications with Argentina.**
Keesing's Contemporary Archives, vol. 18 (4-11 December 1971), p. 24968.
Following discussions in Buenos Aires from 21 to 30 June 1971, between the Argentine and British Governments, attended by two members of the Falkland Islands Legislative Council, a Joint Statement was issued containing proposals for establishing regular sea and air communications between Argentina and the Falklands, and for improving postal, cable, and telephone links. In addition to measures relating

to travel documents, tax and duty exemptions, and military service obligations, the Statement proposed that 'The British Government should arrange for a regular shipping service for passengers, cargo and mail between the islands and the mainland, while the Argentine Government should arrange for a regular weekly air service for the same purposes between the mainland and the Falklands'. It also stated that 'Both Governments should co-operate in simplifying administrative practices, regulations and documentation for sea and air transport, bearing in mind the need to promote and accelerate communications'. The statement ended: 'Since divergencies remained between the two Governments regarding the circumstances which should exist for a definite solution to the dispute concerning sovereignty over the Falklands, nothing contained in the Joint Statement and approved by both Governments on Aug. 5 should be interpreted as (a) a renunciation by either Government of any right of territorial sovereignty over the Islands, or (b) a recognition of or support for the other Government's position with regard to such sovereignty'.

442 **An airline for the Falklands.**
M. J. Hardy. *Air Pictorial*, vol. 44, no. 8 (August 1982), p. 314.

Hardy bases his argument on the overt criticism of Whitehall's failure in the 1960s to understand the importance of adequate communications to Port Stanley, described as 'a deliberate and furtive policy ... aimed at the eventual cutting adrift of the Falklands from British rule'. Hardy claims that 'if the Chileans could build a runway on Easter Island for LAN-Chile's Boeing 707 services from Santiago to Papéeté (Tahiti), then surely the much more populous Falklands could support one jet service a fortnight from Port Stanley to London'.

443 **The Flexiport: a triumph for British initiative, design and cooperation.**
Falkland Islands Newsletter, vol. 20 (August 1984), p. 2-4.

On 26 April 1984 Major-General Keith Spacie, Military Commissioner and Commander British Forces Falkland Islands, took delivery on behalf of the Ministry of Defence of a new £20 million floating port and warehouse complex known as Flexiport. The Falklands Intermediate Port and Storage System (FIPASS), to give it its proper name, consisted of six linked standard North Sea Oil rig support barges, each measuring 300 feet by 90 feet, moored to a quay. Four of the barges contained warehouses offering 10,000 cubic feet of space for 16,000 different items of stores. Its purpose was to reduce the number of cargo and storage ships supporting the military garrison by eliminating vessels lying idle at Stanley and to turn round quickly those delivering supplies and stores, saving time, armed services labour and demurrage. A saving to the British taxpayer of £12-15,000 a day was reported.

444 **Falklands helicopter operations.**
Eric Beech. *Flight International*, vol. 131, no. 4062 (16 May 1987), p. 20-23.

The rotary-wing aircraft deployed on the Falklands, their supplying and personnel transporting operations, the use of chartered civil helicopters, and the airborne equipment installed, are the main topics touched upon in this illustrated article.

Stanley Airport.
See item no. 337.

Agriculture, Forestry and Fisheries

Agriculture

445 Introduction of stock to the Falkland Islands.
Ian J. Strange. *Falkland Islands Journal*, no. 7 (1983), p. 7-12.
In 1764 Antoine de Bougainville established a settlement at Port Louis, where he transported seven heifers, two bulls, a few pigs and sheep, three horses, and a goat. This account traces the growth of the herds up to 1842 and also chronicles the Falkland Islands Company's ultimately successful legal action to have the cattle declared *ferae naturae*. A list of Spanish terms used for horses and cattle is included.

446 Cattle country: a report made in 1859.
Falkland Islands Journal, no. 4 (1970), p. 17-19.
Reproduces the report made by Arthur Bailey, Surveyor General to Governor Captain T. C. L. Moore, on 5 February 1859, after a tour of the Islands to estimate the numbers of wild cattle, and to report on the general character of Crown Lands.

447 Annual reports on the state of the colonies 1861-63.
In: *British parliamentary papers: colonies general 10.* Shannon, Ireland: Irish Universities Press, 1970, p. 606-07.
Governor Moore's despatch to the Duke of Newcastle, dated 13 February 1861, reported on the current state of the sheep industry in the Islands: 'The tables of agriculture show that there are now in the colony about ten thousand sheep, some of which are of the best English breeds, and almost all of them crossed with those breeds. From this stock the increase will be rapid, and the annual clip of wool will yield large profits to the sheep farmer, independent of the supply of mutton, and of live sheep for sea stock, to the shipping and colonists at Stanley. It will be difficult, however, for persons without capital to establish sheep-farms here for some time, as the first purchase of sheep must involve a heavy outlay'. *Annual Report 1861* was issued by HMSO in 1862.

448 **Annual reports on the state of the colonies 1877-78.**
   In: *British parliamentary papers: colonies general 18.* Shannon,
   Ireland: Irish Universities Press, 1970, p. 33-43, 856-71.

Two important reports on sheepfarming were included in Governor T. F. Callaghan's despatches to the Earl of Carnarvon, dated 19 March 1877 and 21 March 1878. In the first despatch an increase of 86,000 in the number of sheep on the Islands was reported for the year, rising to 271,000 in 1876, along with remarks on the very severe ravages of scab. Many sheep farmers were calling for stringent ordinances to be enforced by a Government Inspector but strong opposition to this from the larger proprietors on East and West Falkland was thought likely. *Annual Report 1876* and *Annual Report 1877* were first published by HMSO in 1877 and 1878 respectively.

449 **Annual reports on the state of the colonies 1878-79.**
   In: *British parliamentary papers: colonies general 19.* Shannon,
   Ireland: Irish Universities Press, 1970, p. 549-63.

A review of sheepfarming in the Colony since its introduction in about 1852 by G. M. Dean, one of the largest sheepfarmers in West Falkland, was included in Governor T. F. Callaghan's despatch of 13 May 1879 to Sir Michael Hicks Beach. Dean touched upon the practice of breeding sheep especially for their fleece (from 1867); the heavy expense of conveying produce and stores to and from Stanley; and the drawback of not being able to ascertain in time the state of the home market. Another sheep farmer reports that lime and sulphur dipping at the end of March has cured scab and would not retard wool growth. *Annual Report 1878* was first published by HMSO in 1879.

450 **From the Falklands to Patagonia: the story of a pioneer family.**
   Michael James Mainwaring. London: Allison & Busby, 1983. 288p.
   maps on endpapers. bibliog.

A clear picture of the social and economic standing of sheepfarming in the Falklands during the late nineteenth century is presented in the first chapter of this book which, based on family documents, and illustrated with contemporary photographs, relates how William Halliday, a shepherd, gave up his job and emigrated, with his wife and seven children, to start his own sheep station in Patagonia in 1885.

451 **Annual reports on the state of the colonies 1898-99.**
   In: *British parliamentary papers: colonies general 36.* Shannon,
   Ireland: Irish Universities Press, 1971, p. 151-73.

A stock report, signed James Robertson, Acting Chief Inspector of Stock, was submitted by the Colonial Administrator, F. Craigie Halkett, to Mr Joseph Chamberlain on 25 June 1897. Contrary to previous thinking, an amended and more stringent Scab Ordinance had proved necessary. Twenty stations had been put in quarantine, four prosecutions incurring the maximum penalty had taken place during the year, and extra assistant inspectors had been appointed for short periods.

452   **A shepherd abroad.**
William Alexander Blain.   *Blackwood's Magazine*, vol. 328, no. 1977
(July 1980), p. 15-26.
Also appearing in the *Falkland Islands Journal* (1981), p. 15-22 in a condensed form,
this is the story of a Scottish shepherd who spent five years working on a West
Falklands sheepfarm in the last years of the nineteenth century. He vividly describes
his voyage to Stanley in *The Vicar of Bray* and his experiences on the camp.

453   **Anson – the government experimental farm 1926-8.**
Sydney Miller.   *Falkland Islands Journal*, no. 15 (1981), p. 11-14.
On the initiative of the Governor, Sir John Middleton, the Falkland Islands
Government obtained the services of Mr Hugh Munro, the Principal District Officer of
the New Zealand Department of Agriculture, to visit the colony and to report on its
farming industry. After an eight-month stay he recommended that an experimental
farm should be established. This paper reviews the farm's activities which included:
regrassing hard camp by surface sowing; growing root and other forage crops on an
extensive scale; and draining a limited area of waterlogged land for surface sowing
and cultivation.

454   **The grasslands of the Falkland Islands.**
William Davies.   Stanley: Government Printer; London: Crown
Agents for the Colonies, 1939. 86p. 2 maps. bibliog.
During the course of a comprehensive survey, from 20 November 1937 to 11 March
1938, Davies visited every station on East and West Falkland, as well as a large
number of others on the outlying islands, covering 100 miles on horseback, and 1,000
miles by sea in Falkland waters. This study is the result of observations he made and
encompasses the Islands' natural pastures, pasture improvements round the
settlements, seed mixtures, rotational grazing, the fencing and sub-division of
paddocks, seed production, soil fertility, and the reclamation of sand drifts. At the
time Davies was Senior Grassland Investigator of the Welsh Plant Breeding Station in
Aberystwyth.

455   **Abstract of report on the work and findings of the Department of
Agriculture 1937 to 1946.**
J. G. Gibbs.   Stanley: Government Printing Office, 1947. 14p.
The Department of Agriculture was established in 1937 'to administer the Ordinances
and Regulations relating to agriculture, to accumulate by experiment and other means,
useful knowledge on agricultural subjects, and to distribute this knowledge among the
people of the Colony'. Its various services are evaluated: stock (animal quarantine,
economics of sheepfarming, dairying); pasturage; supplementary crops and
cultivation; vegetable products; shelter plants; and rural economy.

456   **Sheep farming in the Falkland Islands.**
Raymond Adie.   *Farm*, vol. 4, no. 5 (May 1951), p. 2-3, 5-6.
Based on a four-month stay on the Falklands, in 1946-47, this study of a typical
sheepfarm's operations discusses the breeds most suitable for the harsh climate
(Corriedales and Romney Marsh), lambing, the optimum size of farms, the desirability
of importing rams for breeding, sheep gathering, shearing, and the sheep stations.

457 **An ecologist in the Falkland Islands.**
J. B. Cragg. *Listener*, vol. 59, no. 1514 (3 April 1958), p. 574-77.

Concentrating on the uncontrolled grazing threatening the Islands' herbage, Cragg recalls the 1938 recommendations of William Davies, which included the use of fertilizers; re-seeding of large areas of land; greater sub-division by fences; and controlled grazing. Cragg perceives the Falklands as a paradigm of a world problem, that of producing food either as plant or animal crops, from marginal areas, in other words, those which are too difficult or too remote to maintain by techniques proven to be profitable in more temperate climates.

458 **The cultivation of tussac grass.**
D. W. H. Walton. *Falkland Islands Journal*, no. 19 (1985), p. 38-42. bibliog.

'Since the early reports on the value of tussac grass . . . in the mid-nineteenth century there have been various attempts to cultivate the grass both in the Falkland Islands and elsewhere. Its value to grazing stock and as conserved fodder was recognised by all the early settlers in the Islands. Uncontrolled grazing and fire since then has resulted in the the loss of much of the original tussac areas but attempts have been made periodically to re-establish it'. This paper is an authoritative account of those attempts.

459 **The United Kingdom Falkland Islands Trust: a biological husbandry project.**
Falkland Islands Newsletter, no. 43 (June 1990), p. 11.

A pilot plant was established in February 1990 at the Market Garden in Stanley to produce liquid seaweed extract to be used for trials on trees and pasture.

460 **The Upland Goose.**
R. W. Summers, J. H. McAdam. Belfast: Department of Agricultural Botany, Agriculture and Food Science Research Centre, 1992. 162p.

With the development of sheepfarming in the Falklands farmers have constantly complained about the depredations of upland geese in consuming the best grasses needed for their flocks. No less than four million birds were shot when bounty payments were introduced. This important study describes the biology of upland geese and assesses their feeding and reproductive habits in relation to farm management. The effectiveness of control measures in the light of farm profits also comes under scrutiny.

461 **Corrals and gauchos: some of the people and places involved in the cattle industry.**
Joan Spruce. Bangor, Northern Ireland: Peregrine Publishing for Falklands Conservation, 1992. 48p. map.

Illustrated by eight full-page colour photographs of Dale watercolours, now in the Falkland Islands Museum, this attractive historical booklet describes the wild cattle, the legendary 'gauchos' (cattle-hands) of the last century, their life in the Camp, and the stone and turf corrals they constructed. A location map of surviving corrals occupies the two central pages.

462 **Farming on the world's edge.**
Alistair McNaught. *Geographical*, vol. 65, no. 8 (August 1993),
p. 47-51.
Following a description of the physical environment of the Falklands and an outline of
their ecology, McNaught examines the history of farming on the Islands. He looks at
the reasons for the large-scale sub-divisions of land which was common in the 1970s
and 1980s and assesses their economic implications. His points are given force by a
case-study of Lake Sullivan Farm at Fox Bay West comprising 63,000 hectares, which
in 1986 was divided into six smaller farms.

463 **United Kingdom Falkland Islands Trust agricultural initiatives.**
David Strickland. *Falkland Islands Newsletter*, no. 57 (November
1993), p. 14.
With the objective of enabling farmers to make more money, and to produce crops
other than wool, using all the natural resources available, the Trust investigated the
possibilities of turning peat into good arable soil. They also considered the potential
for grass improvement by means of a liquid seaweed preparation, of carrot growing,
and of the organic wool market.

Forestry

464 **The Falkland Islands.**
William Dallimore. *Kew Bulletin*, no. 5 (September 1919), p. 209-21.
'The records of the Royal Botanical Gardens, Kew, indicate that on several occasions
between 1842 and the present date correspondence has taken place between the
Governor of the Falkland Islands and other individuals, the Colonial Office, and the
Director of the Royal Botanical Gardens, Kew, respecting trees suitable for
experimental planting in the Islands, and the advisability of planting the Falkland
Islands Tussocks [Tussac] Grass extensively in certain parts of the British Isles;
therefore, in view of recent interest in the two subjects, the following notes have been
prepared. . .'. Dallimore principally looks at the prospects of establishing trees in the
Falklands and includes a list of the trees and shrubs sent from Kew on 27 December
1848.

465 **Trees for the Falkland Islands.**
William Dallimore. *Kew Bulletin*, no. 10 (December 1920), p. 377-78.
Constitutes a list of plants, cuttings, and seeds, supplied by Messrs Dicksons of
Chester, and by the Royal Botanical Gardens in Kew, and sent out to the Islands with
James Reid, the newly appointed Forestry Officer for the Falklands, who sailed from
England on 20 November 1920.

466   **The Falkland Islands.**
Kew Bulletin, no. 1 (February 1927), p. 1-3.

This short account of forestry experiments since the appointment of James Reid as Forestry Officer in 1920 describes how the attempt to establish trees on Mount Low, East Falkland, had been abandoned to concentrate on Hill Cove, West Falkland. Plants, seedlings and seeds had come from England, Scotland, South America, the Scilly Isles, and New Zealand.

467   **Trees for the Falkland Islands.**
P. J. Stewart. *Commonwealth Forestry Review*, vol. 61(3), no. 188 (September 1982), p. 219-25. bibliog.

For the general purposes of soil improvement, and the provision of shelter, Stewart recommends that fifteen species of trees and shrubs from Britain, South-western Scandinavia, British Columbia, and Southern Chile (in other words, regions of cool temperature exposed to maritime winds) should be introduced to the Falklands. He proposes that as a first step a tree nursery and an experimental plantation should be established near Port Stanley.

468   **Recent tree planting trials and the status of forestry in the Falkland Islands.**
J. H. McAdam. *Commonwealth Forestry Review*, vol. 61(3), no. 189 (December 1982), p. 259-67. bibliog.

The sparsity of trees on the Falkland Islands is put down to a combination of undeveloped soils and the lack of advice and encouragement. An updated list of species currently growing in the Islands is presented and there is also a description and an analysis of the important plantation at Hill Cove.

469   **Tree planting in the Falkland Islands.**
Alan J. Low. *Forestry*, vol. 59, no. 1 (1986), p. 59-84. map. bibliog.

Following a recommendation in the 1982 Shackleton Report that advice on tree planting should be sought from the Forestry Commission, the author spent three weeks in the Falklands in September 1982 examining the results of earlier programmes of tree planting, assessing climatic conditions, and other limiting factors on tree growth, and how far these could be overcome by using modern forestry techniques developed for difficult, exposed upland sites in North Britain. In this paper, which is undoubtedly the most accessible, comprehensive, and up-to-date report on forestry in the Falklands, Low reviews previous attempts to introduce trees to the Islands and the present location and nature of tree growth with a description of the plots and plantations in Stanley and elsewhere. He considers the reasons for tree planting successes and failure and outlines the prospects for shelterbelt planting, planting for wood production, and amenity planting for houses and gardens. His recommendations for new trials are printed and there is a table of trees and species of tall shrub found in the Islands giving their botanical and common name with some remarks. *Forestry* is the journal of the Institute of Chartered Foresters.

470   **United Kingdom Falkland Islands Trust tree planting and establishment.**
       Michelle Lovett. *Falkland Islands Newsletter*, no. 56 (August 1993), p. 13.

This is an account of a project which started in 1989. Funded by the Falkland Islands Development Corporation, and with a donation by the Standard Chartered Bank, trials were held initially at Keppel Island, Fitzroy, and Stanley Market Garden, with the objective of determining 'the most suitable method of planting and establishing trees on a range of Camp sites in the Islands and to provide information on species suitability for various locations'. At each site a group of Lodgepole Pines and Sitka Spruce was planted. Although a ten per cent loss rate was recorded, 'overall, the project has shown that provided ground preparation and nutrition are attended to trees can be established in a wide variety of situations'.

Fishing, whaling and sealing

471   **Some aspects of the origin and implementation of the eighteenth century Falkland Islands sealing industry.**
       Anthony Dickinson. *International Journal of Maritime History*, vol. 2, no. 2 (December 1990), p. 33-68.

A masterly exposition, thoroughly researched, and extremely well documented, this academic paper relates the full story of the early Falkland Islands sealing industry. Among the topics discussed are the five pinniped (finned creature) series which sporadically visit or breed on the Islands, the hunting and killing methods employed, the classification of skins devised, oil extraction processes, and a chronological account of the American and British southern hemisphere whaling industry. The *International Journal of Maritime History* is published by the Maritime Studies Unit, Memorial University of Newfoundland, St. Johns.

472   **Sealing industries of the Falkland Islands.**
       Ian J. Strange. *Falkland Islands Journal*, no. 6 (1972), p. 9-17. bibliog.

A chronological account of the seal industry from the landing of 13,000 skins at Boston in 1784 to Dr M. A. Laws' survey of the fur-seal population in 1951.

473   **Fur sealing in the Falkland Islands in the 1820s and 1830s.**
       A. G. E. Jones. *Falkland Islands Journal*, vol. 6, no. 1 (1992), p. 39-47. bibliog.

Largely because countless log-books have long since been destroyed, very little is known of the ships and shipowners engaged in the early nineteenth-century fur-seal trade in the Antarctic, and even less about their masters and seamen. Jones provides details of five sealers, *Adeona, Dart, Uxbridge, Susanna Ann*, and *Exquisite*, investigates the profitability of the sealing trade, outlines what few source materials remain, and tabulates the figures showing the import of seal skins into England.

474   **The story of the New Islands whaling venture.**
Christian Salvesen Ltd.   *Falkland Islands Journal*, no. 16 (1982),
p. 6-12.

This is a brief outline of C. A. Larsen's whaling venture, which was funded by the
Compañía Argentina de Pesca, based on New Island, in 1907-15. The story of
Larsen's negotiations with the Colonial Office is set in the context of the development
of the southern whaling industry.

475   **The whale fisheries of the Falkland Islands and Dependencies.**
Theodore E. Salvesen.   In: *Report on the scientific results of the
Scottish National Antarctic Expedition: vol. 4.*   Edinburgh: Scottish
Oceanographical Laboratory, 1914. p. 479-86. map. 10p. of plates.

Contributed by a leading member of the famous whaling firm of Christian Salvesen, of
Leith, this authoritative study describes in some detail the whaling equipment and
methods of the time, the species hunted in the South Atlantic, factory operations, and
whale products. Also included is a list of whaling companies operating in the Falkland
Islands and South Georgia giving their home ports, when they were established, their
shore stations, and the number of ships they employed. Eighteen photographs of
genuine historical interest attractively complement Salvesen's text. This paper was
issued separately in May 1914.

476   **Fishing the Falklands.**
Gordon Eddie.   *Fishing News International* (21 October 1982),
p. 34-37.

Concentrating on salmon ranching and fisheries prospects in coastal and inshore
waters, the offshore areas, and the Southern Ocean off South Georgia, this review
article on Lord Shackleton's second report also looks back at the recommendations of
the Overseas Development Administration's fisheries adviser in 1978 who proposed
that a pilot scheme be set up at Darwin, on the Ceritos, and Camilla Arroyos. Nothing
came of this proposal although Shackleton revived it. A survey of shellfish resources
around the islands, at a cost of £750,000 over three years was also suggested.

477   **The Falkland Islands.**
R. N. Spafford.   *World Fishing*, vol. 33 (October 1984), p. 10-12.

Denounces the Government's inaction on declaring a 200-mile fishing zone around the
Falkland Islands and their Dependencies, resulting in severe overfishing and the loss
of substantial revenue to the Islands' economy. Among the salient points discussed are
the exploitation of squid off South Georgia by foreign fishing fleets; the necessity for
an efficient licensing, surveillance, and policing system; the plans of J. Marr & Son to
conserve fish stocks; the certain burgeoning of the Islands' income should a system be
initiated; and the relatively new krill fisheries.

478   **Last great free-for-all at sea.**
Jeremy Cherfas.   *New Scientist*, vol. 108, no. 1487 (7 November
1985), p. 18-19.

Cherfas underlines the need for swift action to control the fisheries around the
Falklands. The British Government was reluctant to impose controls unilaterally and

preferred an international multilateral agreement under the aegis of the Food & Agricultural Organization.

479 Falkland farming and fishing.

W. R. P. Bourne. *Marine Pollution Bulletin*, vol. 18, no. 1 (January 1987), p. 1-2.

The concern with Falkland farming is mainly confined to the incidence of unsupervised large fires designed to dispose of the whitegrass, *Cortaderia pilosa*, which during unusually dry summers occasionally get out of control to the detriment of the underlying peat. Concern is also reported on the concentrated fishing of a limited area along the continental shelf to the south and east of the Islands. 'It is increasingly clear that if Britain wishes to maintain a credible claim to the Falklands . . . she will have to put her affairs there in better order, starting with the regulation of the great fisheries around the islands, where a previous generation of our best scientists sat and watched the whales being exterminated'.

480 The Sino-Argentine 'Squid War' of 1986: its implications for fisheries policy making.

Nien-Tsu Alfred Hu. *Marine Policy*, vol. 11, no. 2 (April 1987), p. 133-42.

A serious fisheries incident between the Republic of China and Argentina, which culminated in bloodshed, occurred on 28 May 1986 in Latitude 49° 16'S, Longitude 61° 02'W when the coastguard ship *Prefecto Derbes* chased and fired upon the fishing vessel *Chii Fu 6*. The whole question of conflicting claims to sovereignty and the exploitation of maritime national resources was reopened in dramatic fashion.

481 Falklands update.

R. N. Spafford. *World Fishing*, vol. 36, no. 4 (April 1987), p. 2-4.

In this article, Spafford describes the frantic activity that followed the announcement in London of an 150-mile Fishing Zone round the Falkland Islands at the end of October 1986. This covered the vessels chartered from J. Marr & Sons of Hull; the Dornier 228 aircraft employed; the administrative costs; the international compliance to the regulations; the number of applications for licences and the number granted (215 out of 400); the licensing costs (ranging from £26-80,000 depending on tonnage); and the profit accruing to the Falkland Islands Government.

482 Fishy events in the Falklands.

K. Patterson. *New Scientist*, vol. 114, no. 1562 (28 May 1987), p. 44-48. map.

Expresses concern that by late 1986 the situation for the Falkland fisheries appeared bleak. Stocks were on the verge of being overfished but the authorities had no plans to check the continued expansion of the fishing industry because of the political and legal problems that hindered the British declaration of a fishing zone. Despite this the Falkland Islands Government was setting up a fisheries department to police the fisheries and administer licences. Patterson's account also contains vivid descriptions of Japanese squid jiggers and trawlers and their fishing methods. 'Researchers are interested in squid and other cephalopods because they could prove to be one of the world's greatest sources of untapped protein'.

483 **Falklands fishing.**
J. A. Gulland. *Marine Policy*, vol. 11, no. 3 (August 1987), p. 240.

Argues that the British Government's decision to enforce control over the fisheries around the Falklands would probably be welcomed by most of the fishing fleets: 'most participants would accept . . . controls, provided they were imposed reasonably since this would give them a future in which there is less chance of the stocks collapsing'. Problems envisaged were the sovereignty issue, the benefits to coastal states, and the development of appropriate shore facilities.

484 **Falkland Islands – Declaration of FICZ – Report on future development.**
Keesing's Record Of World Events, vol. 33, no. 10 (October 1987), p. 35454-55.

A report principally concerned with the declaration by the British Government that a Falkland Islands Interim Conservation and Management Zone (FICZ) was to be created covering a radius of 150 miles round the Islands. 'The FICZ was to come into effect on Feb. 1 1987; thereafter, every fishing vessel wishing to fish within the designated zone would be required to obtain a licence costing as much as £120,000. Enforcement of the FICZ . . . was to be undertaken by the Falklands Fisheries Protection Force, comprising two UK former deep sea trawlers and a Dornier aircraft. The vessels would be unarmed, but Royal Navy vessels would assist if necessary'.

485 **The British 150 mile fishery conservation and management zone around the Falkland (Malvinas) Islands.**
Yann-Huei Song. *Political Geography Quarterly*, vol. 7, no. 2 (April 1988), p. 183-96. map. bibliog.

Six reasons are adduced for what the author describes as 'a belated declaration of a 150 mile fishing zone': the geographical and economic disadvantages of the Falkland Islands; the development of Exclusive Economic Zones elsewhere; the problem of over-fishing; the 1982 war, the Shackleton Report, and the United Nations Convention on the Law of the Seas; unsuccessful bilateral and multilateral efforts at fishery conservation; and an increase in Argentina's diplomatic offensive.

486 **The Falklands fishing zone: legal aspects.**
R. R. Churchill. *Marine Policy*, vol. 12, no. 4 (October 1988), p. 343-60.

After eighteen months of negotiation and deliberation the British Government finally announced on 29 October 1986 that a Falkland Islands Conservation and Management Zone would operate as from 1 February 1987. This article explains why the zone was established, and examines the legal aspects raised. Amongst these are the legal obstacles to its establishment, the question of delimitation, the criteria for the access of foreign vessels, its enforcement, and the management of joint stocks of fish. The potentially far-reaching political and economic implications of the zone are also subjected to scrutiny.

487   **The squid of the Falkland Islands fishery: a profile.**
Emma Hatfield.   *Falkland Islands Foundation Newsletter*, no. 10
(October 1990), p. 2-4.

Deals with the Falkland Islands fishery which supports a total annual catch of about
200,000 tonnes with an estimated market value of £235 million. Two species of squid
form the principal catch: the Argentine Shortfin Squid which is heavily in demand
from Japanese, Taiwanese, and Korean vessels, and the Patagonian Squid favoured by
Europeans. To help preserve stocks of squid the British Antarctic Survey is currently
researching into the lifespans of the squid, their growth rates, and the timing of
reproduction.

488   **Stock assessment and the provision of management advice for the
short fin squid fishery in Falkland Island waters.**
J. R. Beddington, A. A. Rosenberg, J. A. Crombie, G. P. Kirkwood.
Fisheries Research, vol. 8, no. 4 (1990), p. 351-65.

This scientific paper outlines the policies adopted to regulate the short fin squid
industry and explains how each year's level of fishing is calculated. The results of the
policies described are given for 1987 and 1988, the first two years of regulated fishing.

489   **So what is AFIFI?**
Falkland Islands Newsletter, no. 47 (May 1991), p. 12.

'Any company that is involved in the fishing industry in any way at all and which is
"majority beneficially owned and controlled by Falkland Islands residents" is eligible
for membership of the Association of the Falkland Islands Fishing Industry'. Members
include: Beauchene (FI) Fishing and Trading Co.; Goodwin Offshore; Meredith
Fishing Co.; SFS Navagantes; Stanley Trawlers; Fortuna; JBG Falklands; Polar; South
Atlantic Marine Services; and Stevedore and Fisheries Services. This feature explains
why it was thought necessary to form the Association and why it is important that the
colony supports its own industry and doesn't leave the exploitation of its fisheries to
foreign fleets.

490   **The 1994 fishing agreement.**
P. J. Pepper.   *Falkland Islands Newsletter*, no. 57 (November 1993),
p. 3.

Following a meeting in Argentina on 18-19 October 1993, it was agreed that in 1994
Argentina would have the right to license eighty foreign vessels and to fish a total of
220,000 tonnes of squid in waters south of the forty-fifth parallel; the Falklands would
fish 150,000 tonnes. This report notes a massive increase in the Argentine quota, the
fact that no long-term agreement was signed, the reaction in Argentina, and the
signing of an Argentine-European Community fishing treaty.

Conservation and Environmental Management

491 **Profile William Lamond Allardyce: 1861-1930 pioneer Antarctic conservationist.**
Henry R. Heyburn. *Falkland Islands Journal*, no. 13 (1980), p. 24-28.

Governor from 1904 to 1915, Allardyce was active from the first in regulating the burgeoning whale industry on South Georgia. Aware that whaling boosted the Falklands economy he consistently attempted to enforce conservation measures: 'the policy of this Government will continue to be that of endeavouring to establish a permanent industry rather than the rapid collection of a large revenue'.

492 **Sand-binding grasses in the Falkland Islands.**
C. E. Hubbard. *Kew Bulletin*, no. 4 (June 1937), p. 274. 1p. of plates.

An account of the planting of marram grass for the consolidation of drifting sands around the Board of Trade lighthouse, Cape Pembroke, near Stanley, to halt and repair the destruction of practically all vegetation on that long peninsula.

493 **The conservation of wild life in the Falkland Islands.**
Ian J. Strange. *Falkland Islands Journal*, no. 1 (January 1967), p. 21-28.

Current conservation practices and their effects on both Crown and private property are set out in this article, which has five appendices: the International Union for the Conservation of Nature Policy's statement of purpose; Falkland Islands birds and mammals; census reports on individual species; the species of special interest in the Falklands (that is, those in need of conservation); and the Islands of special interest for future conservation.

494   **The wise men of West Point.**
Ian J. Strange.   *Animals*, vol. 11, no. 60 (February 1969), p. 458-62.
Based on detailed information supplied by the owner of West Point Island (formerly Albatross Island), in the north-west corner of the Falklands archipelago, this illustrated article relates how the soil erosion caused by unrestricted sheep grazing on tussac grass, and its consequent effect on the Island's ecology, was repaired by the replanting of tussac grass and other vegetation in a practical programme of conservation. The preservation of the grass encourages thousands of Magellan Penguins to return to their traditional nesting areas. The other main topic treated is the study of the Black-Browed Albatross, initiated by the author, which became an official part of the United States Antarctic Research Program in 1960.

495   **Wildlife in the Falklands.**
Ian J. Strange.   *Oryx*, vol. 11, no. 4 (1972), p. 240-57. map.
Discussion of the continuous supply of marine food, the various species of breeding birds and mammals, early and modern depredations, and threats to the Islands' ecology, precedes an optimistic account of the steps taken towards conservation of their fauna in this authoritative paper. Nevertheless, it is warned that 'very careful handling and continued study must be paramount if the Falkland Islands' most valuable natural asset is to survive'.

496   **The silent ordeal of a South Atlantic archipelago.**
Ian J. Strange.   *Natural History*, vol. 82, no. 2 (February 1973),
p. 30-39.
In this illustrated feature Strange chronicles the threats to the varied wildlife of the Falklands over two centuries. He reports on the promulgation of two Ordinances in 1964 for the protection of birds and animals and for the establishment of wildlife reserves. By 1970 there were seventeen sanctuaries and four wildlife reserves. But, 'the surrounding seas are being opened up to the world's fishing fleets, a new form of exploitation aimed at the food so much of the islands' bird and animal life depends upon. It is not known whether the Falklands can face or survive another round of exploitation'.

497   **Ravaged Falkland Islands.**
Ian J. Strange.   *Geographical Magazine*, vol. 48, no. 5 (February
1976), p. 297-304. 2 maps.
Relates the measures taken to safeguard the environment and to avoid ecological disasters similar to those that occurred when the whaling and sealing industry was at its height. In 1964 the Falkland Islands Government effected ordinances for the establishment of nature reserves – four were on a sound footing by 1970 – and existing laws were amended to give more protection to wildlife. Remaining concerns were soil erosion and the disappearance of tussac (tussock) grass, reckless harvesting of the sea, and the possible effects of the discovery of oil.

498 **The status and conservation of seabirds at the Falkland Islands.**
J. P. Croxall, S. J. McInnes, P. A. Prince. In: *Status and conservation of the world's seabirds.* Edited by J. P. Croxall, P. G. H. Evans, R. W. Schreiber. Cambridge, England: International Council for Bird Preservation, 1984, p. 271-91. 10 maps. bibliog.

Concerned with the distribution and abundance of seabirds on the Falklands, this academic paper, contributed to the ICBP Seabird Conservation Symposium, held in Cambridge in August 1982, includes the sources of its data; a table of the status and distribution of breeding pairs; maps of breeding sites; notes on each species; historical and current population trends; threats (competition with commercial fisheries, pollution and poisoning, habit destruction and disturbance, and predators); conservation action and requirements; and an extensive list of references.

499 **Conservation problems in the Falkland Islands and the role of the Falkland Islands Foundation.**
Simon Lyster. *Sea Swallow*, vol. 35 (1986), p. 21-23.

The Honorary Secretary of the Falkland Islands Foundation reports on the establishment of a two-year research project into the diet and numbers of Falklands seabirds in order to assess the threats from commercial fisheries.

500 **Tussac grass in the Falklands: an assessment of the potential for competition between the seabirds and fisheries in the Falkland Islands.**
Ian J. Strange, C. J. Parry, M. C. Parry, Robin Woods. Stanley: Falkland Islands Foundation Project in collaboration with the Falkland Islands Government, 1988. variously paginated.

Funded by the Falkland Islands Government, this is really a series of four reports brought together in the same cover. Cumulatively, the separate reports present a detailed view of the current status of tussac grass which also charts its dramatic historical and continuing decline. Ian Strange is responsible for the 'Tussac grass survey', a historical and ecological study, and a 'List of Islands', which offers a physical description and location of the islands, whilst Robin Woods carried out a tussac distribution survey. Another section is devoted to patterns of change, showing tussac cover, and examples. The survey arose from a concern over the general decline of tussac which prompted the Falkland Islands Government in January 1986 to instigate a thoroughgoing investigation which would lead to the development of guidelines for legislation for grazing management and for total protection on some islands. A summary of the report, with an explanation of the methods used to compile it, and progress since its publication, can be found in 'Tussac Grass in the Falklands', *Falkland Islands Foundation Newsletter*, no. 9 (November 1989), p. 3-7.

501 **Time to act: a replanting strategy for Tussac Grass.**
Gerry Hoppé. *Warrah*, no. 2 (May 1992), p. 4-5.

This paper by an officer of the Falkland Islands Government Department of Agriculture draws attention to previous attempts to restore the tussac grass habitat, to the greater recognition of its conservation value following recent changes in land ownership, to a replanting strategy, and to a series of field trials designed to identify practical methods for tussac establishment and maintenance.

502   Wetlands conservation in the Falklands.

Kate Thompson.   *Warrah*, no. 3 (December 1992), p. 4.

Thompson describes recent developments in wetlands conservation and possibilities for the future following the Convention on Wetlands of International Importance held in Ramsar (Iran) in 1971. A study commissioned by the Department of the Environment, jointly undertaken by the International Waterfowl and Wetlands Research Bureau and the NGO Forum for the UK Dependent Territories subcontracted to Falkland Conservation, highlights the predominance and conservation significance of wetland sites in the Islands.

503   Soil erosion in the Falkland Islands: an assessment.

Peter Wilson, Richard Clark, James H. McAdam, Elizabeth A. Cooper. *Applied Geography*, vol. 13, no. 4 (October 1993), p. 329-52.

'Observations and data concerning soil erosion on clay-rich, sand-rich and organic soil materials are reported. . . The most extensively eroded areas are located on coastal sand deposits and where sandy soils occur at inland sites. There is evidence that soil erosion is of more recent origin and can be associated with land management practices, principally grazing management, stocking rates, and the frequency and intensity of pasture burning' (Abstract). There are extensive references.

504   Welcome to the new battle of the Falklands.

Nick Nuttall.   *The Times Weekend* (31 December 1994), p. 14.

This is an up-to-the-minute report on the commercial pressures putting the Islands' wildlife at risk from oil exploration and the activities of the fishing fleets. The social and economic consequences of conservation, and the tension between farmers and landowners on one side, and the conservationists on the other, are also outlined.

Natural history of an unlikely battlefield.
See item no. 109.

The bird man.
See item no. 351.

Falkland Islands Foundation Newsletter.
See item no. 542.

The Warrah.
See item no. 543.

Falkland Islands Foundation.
See item no. 546.

United Kingdom Falkland Islands Trust.
See item no. 547.

Falkland Islands Trust.
See item no. 548.

Conservation and Environmental Management

Falklands Conservation.
See item no. 551.

Philately and Coinage

505 The letters from the Falkland Islands.
  C. S. Morton. *Stamp Collecting*, vol. 24, no. 605 (16 May 1925),
  p. 162-63.

Outlines the history of the Falkland Islands postal system including the shipping of
mail from Stanley to Montevideo by the Falkland Islands Company. Morton
encompasses the early arrangements for mail to West Falkland, and the Postal
Ordinance of 1880, which required the masters of all vessels leaving the Colony to
attend the Collector of Customs and to receive on board any mail handed to him for
which he should provide 'a dry and secure place'.

506 Some notes on the early stamps of the Falkland Islands.
  David Nabarro. *London Philatelist*, vol. 41, no. 482 (February 1932),
  p. 30-35.

In this authoritative study Nabarro investigates the number of stamps printed for all
denominations of each issue, and examines whole sheets of each printing, noting their
paper, watermarks and perforation. He concludes with a table of consignments from
London from 1878 to 1891, giving such details as the printers' date of delivery, the
stamps' face value, the numbers printed, and their colour.

**507 Argentina's claim to the Falkland Islands: commemorative stamps
  not to be recognised.**
  Eric R. King. *London Philatelist*, vol. 42, no. 497 (May 1933),
  p. 112-13.

A report on Argentina's decision to surcharge all correspondence from the Falklands
franked with the Centenary stamps commemorating the British reoccupation of the
Islands, 3 January 1833. 'As far as the writer is aware, this is the first occasion on
which a member of the International Postal Union has refused to recognise the postal
emissions of another member. Should the Argentine government carry out its intention
of surcharging correspondence from the Falklands bearing the commemorative
stamps, some most interesting entires will be created'.

508 **The postmarks of the Falkland Islands and Dependencies.**
S. H. Creese. *Philatelic Journal of Great Britain*, vol. 46, no. 543 (March 1936), p. 46-49.
The postmarks of the Falkland Islands.
James Andrews. *Philatelic Journal of Great Britain*, vol. 47, no. 555 (March 1937), p. 48-49, 55.

Creese's article is an illustrated account of five categories of postmarks: cork cancellations; Falkland Islands obliterations; circular postmarks; ship cancellations; and postmarks used in the Dependencies. Andrews adds 'a few supplementary notes' mainly on circular postmarks. Geoffrey Moir's '20th century cancellations of the Falkland Islands', *Gibbons Stamp Monthly*, vol. 26, no. 3 (August 1995), p. 67–71, brings the story up to date.

509 **On the fringe of the Antarctic (peoples and posts of the Falkland Islands).**
Harold G. D. Gisburn, Kay V. Lellman. *Philatelic Magazine*, vol. 54, no. 24 (29 November 1946), p. 576-77.

The authors present a good outline of the internal and external postal services of the Falklands soon after the Second World War, when external communications depended upon an irregular cargo vessel service to Montevideo, Buenos Aires, or Magellanes in Chile. The establishment of the General Post Office in Stanley consisted of the postmaster and three clerks; there was no postal delivery in the town (residents called for their mail); whilst in the Camp direct delivery often relied on farmowners.

510 **The postage stamps of the Falkland Islands and Dependencies.**
B. S. H. Grant. London: Stanley Gibbons, 1952. 138p. map. bibliog.

Generously illustrated, this definitive work on the Islands' postal history covers: franks; the first postage stamps of 1878-79; Victorian provisional and definitive issues; the Edwardian issues of 1904-17; King George V issues, 1912-29; the war stamps of 1918-20; the centenary issue of 1933; other commemorative issues; the 1952 pictorial issues; postmarks; and proofs, essays, and special stamps. Appendix one is a list of printings for all Falkland Islands stamps giving the value, date of delivery from the printer, the number printed, their colour, and remarks on points of interest to collectors. An earlier study, Bertram W. H. Poole's *The postage stamps of the Falkland Islands* (London: D. Field, 1909), contains an enormous amount of historical research, and is still of interest.

511 **The cancellations of the Falkland Islands and Dependencies and the handstruck stamps; with notes on the British, Argentine and Chilean post offices in the Antarctic.**
James Andrews. London: Robson Lowe, 1956. 56p. 4 maps. bibliog.

A short history of postal communications on the Islands and Dependencies, pieced together from old colonial reports and from items in the *Falkland Islands Gazette*, introduces a more detailed study of handstruck town and ship postal cancellation marks. Post Office locations are indicated on the maps of individual territories. Further interesting examples of cancellations occur in R. N. Spafford's 'Falkland Islands: recent postal history finds', *Stamp Collecting*, vol. 147, no. 13 (13 June 1983), p. 405, 407.

512   **The Falkland Islands inter-islands posts.**
Compiled by W. C. Nield from notes collected by C. Stewart Douglas.
Gibbons Stamp Monthly, vol. 41, no. 8 (April 1968), p. 135-38.

This illustrated account ties together what little is known of the transport of mail in the early days of the Colony, from Captain Hanson's schooner, *Foam*, perhaps as early as 1866, to the Falkland Islands Company's *Fitzroy* in the 1930s. Other ships mentioned include the Kosmos Company's *Malvinas*, Salvesen's *SS Columbus*, the Falkland Islands Transport Company's *Wheatsheaf*, and the *RMS Falkland*, and *HMCS Afterglow*.

513   **The postal service of the Falkland Islands including South Shetlands (1906-1931) and South Georgia.**
Robert Barnes.   London: Robson Lowe, 1972. 96p. bibliog.

Sponsored by the Falkland Islands Philatelic Study Group, this authoritative work covers postal legislation, overseas communications, Falkland Islands postmasters, and the post offices at Stanley, Fox Bay, New Island and South Georgia. Barnes also discusses overseas and inland postal rates, overseas and inland air mail services, and the Battle of the Falklands. Overseas mail contracts with Kosmos (1880-1900) and with the Pacific Steam Navigation Company (1900-17) are appended.

514   **The 1933 centenary issue of the Falkland Islands.**
R. N. Spafford.   Chippenham, England: Picton Publishing, 1972. 84p.
maps on endpapers. bibliog.

Published in a limited edition of 1,000 copies, this specialist account contains chapter-length studies of each of the stamps in the centenary issues, a chapter on the Colony's heraldic arms, and another on the stamps' production. There are also two short biographical sketches, on George Roberts, the designer of most of the centenary stamps, and Ellen Maude Carey, the Colonial Postmaster between 1934 and 1947. The centenary issue also figures prominently in G. D. Moir's 'Falkland Islands: the stamps of King George V', *Gibbons Stamp Monthly*, vol. 25, no. 11 (April 1995), p. 29-32, where it is described as 'almost certainly the most attractive set of twelve stamps ever produced throughout the British Empire and, possibly, the world'.

515   **The Falkland Islands philatelic digest no. 1.**
Edited by M. D. Barton.   Batley, England: Falkland Islands Philatelic
Study Group, 1975. 182p. map. bibliog.

Features originally published in *Falkland Islands Philatelic Study Group Newsletters*, nos. 1-8 (October 1969-June 1971) and in *Upland Goose*, nos. 1-4 (September 1971-June 1972) are contained in this volume. Topics covered include postal rates; the Falkland Islands 1912-20 issue; war stamps; the 1933 centenary issue; printing and sales figures; Falkland Islands postal stationery; formula registered envelopes; specimen stamps; registration labels; New Island, South Georgia and Port Foster overprints; and forged postmarks.

516 **Catalogue of the award-winning collection of Falkland Islands offered by order of Mr John F. Ayre of Newfoundland and the selected properties of other owners: to be sold by public auction in two sessions on Tuesday, October 2, 1979.**
London: Harmers, 1979. 40p. 24p. of plates.

Stamp auction catalogues are valuable for their annotations on the rare stamps, franks, cancellations, watermarks, letters, and postal stationery on offer. This illustrated catalogue is representative of a number of others issued by Harmers, who also disposed of the collections of B. S. H. Grant, C. Stewart Douglas, A. G. Carpenter, and F. E. Baker. A notable evening sale at Harmers of 'Falkland Islands 1872 to 1981', which also included much rare material, took place on 8 November 1983.

517 **The Falklands Task Force: a postal history.**
Peter High. *Stamp Collecting*, vol. 145, no. 21 (19 August 1982), p. 883-85.

Examines the cancellations of *HMS Endurance*, other naval vessels, merchant vessels, and of the British Forces Post Offices on the Falklands, during the 1982 South Atlantic War.

518 **Falklands: 150 years.**
R. N. Spafford. *Philatelic Magazine*, vol. 91, no. 4 (January 1983), p. 172-73; no. 5 (February 1983), p. 228-29.

In this feature Spafford considers the subjects featured on long-term commemorative issues marking the 150th anniversary of British administration in the Falklands: the raising of the flag at Port Louis; Chelsea pensioners and barracks (1849); the development of the wool trade (1874); the ship repairing trade (1850-80); Government House (early twentieth century); the Battle of the Falklands (1914); the Centenary (1933); the contribution to the war effort (1938-46); the Duke of Edinburgh's visit (1957); and Royal Marines (1833-1983).

519 **Argentina's philatelic annexation of the Falklands.**
Peter J. Beck. *History Today*, vol. 33, no. 2 (February 1983), p. 39-44. bibliog.

Argentine postage stamps depicting maps showing the Falklands as Argentine possessions, and propaganda postcards, regarded as 'Argentina's cartographical wish-fulfilment', are described and illustrated here. British Foreign Office unease about Crown Colony commemorative stamps is also recounted.

520 **The Falklands War: postal history and stamps of the Argentine occupation of 1982.**
J. D. Davis. Andover, England: J. D. Davis, 1983. 85p.

On being sent to the Falklands by the Ministry of Defence at the end of June 1982, Davis determined to investigate the philatelic history of the short-lived Argentine occupation. In this admirably clear and concise study he concentrates on the despatch of private and official mail from the mainland and its handling at the Buenos Aires post office. He also focuses on the involvement of all levels of Argentine officialdom in extending the propaganda campaign; postal operations at Stanley including stamps and cancellations; internal and external mail services from Stanley and Fox Bay; commercial activities including dealers' covers and special event cancellations; and the problems for the post office as Stanley returned to normal.

521　**The Forces postal history of the Falkland Islands and the Task Force.**
John A. Daynes.　Burnham-on-Crouch, England: The Forces Postal History Society, 1983. 162p. maps.

Spiral bound, and reproduced from typescript, this specialist study covers all periods of modern Falklands military history from the naval battle of 1914, continuing to the Battle of the River Plate in 1939 and World War Two, the post-war period, Royal Navy ships, 1955-82, and the 1982 war. In the most recent conflict the whole philatelic scene is encompassed: the Forces Postal Service; the Task Force at sea; Spanish-language leaflets dropped by RAF Harriers encouraging the Argentine forces to surrender; covers, postmarks, censor marks, and handstamps. Nothing is overlooked or forgotten.

522　**War in the Falklands.**
Ronnie Spafford.　*Supplement to Philatelic Magazine*, vol. 92, no. 2 (November 1983), 26p.

Essential reading for all collectors of Falkland Islands stamps, this invaluable study first looks back to the brouhaha of the 1933 centenary stamps, the subsequent Argentine political map stamps, the 1971 communications agreement, and to Falklands anxieties and Argentine disquiet regarding the 1983 celebrations. The Argentine invasion and occupation is considered next, and includes a consolidated and definitive list of the stamps put on sale in Stanley, 29th April 1982, followed by the postal history of the recapture of the Islands. Lastly, Spafford outlines the immediate post-war scene, ending with a list of mail deliveries for Royal Navy and Mercantile Marine ships passing through British Field Post Office 666. The author's 'The Falklands today: Port Stanley Post Office', *Philatelic Magazine*, vol. 91, no. 9 (June 1983), p. 451, describes the possibly unique occurrence of civil and military postal workers sharing the same counter.

523　**Postcards of the Falkland Islands: a catalogue 1900-1950.**
Henry Heyburn, Frances Heyburn.　Chippenham, England: Picton Publishing, 1985. 255p. maps on endpapers. bibliog.

Over 340 cards are listed in this scholarly history of the first half-century of Falkland Islands postcards. Arranged as nearly as possible in chronological order, the information for each card includes the scene and locality, publisher (if known), lettering, reproduction, and an extensive annotation providing details of the historical, social and economic background to the scenes depicted. Two thirds of the postcards are illustrated in the work and there are title, subject, and publisher indexes. *Supplement to postcards of the Falkland Islands: a catalogue 1900-1950,* 109p., bibliog., was published in 1989.

524   **Stanley Gibbons Falkland Islands and British South Atlantic Islands stamp catalogue.**
London: Stanley Gibbons Publications, 1985. 2nd ed. 105p.

Falkland Islands and Falkland Islands Dependencies stamps for the period 1869-1984 take up the first thirty-four pages of this catalogue. The information for each set of stamps issued includes the date of issue, names of the designer and printer, method of printing, details of watermarks and perforations, and, for Elizabethan issues, sheet sizes, quantities sold, and withdrawal dates. Prices are quoted for stamps in mint and used condition. A note on the Argentine occupation, from 2 April to 15 June 1982, is also included. Information on later issues can be found in *Stanley Gibbons Commonwealth two reigns stamp catalogue Falkland Islands and Antarctica* (1988. 33p.) and in *Stanley Gibbons stamp catalogue part 1: British Commonwealth* which is published annually. In the 1993 edition Falkland Islands occupies p. 331-41 and Falkland Islands Dependencies p. 342-44.

525   **The De La Rue definitives of the Falkland Islands 1901-1929.**
John P. Bunt.   Truro, England: published by the author, 1986. 100p. bibliog.

Published in a limited edition of 600 copies, this detailed study of all De La Rue-printed definitive stamps includes chapters on Thomas De La Rue and his family, De La Rue technology, Edward VII and George V definitives, War Stamp overprints, and the 1923-28 provisionals.

526   **The development of the external air mail service of the Falkland Islands.**
Geoffrey D. Moir.   *Gibbons Stamp Monthly*, vol. 19, no. 10 (March 1989), p. 30-32; vol. 20, no. 1 (June 1989), p. 30-32.

By an Order in Council on 16 August 1944, the Falkland Islands Government decided that postal material for onward transmission from Montevideo would be accepted at Stanley and Fox Bay post offices where air mail labels would be available. In these two illustrated articles Moir surveys the development of the air mail service in some detail including postal stationery, the pioneering direct air link between Southampton and Stanley in 1952, the Argentine air service to Stanley, and the vastly improved service from Mt. Pleasant airport after the war. He also includes a table of air mail postage rates for the period of September 1971 to April 1986.

527   **Falkland Islands mails: the Kosmos years 1880-1900: a history of the mail contracts with the Deutsche Dampfschiffahrts Gesellschaft Kosmos of Hamburg.**
J. W. T. Howat.   London: British Philatelic Trust, British Philatelic Centre, 1989. 146p. maps.

Complementing Howat's earlier self-published work, *South American packets* (1985), which in part deals with the branch packets running between Montevideo and Port Stanley in 1852-1880, this study traces the development of postal communication between the Falklands and the outside world. A series of appendices provides the text of five mail contracts, financial information, details of the ships employed, and data on over 180 recorded items of mail carried. Considering that Kosmos' archives were lost during the Second World War, this is a remarkably complete history.

528 **The internal mail of the Falkland Islands.**
Geoffrey D. Moir. *Gibbons Stamp Monthly*, vol. 20, no. 11 (April 1990), p. 46-47, 52.

Early communications between East and West Falkland; postal rates; the visits of the Kosmos vessels; the first internal air service; the Argentine stamps used during the brief occupation in 1982; and internal communications on the Camp, are all features in this typically enthusiastic illustrated article.

529 **Specialised stamp catalogue of the Falkland Islands and Dependencies including postal history and cancellations, 1800-1990.**
Stefan Heitz. Stockholm: published by the author, Box 26048, S-100 41 Stockholm, 1990. 2nd ed. 240p.

Heitz includes chapters listing the stamps and covers of the Falkland Islands, the Dependencies, and British Antarctic Territory; the cancellations of all three territories; and a miscellaneous chapter encompassing postal stationery, registration labels, cachets, privileged mail, censored covers, and listing of postal rates from 1850 onwards. The work was first published in 1988.

530 **The posties went to war.**
Ian Winfield. Worcester, England: Square One Publications, 1990. 95p. map.

Major Winfield of 2 Postal and Courier Regiment, Royal Engineers, sailed with his unit in the 1982 Task Force. This story of the Falklands war postal service, which was so vital to morale, is based on his journal, relating events from 4 April to 10 September 1982.

531 **The surface mail of the Falkland Islands 1833-1900, 1900-1928, 1928-1971.**
Geoffrey D. Moir. *Gibbons Stamp Monthly*, vol. 21, no. 8 (December 1990), p. 31-33; no. 11 (April 1991), p. 83-85; vol. 22, no. 4 (September 1991), p. 49-51.

No aspect of Falkland Islands surface mail escapes Moir's expert attention. Writing with his customary authority and enthusiasm he passes in review its entire history, starting in 1832 with the regular monthly packet service from England to Rio de Janeiro and with connecting links to Montevideo, for passing ships to pick up mail en route to Stanley. The Kosmos and Pacific Steam Navigation Company services, the first stamps, surcharges and cancellations, ship arrivals, disrupted services during the two world wars, the beginnings of a postal service from South Georgia, and the 1933 centenary issue, all fall under his expert eye.

532 **'The Falkland Islands conflict' April-June 1982.**
Geoffrey D. Moir. *Gibbons Stamp Monthly*, vol. 22, no. 12 (May 1992), p. 47, 50-53.

Earlier Argentine attempts at invasion, the work of Stanley post office during the occupation, the use of Argentine stamps, the military mail of both sides, the work of the Army Field Post Office, and the post-war restoration and redevelopment of services, are the main themes in this account of a difficult and unusual period in Falklands philatelic history.

533 **The history of the Falkland Islands.**
Geoffrey D. Moir. *Gibbons Stamp Monthly*, vol. 23, no. 3 (August 1992), p. 94-96; no. 6 (November 1992), p. 50-53; no. 9 (February 1993), p. 29-32.

Marshalled here are the principal maritime, diplomatic, and military incidents in Falkland Islands history as depicted on various postage stamp issues. Economic and religious affairs, internal and external communications, the Shackleton Report, the development of tourism, and the Islands' future under the British flag, also feature in this wide-ranging essay.

534 **The history of the Falkland Islands on stamps.**
London: Stanley Gibbons, 1994. 2 vols.

Two specially designed and handsomely bound, descriptive illustrated albums in blue leatherette have spaces for all the Falkland Islands stamps issued between 1878 and 1993, and for Falkland Islands Dependencies (including British Antarctic Territory) issues 1944-93. The Falklands' national crest is embossed on their spines and front covers. Gibbons' Falkland Collectors Club issues regular newsletters and sends quarterly selections of stamps to club members at special club prices.

535 **The Victorian posts of the Falkland Islands.**
Geoffrey D. Moir. *Gibbons Stamp Monthly*, vol. 24, no. 6 (November 1993), p. 29-32. bibliog.

The indefatigable Moir turns his attention here to the earliest Falkland mails, postage rates, mail contracts, the black and red franks, and early cancellations. He also reproduces two London General Post Office notices regarding mail and postage rates from England. An earlier essay 'The Queen Victoria issues of the Falkland Islands', *Gibbons Stamp Monthly*, vol. 24, no. 3 (August 1993), p. 28-29, 31, examines the first stamp issues, bisects, printings, and colour shades and changes.

536 **Falkland Islands coinage and currency 1825-1975.**
Ian J. Strange. *Falkland Islands Journal*, vol. 8 (1974), p. 27-31.

The first recorded Falklands currency were the notes issued by the Argentine Governor, Vernet. This brief sketch of the paper currency employed on the Islands ends with the issue of gold, silver, cupro nickel, and bronze coins on 18 December 1974. It had been decided that commemorative coins might prove a useful means of raising revenue.

Falkland Islands cartographers.
See item no. 88.

Maps on postage stamps as propaganda.
See item no. 96.

Birds of the South Atlantic.
See item no. 140.

Southern Elephant Seal.
See item no. 147.

Cape Horners of the Falkland Islands.
See item no. 176.

Falkland Islands history through philately.
See item no. 201.

Upland Goose.
See item no. 540.

Falkland Islands Philatelic Study Group.
See item no. 544.

The Press

537 **Falkland Islands Gazette.**
Stanley: Falkland Islands Government, 1891- . irreg.
Falkland Islands Government business and activities are advertised and promulgated
in this official gazette: mining and land leases, whaling and sealing regulations,
government appointments, cost of living increases, naturalization applications, new
place names, and countless other items are printed. Substantial items like Government
Ordinances and Regulations, or the annual Taxes Bulletin, are printed in *Falkland
Islands Gazette Supplement* which appears as and when necessary.

538 **Falkland Islands Focus.**
London: Falkland Islands Government, 1959- . quarterly.
This publication is a news digest compiled by the Falkland Islands Government
London Office. Issue no. 51, April 1994, included paragraphs on the visit of Douglas
Hurd to Stanley, prospects for the oil industry, the re-arming of the Argentine Air
Force, the burial of Argentine war dead on Pebble Island, the visit of a Chilean
parliamentary delegation, and numerous other items.

539 **The *Falkland Islands Journal*.**
D. W. H. Walton. *Polar Record*, vol. 22, no. 140 (May 1985),
p. 537-38.
Founded in 1967, the *Falkland Islands Journal* set out 'to promote interest in the
Falkland Islands and their history. Editorial policy is to publish items of interest from
the past and present. Politics do not come into it'. Printed on the islands for the first
ten years, copies were comparatively rare but they were reprinted in hardback in two
volumes by Bluntisham Books in 1985. Walton's 'Historical vignettes – 25 years of
the Falkland Islands Journal', *Falkland Islands Journal*, vol. 6, no. 1 (1992), p. 64-66,
highlights the articles printed that he considers of most interest, and the topics he
looks forward to finding in future issues: the farming industry; the fisheries; and the
social aspects of Falklands life.

540 **Upland Goose.**
Place of publication varies: Falkland Islands Philatelic Study Group,
1970- . quarterly.

Although *Upland Goose* is the official journal of the Falkland Islands Philatelic Study
Group it would be a mistake to regard it as containing strictly philatelic information
since few aspects of the Falklands are very far away from a definitive or
commemorative issue of postage stamps. Consequently the information to be found,
especially on the Islands history and wildlife, is almost limitless. The compiler of this
present bibliography had to exercise immense self-discipline to avoid excessive use of
items culled from its pages.

541 **The Penguin News: Voice of The Falklands.**
Stanley: Media Trust (Penguin News), 1979- . weekly.

Published fortnightly until 5 February 1993, but now firmly secured as a weekly
publication, *Penguin News* is the Islanders local newspaper. Its columns represent
their news on such matters as politics, keeping the Falklands British, economic
development, and relations with the military garrison. No one wishing to keep up to
date with Falkland Islands affairs can afford to miss it.

542 **Falkland Islands Foundation Newsletter.**
London: Falkland Islands Foundation, 1983-90. irreg.

Running for just ten issues, the Newsletter was 'designed to provide some interesting
reading about the natural and maritime history of the Falklands as well as to let
members know what the Foundation is doing'. It was succeeded by *The Warrah*.

543 **The Warrah: Newsletter of Falklands Conservation.**
London: Falklands Conservation, 1991- . irreg.

Organized very much in the same pattern as its predecessor, the *Falkland Islands
Foundation Newsletter*, *The Warrah* carries updating articles on the conservation of
Falklands wildlife, book reports, and news reports. Five issues were published
between November 1991 and April 1994.

Groups and Institutions

544   The Falkland Islands Philatelic Study Group.
1970-   .

The objectives of the Group are to research into all aspects of philately relating to the Falkland Islands and their former Dependencies and to publicize its findings. It also aims to foster Falkland Islands philately and to provide the means whereby members may exchange views and exchange or otherwise acquire related material. The group publishes the journal *Upland Goose* (*see* item 540).

545   The Falkland Islands Association.
2 Greycoat Place, London, SW1P 1SD. 1977-   .

Formed in 1977 to provide a means of mutual communication for individuals sharing an interest in affairs and subjects pertaining to the Islands, and to support, and initiate, such measures as would result in the maintenance and development of the British settlement, the Falkland Islands Association continues to exert a powerful influence on behalf of the Islanders. 'If success is measured by achievement of those matters for which we have campaigned, then the Falkland Islands Association believes that it has taken its full part in changing the Falkland Islands for the better, and the Falkland Islands remain firmly British'. ('Representing the Islanders over fifty issues', *Falkland Islands Newsletter*, no. 50 [February 1992], p. 1). The full story of its progress from the Falkland Islands Emergency Committee (1968), and the Falkland Islands Research and Development Association (1977-84), is well told in Clive Ellerby's 'The role of the Falklands lobby 1968-1990'. In: *International perspectives on the Falklands conflict*. Edited by Alex Danchev. London: Macmillan, 1992, p. 85-106.

546   The Falkland Islands Foundation.
1979-91.

The Falkland Islands Foundation for the conservation of wildlife, wrecks, and places of historical interest was founded as a United Kingdom registered charity in 1979. It acquired eighteen small islands, either by purchase or by lease, to further its nature reserves programme, and maintained close links with the Falkland Islands Trust. An attractive and informative *Newsletter* was also published (*see* item no. 542). 'The Falkland Islands Foundation', *Popular Archaeology*, vol. 4, no. 2 (August 1982), p. 18, is instructive reading. In 1991 the Foundation merged with the Trust to form Falklands Conservation.

547 The United Kingdom Falkland Islands Trust.
2 Greycoat Place, London, SW1P 1SD. 1980-   .

Not to be confused with the Stanley-based Falkland Islands Trust, UKFIT was established as a charity by the Falkland Islands Association in 1980 to support a broad range of activities in the Falklands, notably in the field of education, and in promoting study and research into the development of agriculture and other industries. A biological husbandry project, a tree-planting project, and agricultural initiatives, are already numbered amongst its successes. Nigel St. G. Gribbon's 'The United Kingdom Falkland Islands Trust', *Falkland Islands Newsletter*, no. 55 (June 1993), p. 16, presents its structure, its personalities, its relationships in the Islands, its projects, and its future, whilst his 'Taking stock: the UKFIT 1981-1993', *Falkland Islands Newsletter*, no. 58 (February 1994), p. 16, is a résumé of its educational and civic projects.

548 Falkland Islands Trust.
1981-91.

According to Tom Davies' 'The Falkland Islands Trust', *Falkland Islands Foundation Newsletter*, no. 1 (December 1983), p. 6, the Trust's objectives were 'to take an interest in, and promote the conservation of, all aspects of the Falkland Islands heritage – the flora and fauna, the historic buildings and sites, the maritime history and relics'. Their aims were virtually identical to those of Falkland Islands Foundation, and the two organizations merged in 1991 to form Falklands Conservation.

549 Falkland Islands Development Corporation, Stanley.
Falkland Islands Government Office, 14 Broadway, London,
SW1H 0BH, 1983-

Constituted under the Falkland Islands Development Corporation Ordinance of 1983, 'to encourage and assist in the economic development of the Falkland Islands', FIDC works within the constraints of a predominantly single-source economy, a limited working population, very restricted private investment capital, and limited internal and external transport facilities. To address these issues its objectives are: to diversify potential sources of income and most particularly where there are export or import substitution opportunities; provide opportunity to local people and encourage controlled immigration where there is unfulfilled need; increase the level of local expertise in all sectors through the provision of training, opportunity and information; create a pool of investment capital outside of Government sources; promote a rural development policy which will encourage Camp-based economic activity; promote the long term capability of the Falkland Islands to achieve self-sufficiency; and ensure that the social and environmental impact of development is positive. An annual Report and Accounts is published and an updated account of its activities appears in successive issues of the *Falkland Islands Newsletter*.

550 **Falkland Islands Agency.**
Falkland House, 3 Tucker Street, Wells, Somerset, BA5 3DZ. (Tel: 01749 677902). 1987- .

Officially opened by Sir Rex Hunt on 21 May 1987, the Agency now markets all Falkland Islands Association products: Falkland Islands wool and woollen sweaters; watercolours of Falkland Islands wildlife and scenery; philatelic items; crests and badges; picture postcards and greetings cards, and a wide selection of books.

551 **Falklands Conservation.**
1 Princes Avenue, Finchley, London, N3 2DA, 1991- .

Formed by a merger of Falkland Islands Foundation, and the Falkland Islands Trust, based in Stanley, and launched at a press conference at the Royal Geographic Society, Falklands Conservation aims to promote the conservation of wildlife, wrecks and places of historical interest in the Islands. A key objective is to substantially increase direct local involvement in conservation work, taking advantage of modern telecommunications. During the first five years its operations will include a sea-bird monitoring programme, a sea-lion research project, a survey of tussac islands, the production of conservation education materials, archaeological surveys of historical sites, and the stabilization of hulks in Stanley Harbour. For more details refer to 'Merger of Falkland Islands Foundation and Falkland Islands Trust', *Falkland Islands Newsletter*, no. 48 (August 1991), p. 15, and Kate Thompson's 'Falklands Conservation launched', *Warrah*, no. 1 (November 1991), p. 2.

Directories

552 The Falkland Islands business directory.
Edited by Nicola Summers. Stanley: Falkland Islands Government,
1990. 94p.

Includes sections on Arts and crafts; Useful information (harbour dues, import duties,
postal rates, public holidays, etc.); Fisheries; Government departments; Hotel and
catering services; General services (from banking to vehicle repairs); Manufacturing;
Professional services; Retailing; Utilities; and a list of ninety-six farms on East and
West Falkland. Some 300 companies and associations are mentioned.

553 The Europa world year book 1995.
London: Europa, 1995. 36th ed. 2 vols.

The mystery is why Europa's regional survey, *South America, Central America and
the Caribbean,* can find only one page for the Falklands whereas the *World Yearbook*
devotes four pages to the Islands. An introductory survey includes general information
(such as location, climate, language, religion and flag), recent history, government,
defence, economic affairs, social welfare, education, public holidays, and weights and
measures. The directory proper provides details of the Falkland Islands constitution
and names and addresses of the government, executive and legislative councils,
government offices, political organization, judiciary and court of appeal, religious
denominations, the press, radio, financial institutions, trade and industry (employers'
association, trade union, and co-operative society), transport, and tourism.

554 Whitaker's almanack 1995.
London: J. Whitaker, 1994. 127th ed. 1280p.

Presenting 'a vast amount of information respecting the government, finances,
population, commerce, and general statistics of the various nations of the world', the
section for British Dependent Territories contains brief information on the government
of the Falkland Islands (p. 1069) and on South Georgia and The South Sandwich
Islands (p. 1075).

555 **South America, Central America and the Caribbean 1995.**
London: Europa, 1994. 5th ed. 702p. (Regional Surveys Of The
World).

Just one page is allocated to the Falklands in this massive regional survey. The
summary factual account provides general and statistical information (livestock, wool,
government, cost of living figures) and sections on government, banking, trade and
industry, transport, and tourism. The survey is revised biennially.

556 **The statesman's yearbook: statistical and historical annual of the
states of the world for the year 1994-1995.**
Edited by Brian Hunter. London: Macmillan, 1994. 131st ed. 1709p.
maps. bibliogs.

The entry for the Falkland Islands (p. 532-35) contains official information, arranged
in ten (subdivided) sections: History; Area and Population; Climate; Constitution and
Government; Defence; Economy (Policy, Budget, Currency, Banking, Oil,
Agriculture, Fisheries); Trade; Communications (Roads, Civil Aviation, Shipping,
Telecommunications); Justice, Education and Welfare; and Wild Life.

557 **The world factbook 1994-95.**
Central Intelligence Agency. Washington, DC: Brasseys, 1994. 489p.
maps.

Produced annually by the CIA, this factbook, which is designed for the specific
requirements of various United States government agencies, is commercially
published by Brassey's to extend its otherwise limited audience. It provides an outline
of the area, climate, recent international disputes, natural resources, environment,
population, inflation rate, gross domestic product, agriculture, industries, defence
expenditure, national holidays, literacy rate, religion, legal system, government and
constitution, economy, and communications of 266 nations, territories, islands, and
ocean regions, including the Falkland Islands (Islas Malvinas) (p. 125-26) and South
Georgia and the South Sandwich Islands (p. 357-58). The cut-off date for information
is 1 January 1993 for this edition.

Bibliographies

558 **Bibliografía de Las Malvinas: obras, mapas y documentos.**
(Bibliography of the Falkland Islands: works, maps and documents.)
José Revello de Torre.   Buenos Aires: Imprenta de la Universidad,
1953. 260p. maps. (Publicaciones del Instituto de Investigaciones
Históricas, no. 99).

In this authoritative bibliography 1,702 annotated entries are arranged in three sub-divided sections: Historia (bibliografías y catálogos de obras; colecciones de documentos; obras generales; obras sobre las islas Malvinas; artículos en publicaciones periódicas); Geografía (catálogos y relaciones de mapas; planos etc., viajes; cartografía; selección de mapas generales en los figuran las islas Malvinas 1518-1829; mapas, planos, vistas referentes a las islas Malvinas; descripciones, geografía y geología); and Catálogo de documentos editos. There are indexes for geographical names, ships, persons and illustrations. Very few English-language items are entered, and then only briefly, with the exception of Goebel's *Struggle for the Falkland Islands* which is given almost two pages. The work is updated by Abel Rodolfo Geoghegen's 'Bibliografía de las Islas Malvinas; suplemento a la obra de José Torre Revelo, 1954-1975', *Historigrafia*, vol. 2 (1974), p. 165-212, which includes a further ninety-five items.

559 **An annotated bibliography of the Falkland Islands and the Falkland Island Dependencies.**
Margaret Patricia Henwood Laver.   Cape Town: University of Cape
Town Libraries, 1977. 239p.

Submitted for the Final Diploma in Librarianship of the University of Cape Town, Republic of South Africa, 1974, this bibliography contains 1,539 entries, divided into sixty-three alphabetically classified sections, and an index of authors and selected titles. From a fledgling librarian it is an impressive compilation. If a word can be levelled in criticism it is that in her enthusiasm she occasionally includes items that contain only passing references to the Falklands. Meg Laver twice visited the Islands in her search for material not generally available elsewhere. Her 'My bibliography of the Falklands', *Falkland Islands Journal*, no. 10 (1976), p. 17-23, makes very interesting reading.

560 **Islas Malvinas reseña geográfica: bibliografía (1955-1982).**
(Falkland Islands geographical review: bibliography [1955-1982].)
Federico A. Daus, Raúl C. Rey Balmaceda.   Buenos Aires: OIKOS
Asociación para la Promoción de los Estudios Territoriales y
Ambientales, 1982. 242p. map.

Daus' geographical survey of the Islands includes their position *vis à vis* the continental shelf, their geological character, which closely resembles that of Argentina, their physical and zoological geography, and their external communications. An appendix to this edition centres round a discussion of the moral problem of colonial exploitation, the future of the Islands, and the events of 1982. 'Equivalencias Toponomasticas' (Toponomastical equivalents) lists new Argentine and old English place-names. Balmaceda's 'Bibliografía sobre Las Islas Malvinas' (p. 95 onwards) presents 500 references to books, journal and newspaper articles, arranged A-Z by author. It begins with a useful review of earlier bibliographies.

561 **A selective listing of monographs and government documents on the Falkland/Malvinas Islands in the Library of Congress.**
Everette E. Larson.   Washington, DC: Library of Congress, 1982.
28p. (Hispanic Focus, no. 1).

Listing 196 items including histories, travellers' accounts, and population data, this replaces two unpublished lists previously available in the Library of Congress' main reading room. These were H. F. Conover's *The Falkland Islands and its dependencies: a list of recent references* (1944) and *Antarctica and the Falkland Islands: a list of recent references* (1955).

562 **The Falkland/Malvinas Islands: a bibliography of books (1619-1982).**
Sara de Mundo Lo.   Urbana, Illinois: Albatross, 1983. 65p.

With over 480 items listed, including twenty-three relating to the 1982 war, arranged alphabetically by author, and with a selective subject index, this is described as a digest of previous bibliographies. Reproduced from typescript it shows signs of hasty preparation and it cannot compare with the author's other published bibliographical works.

563 **Scientific papers and publications relevant to the Falkland Islands.**
Edited by J. H. McAdam.   *Falkland Islands Journal*, 1984-   .

Arranged alphabetically by author and providing date, title, journal, pagination, and a brief annotation, this feature has been included in every issue of the *Falkland Islands Journal* since 1984 with the exception of 1990. Entries are collected in four sections: General science; Fisheries; Agriculture and forestry; and Biological sciences.

564 **Catalogue of Admiralty charts and other hydrographic publications.**
Taunton, England: Hydrographer Of The Navy, 1985. 176p.
59cm × 42cm. maps.

The chart number, title, scale, and date of publication, is provided for all Admiralty charts in this regionally arranged catalogue. Those for Antarctica and the Falkland Islands, with location maps, are listed on p. 132-33.

565 **Since the war: an annotated bibliography of English language books on the Falkland Islands and their Dependencies published since June 1982.**
Thomas G. Reid. *Falkland Islands Journal*, vol. 5, no. 4 (1990),
p. 33-50. 1991 supplement, vol. 5, no. 5, p. 45-51. 1992 supplement,
vol. 6, no. 1, p. 26-30. 1993 supplement, vol. 6, no. 2, p. 119-23. 1994
supplement, vol. 6, no. 3, p. 108-16.

Listed alphabetically by author, 142 items are entered in the 1990 base bibliography with a further twenty-eight in the first supplement, twenty-one in the second, and seventeen in the third, all numbered in one sequence (i.e., nos. 1-181). Each item includes details of the author, title, place of publication, publisher, date and International Standard Book Number. The annotations are crisp, informative, and perennially suspicious of left-wing or pro-Argentine influence.

566 **Polar And Glaciological Abstracts.**
Cambridge, England: Scott Polar Research Institute, 1990-
quarterly.

Compiled from the Scott Polar Research Institute Library database this abstracts service replaces *Recent Polar and Glaciological Literature* (1981-89) which, in turn, absorbed *Recent Polar Literature* (1949-80) and *Glaciological Literature* (1949-79). References are grouped in broad subject categories (defined in the list of subject headings) and within each category the items are listed alphabetically by author. Each issue contains author and subject/geographical indexes and cumulative indexes are included in the last (October) issue of the year.

567 **Miles apart: new and second hand books on the South Atlantic islands.**
Newmarket, England: Ian and Allison Mathieson, 1995. 4th ed. 27p.

Miles Apart provides a mail order service for new and second-hand books mainly centred on the United Kingdom dependent islands in the South Atlantic. This fourth list contains a greatly expanded section on Falklands' material, including some rare reports, maps of all the islands, postcards, and videos.

Falkland Islands: a bibliography of 50 examples of printed maps bearing specific reference to the Falkland Islands.
See item no. 86.

A selected bibliography of Falkland Islands birds.
See item no. 138.

Insects of the Falkland Islands: a checklist and bibliography.
See item no. 151.

Bibliography of the 1982 Falklands War.
See item no. 318.

The Falklands War: background, conflict, aftermath: an annotated bibliography.
See item no. 328.

The Falklands/Malvinas campaign: a bibliography.
See item no. 330.

South Georgia

Discovery and early voyages

568 **The supposed discovery of South Georgia by Amerigo Vespucci.**
E. W. H. Christie. *Polar Record*, vol. 5, no. 40 (July 1950),
p. 560-64. bibliog.
'This summary of the latest research into the achievements of the expedition in 1501
shows that expert opinion on the subject, while not in complete accord on all points, is
at least unanimous in ruling out the possibility of any discovery of insular land in the
South Atlantic. There is thus no reason whatsoever for naming Amerigo Vespucci as
the discoverer of South Georgia'.

569 **The journals of Captain James Cook on his voyages of discovery:
the voyage of The *Resolution* and *Adventure* 1772-1775.**
Edited by James Beaglehole. Cambridge, England: Cambridge
University Press for the Hakluyt Society, 1969. 1028p. 10 maps.
bibliog.
This second volume of four, comprising Beaglehole's edition of Cook's *Journals*,
includes passages relating to his discovery of South Georgia and the South Sandwich
Islands, his course and bearings, notes and observations on sea birds, his naming of
topographical features, and his account of his landing on South Georgia in three
different places. He displayed his colours and took possession of the island in the
King's name 'under a descharge of small arms' on 17 January 1775. Cook's own
official account of his second voyage was printed in *A voyage towards the South Pole
and round the world: performed by His Majesty's Ships Resolution and Adventure, in
the years 1772, 1773, 1774 and 1775* (London: W. Strahan & T. Cadell, 1777. 2
vols.).

570   **The Resolution journal of Johann Reinhold Forster 1772-1775.**
Edited by Michael E. Hoare.   London: Hakluyt Society, 1982. 4 vols.
Forster was the principal naturalist on James Cook's second voyage to the Pacific Ocean. His journal, bound in six quarto volumes, is now in the Manuscript Department of the Staatsbibliothek der Stiftung Preussischer Kulturbesitz in Berlin. In this printed version (vol. 4, p. 712-20) he records in detail the sighting and circumnavigation of South Georgia, the poor weather and temperatures experienced, the abundant sea birds, and sailing through the South Sandwich Islands.

571   **The voyage of Captain Bellingshausen to the Antarctic Seas 1819-1821.**
Edited by Frank Debenham.   London: Hakluyt Society, 1945. 2 vols.
Appointed to lead an Antarctic exploration expedition by Tsar Alexander I, Bellingshausen sailed from Kronstadt with two sloops, *Vostok* and *Mirnyi* on 16 July 1819. He surveyed the southern coast of South Georgia between 15 and 17 December. His chart, which complemented that of Cook of the northern coastline, was incorporated in the British Admiralty's *The Antarctic pilot* published as late as 1930. Bellingshausen named many islands in the South Sandwich group. The South Georgia episode of his voyage is narrated on p. 88-92 (vol. 1) in this English edition of his account.

572   **Voyages to South Georgia 1795-1820.**
A. G. E. Jones.   *British Antarctic Survey Bulletin*, no. 32 (February 1973), p. 15-22. map. bibliog.
By virtue of unremitting research in old files of *Lloyd's List* and other mercantile journals, Jones retrieved much obscure information on the pioneering sealing voyages to South Georgia waters. From the scanty records surviving he was able to build up a credible outline of the companies, ships and men who engaged in a highly hazardous but profitable venture.

Expeditions

573   **The German station of the first international Polar year, 1882-83 at South Georgia, Falkland Islands Dependencies.**
R. K. Headland.   *Polar Record*, vol. 21, no. 132 (September 1982), p. 287-92. bibliog.
Notes on the Deutsche Polarkommission Expedition's base, personnel, and scientific programme, are followed by remarks upon the activities of subsequent German expeditions, and on a systematic physical examination of the Moltke Harbour station in January 1982. The results of the German expedition were published in *Die Internationale Polarforschung 1882-83: die Deutschen Expeditionen und ihre Ergebnisse* (The international Polar research 1882-83: the German expedition and its results), edited by G. Neumayer (Berlin: A. Asher, 1890-91. 2 vols.).

574 **The winter expedition of the 'Antarctic' to South Georgia.**
J. Gunnar Andersson. *Geographical Journal*, vol. 20, no. 4 (October 1902), p. 405-08.

Relates how a programme of geological, glaciological, botanical, and oceanographical work was undertaken on a winter visit to Jason Bay, Cumberland Bay, and Royal Bay, by the *Antarctic*, the ship of the Swedish South Polar Expedition, 22 April-15 June 1902.

575 **South: the story of Shackleton's last expedition 1914-17.**
Sir Ernest Shackleton. London: Century, 1991. 206p. 4 maps.

Sir Ernest Shackleton was a member of Scott's Antarctic Expedition of 1901-04; in 1907-09 he led an expedition that came within 100 miles of the South Pole, established the position of the Magnetic Pole, and climbed Mt. Erebus. His Transantarctic Expedition of 1914-17, however, came to grief when his ship, *Endurance*, succumbed to the ice in October 1915. The expedition drifted on the ice before taking to the ships boats and heading for Elephant Island which was reached after seven days. From there Shackleton prepared one boat, the *James Caird*, which was loaded with stores to last six men for a month, and set off on a desperate 700-mile voyage to South Georgia to seek help to rescue the party left on Elephant Island. Arriving on the north-west coast of South Georgia, at King Haakon Bay, after sixteen days in an open boat, Shackleton was then faced with crossing the uncharted mountains to the whaling station on Stromness Bay. First published by Heinemann in 1919, *South* was issued in an abridged edition in 1922. Edited by Peter King, this beautifully produced new edition follows the abridged text but, by virtue of a twelve-page introduction, extensive margin notes throughout the text, and by over 100 superb photographs by Frank Hurley, the Expedition's official photographer, it provides a more detailed account than previous editions. Three chapters are devoted to Shackleton's epic mountain crossing: 'The end of the boat journey'; 'King Haakon Bay'; and 'Across South Georgia'. There are also two interesting maps: 'Surroundings of King Haakon Bay' and 'Rough memory map of route across South Georgia'.

576 **Shackleton.**
Roland Huntford. London: Hodder & Stoughton, 1985. 774p. maps. bibliog.

This is surely the definitive biography of Shackleton (1874-1922) for many years to come, superseding H. R. Mills' *The life of Sir Ernest Shackleton* (1923), and Margery and James Fisher's *Shackleton* (1957). Huntford devotes one chapter to his landing in King Haakon Bay on 16 May 1916, after his sixteen-day open boat voyage from Elephant Island, and another to his crossing of South Georgia. Shackleton died of a massive heart attack whilst on yet another Antarctic expedition and is buried on a hillside overlooking Grytviken.

577 **Shackleton Valley, South Georgia.**
G. Hattersley-Smith. *Polar Record*, vol. 28, no. 166 (July 1992),
p. 233. map.
Was Shackleton Valley the passageway to Stromness?
M. K. Burley. *Polar Record*, p. 234-36. map. bibliog.
Husvik or Stromness? A South Georgia enigma.
Michael J. Gilkes. *Polar Record*, p. 236-37.
Three conflicting views on Shackleton's exact route on the last stage of his epic
voyage to safety across South Georgia were published in this issue of *Polar Record*.

578 **The Shackleton controversy continued.**
H. McG. Dunnett. *Polar Record*, vol. 29, no. 169 (April 1993),
p. 164-65.
A resolution to the Shackleton Valley controversy.
J. Meiklejohn, K. I. Skontorp. *Polar Record*, p. 165-66.
Dunnet, Meiklejohn, the founder of the Salvesen Ex-Whalers Club in 1984, and Karl
Skontorp, whose grandfather was manager of the whaling station at Husvik, confirm
that it was Stromness that Shackleton reached after his crossing of South Georgia in
1916. Other relevant articles include Duncan Carse's 'Tracing the limits of
endurance', *Geographical Magazine*, vol. 6, no. 10 (July 1974), p. 561-68; R. T.
Morgan-Grenville's 'Exercise Green Skua: crossing South Georgia', *Polar Record*,
vol. 23, no. 142 (January 1986), p. 73-78; and Angus B. Erskine's 'Shackleton's
landing', *Polar Record*, vol. 28, no. 166 (July 1992), p. 242-44.

579 **Glacier Island: the official account of the British South Georgia
Expedition 1954-1955.**
George Sutton. London: Chatto & Windus, 1957. 24p. 4 maps.
Consisting of a team of four, the South Georgia Expedition of 1954 was the first to
travel to the island specifically to climb its mountains. The team explored the interior
of the island, notably the great Allardyce Range. Their secondary objectives included
glaciological research and the observation of penguins, birds and seals in their natural
habitat.

580 **Combined Services Expedition to South Georgia 1964-65.**
M. K. Burley. *Explorers Journal*, vol. 44, no. 2 (June 1966),
p. 106-18. map.
Lieutenant-Commander Burley was Leader of the 1964-65 Combined Services
Expedition to South Georgia. Here he relates the ascents of Mt. Paget and Mt.
Sugartop, the attempts on Mt. Fagerli and Mt. Paulsen, and the reconnaissance over
the Allardyce Range. He also details the geological, glaciological, zoological, and
botanical work carried out and discusses the survey of the Royal Bay area east of the
Cook Glacier. Much the same ground is covered in P. F. Fagan's article of the same
title printed in *Royal Engineers Journal*, vol. 81, no. 1 (March 1967), p. 56-71.

581   **1982 joint services expedition to South Georgia.**
M. D. R. Kelly.   *Sea Swallow*, vol. 32 (1981/82), p. 4-11. map.

Shortly before the Argentine invasion, a party of fifteen servicemen departed from South Georgia, having spent three months on the island, travelling to its remote southern region, and investigating its bird life. The conclusion they arrived at was that the vast number of birds that congregate around South Georgia feed upon the huge plankton resources attracted there by the ideal conditions caused by certain oceanographic factors.

582   **Summary report of the Dutch South Georgia expedition 1986/87.**
H. D. van Bohemen, D. A. G. Buizer, N. J. M. Gremmen, J. de Korte,
A. F. van Ophen.   *Polar Record*, vol. 25, no. 153 (April 1989),
p. 146-48. 2 maps. bibliog.

The objective of the Dutch South Georgia expedition, which spent four weeks on the island (3 January-30 January 1987), was to collect biological information on the island's ecosystems and the influence of man on them. They also aimed to increase appreciation of the value and beauty of the subantarctic regions and interest in nature conservation. One week (22 December-29 December 1986) was spent on the Falkland Islands collecting conservation, botanical, and marine biological information.

583   **Island at the edge of the world: a South Georgia odyssey.**
Stephen Venables.   London: Hodder & Stoughton, 1991. 177p.
3 maps. bibliog.

Sharply-drawn observations and descriptions of South Georgia's history, natural history, Operation Paraquat, and the new military base at Mt. Pleasant, on East Falkland, are skilfully woven into this account of the 1989-90 Southern Ocean Mountaineering Expedition. During the expedition the author (joint-leader of the expedition) and his four climbing companions travelled along the south-east coast, climbed previously unconquered mountains, and spent three weeks incarcerated in an elaborate ice dug-out. Also worth reading is Venables' 'Peaks, penguins and power games', *Geographical Magazine*, vol. 62, no. 12 (December 1990), p. 30-34, which concentrates on South Georgia's strategic value at a time when a revision of the Antarctic Treaty was fast approaching, on the marine threat to its ecology in the shape of Russian and Japanese trawlers, and on the scientific work of *HMS Endurance*.

584   **Royal Anglian South Georgia Expedition.**
Edited by R. T. Clements.   Uxbridge, England: EDS-Scicon, 1992.
86p.

Consisting of four canoists, and eight mountaineers, this expedition was the brainchild of Major Clements and Captain James Harris, Commanding Officer and Second-In-Command respectively, of the small military detachment at King Edward Point. This account comprises the Expedition's log, running from 28 August to 2 November 1991, together with various reports on its activities.

Geography and geology

Geology and glaciology

585 **Geological observations in South Georgia.**
D. Ferguson. *Transactions of the Royal Society of Edinburgh,*
vol. 50, pt. 4, no. 23 (May 1915), p. 797-876. 8p. of plates. pull-out
geological section.
The geological relations and some fossils of South Georgia.
J. W. Gregory. *Transactions of the Royal Society of Edinburgh,*
p. 817-22. 1p. of plates. pull-out section.
The petrology of South Georgia.
G. W. Tyrrell. *Transactions of the Royal Society of Edinburgh,*
p. 823-36. 1p. of plates.

In 1912 Christian Salvesen, the Leith-based whaling company, sponsored a
mineralogical exploration of South Georgia in the hope of finding viable commercial
minerals, but to no avail. David Ferguson, who conducted the investigation, carried
out a geological survey of the island between 7 January and 19 April of that year. This
first paper describes its physical character, its rocks and their local distribution and
geological age, and reviews previous geological accounts. Gregory's is also a
bibliographic report which concludes that there was no adequate evidence to show
whether South Georgia is a fragment of the Andes or of the mountain loop which once
connected Patagonia and Graham Land. Finally, Tyrrell's paper presents the results of
an investigation of 110 rock specimens collected by Ferguson from the northern coast
of South Georgia.

586 **Topography and geology of South Georgia.**
George Vibert Douglas.
The petrography and geology of South Georgia.
G. W. Tyrrell. London: British Museum (Natural History), 1930.
51p.

Reprinted from 'The report on the geological collections made during the voyage of
the "Quest" on the Shackleton-Rowett Expedition 1921-22', the two reports contained
in this publication review the previous geological exploration of South Georgia and
outline the work of the Quest expedition. They also examine the Island's economic
geology, and make a close study of its igneous and sedimentary rocks, their
geographical distribution, and of South Georgia's stratigraphical and tectonic
relations.

587 **The geology of South Georgia.**
A. F. Trendall.   London: HMSO for The Colonial Office, 1953-59.
2 vols. (Falkland Islands Dependencies Survey Scientific Reports,
nos. 7 and 19).

Trendall's first report includes a topographical outline of South Georgia, a review of previous geological investigations, and detailed studies of its lithology, structure, petrography, and the sedimentary and ignaceous nature of its rocks. Surveys were carried out at Grytviken, Cumberland Bay, New Fortune Bay, Husvik, and the Neumayer Glacier, with a circumnavigation of the Island for brief stops at Wilson and Larsen harbours. The second report embodies fieldwork undertaken on Duncan Carse's second South Georgia expedition, (1953-54) and concentrates on sedimentary rocks, lavas, dykes and minor intrusions. These two general volumes have been followed at intervals by specialized area studies in the same general pattern and format with maps and extensive bibliographies, namely: M. J. Skidmore's *Prince Olav Harbour and Stromness Bay, Barff Peninsula and Royal Bay*; Bryan C. Storey's *Drygalski Fjord*; and B. F. Mair's *Larsen Harbour* (London: British Antarctic Survey, 1972-87).

588 **Glacier problems in South Georgia.**
Jeremy Smith.   *Journal of Glaciology*, vol. 3, no. 28 (October 1960),
p. 707-14. bibliog.

'This paper is a synopsis of *Falkland Islands Dependencies Survey Scientific Report*, no. 29. Glaciological and climatic investigations carried out in South Georgia during the International Geophysical Year are described... The fluctuations of South Georgian glaciers during relatively recent times are briefly discussed' (Abstract). The point is made that 'the scanty literature on the glaciology of South Georgia is mainly descriptive and has arisen from the visits of expeditions whose principal interests were in other fields'.

589 **Antarctic link with the Andes.**
Chalmers M. Clapperton.   *Geographical Magazine*, vol. 44, no. 2
(November 1971), p. 124-30.

Clapperton presents an illustrated study of the geological and glaciological status of South Georgia as a link between the Chilean Andes and the Antarctic Peninsula. Fieldwork in 1968 suggested that, as recently as 10,000 years ago, an ice-cap may have completely covered the island.

590 **Measurement of declination at South Georgia 1700-1984.**
D. A. Simmons.   *Polar Record*, vol. 23, no. 145 (January 1987),
p. 419-26. 2 maps. bibliog.

Values for declination (i.e., the difference between true and magnetic North) for South Georgia are available from 1700 to the present day. This paper describes and catalogues the magnetic measurements made at or near the island, and provides a summary of the results.

591　**South Georgia.**
D. I. M. MacDonald, B. C. Storey, J. W. Thomson.　Cambridge,
England: British Antarctic Survey, 1987. 65p. map. (BAS Geomap).
Drawn on a scale of 1:250,000, this geological map includes in its legend a key to
geological and palaeontological sites, a chronology, and their associated writings. Its
accompanying text has sections on the Island's tectonic setting, on the Drygalski Fjord
and Larsen Harbour complexes, and on the formations of the Annenkov Islands,
Cumberland Bay, Sandebugten, Cooper Bay, Ducloz Head, and the Cumberland Bay
dislocation zone. A final section covers marine geology.

Meteorology and climatology

592　**Comparison between the weather at Bird Island and King Edward
Point, South Georgia.**
P. A. Richards, W. L. N. Tickell.　*British Antarctic Survey Bulletin*,
no. 15 (March 1968), p. 63-69.
'Recent meteorological observations at Bird Island . . . have revealed climatological
differences between it and King Edward Point 67 miles away in Cumberland East
Bay. A comparison of the data from both stations indicates that the drier, warmer and
sunnier weather at King Edward Point is due to the close proximity of high mountain
ranges' (Abstract). Climatological data for the two stations between 1958 and 1964, a
comparison of wind speeds, and humidity values, are presented in tabular form.

593　**Summer weather at Royal Bay, South Georgia, 1882-83 and
1981-82.**
Hamish Greig, John E. Gordon.　*Polar Record*, vol. 26, no. 158 (July
1990), p. 187-94. map. bibliog.
Meteorological readings taken by a Joint Services Expedition in the 1981-82 season
are compared to observations at the German station in Royal Bay during the First
International Polar Year 1882-83. Comparisons between the two sets of figures
confirm the storminess of the climate and indicate that temperatures were slightly
higher in 1981-82.

Maps, charts and surveys

594　**Coast of South Georgia.**
Geographical Journal, vol. 39, no. 1 (January 1912), p. 77-79. 2 maps.
Based on notes and two sketch maps supplied by J. Innes Wilson, stipendiary
magistrate on South Georgia, this is a brief outline of the coast and its harbours north-
westward round the island from Cape Nunes. The maps depict the whaling grounds
and the course usually taken by whales from October to March, and the north-west
part of South Georgia, according to information received from whalers and sealers.

595   **Narrative of hydrographic survey operations in South Georgia and the South Shetland Islands, 1926-1930.**
J. M. Chaplin.   Cambridge, England: Cambridge University Press, 1932. p. 297-344. 4p. of plates. (Discovery Reports, vol. 3).

This survey report ends with four appendices on personnel and equipment, magnetic variation, weather and climate, and a note on kelp. There are three folded charts relating to South Georgia in an end-pocket: Harbours and anchorages (Stromness Bay, Cumberland Bay, King Edward Cove); Harbours and anchorages (Barff Point to Cape George, Stromness, Husvik and Jason Harbours, Pleasant Cove, Maiviken, Elsehul, and Right Whale Bay); and Prince Olaf Harbour Approaches, North Bay, Cape Buller to Cape Constance, Larsen Harbour, Fortuna Bay, Willis and Bird Islands, Undine Harbour and Approaches, Blue Whale Harbour, and Leith Harbour.

596   **The South Georgia survey 1951-52.**
J. B. Heaney.   *Journal of The Cambridge Engineering Society*, vol. 24 (1954), p. 103-11. map.

Heaney was a surveyor with The South Georgia Survey of 1951-52, a small private expedition, sponsored by the Royal Geographical Society, and the Scott Polar Research Institute. Its leader was Duncan Carse and its main task was to survey the south-west coast and to correct two existing maps, both of which were compiled from old sketches and maps drawn by sealing captains, one published by the Admiralty, the other by the Directorate of Colonial Surveys. This article deals with survey methods, the reconnaissance and survey sledging journeys, and the actual survey work.

597   **The survey of South Georgia.**
A. G. Bomford, W. S. B. Paterson.   *Empire Survey Review*, vol. 14, no. 107 (January 1958), p. 204-13; no. 108 (April 1958), p. 242-47.

The authors were both surveyors on Duncan Carse's third and most ambitious survey expedition to South Georgia in 1955-56, which aimed to survey as much of the island as possible according to preconceived standards of accuracy. In the event weather conditions allowed only thirty-nine clear days for surveying and another forty-six for travelling. Nevertheless 240 trigonometrical points were co-ordinated. This report is particularly valuable for its detail on the survey of the coastline. Bomford's 'The South Georgia surveys', *Royal Engineers Journal*, vol. 73, no. 2 (June 1959), p. 180-88, is also of interest.

598   **The survey of South Georgia 1951-57.**
Duncan Carse.   *Geographical Journal*, vol. 125, no. 1 (March 1959), p. 20-37. map.

Carse presents a full account of his team's methods, vicissitudes, and achievements during a three-year survey programme in the 1951-52, 1953-54, and 1955-56 summer seasons. Basically it was a fairly orthodox triangulation survey along the coast, filled in with detail by photo-theodolite, and by plane-tabling and compass traverses. Carse also sketches in the historical background and the expedition's preliminaries. Drawn by Captain A. G. Bomford, RE, the direct result of the survey was a four-colour map of South Georgia on a scale of 1:200,000, published by the Directorate of Overseas Survey in August 1958.

599   **HMS Owen's hydrographic surveys in South Georgia 1960-61.**
      G. P. D. Hall.   *Polar Record*, vol. 11, no. 73 (January 1963),
      p. 423-30. map.

Responding to pressure from the Colonial Office and whaling interests for an improvement to the Admiralty charts of South Georgia, the Hydrographer of the Navy despatched a survey ship during the 1960-61 summer season. It carried out a thorough survey of the waters surrounding the western extremities of the island in order to facilitate the shortest passage possible between the whaling grounds in the west and the whaling stations on the north-east coast. The major part of this paper is taken up with a description of the survey operations and the techniques used.

600   **British Antarctic Territory (north of 75°S) with South Georgia and South Sandwich Islands.**
      London: Directorate of Overseas Surveys, 1963. Single sheet map.
      (DOS 813, Series 3203).

Compiled from published maps and from unpublished material held at the Directorate of Overseas Surveys on 31 May 1963, this map is drawn to the Polar Stereographic Projection on a scale of 1:3,000,000. A copy is lodged in the endpocket of *Antarctic research*, edited by Raymond Edward Priestley, Raymond John Adie, Gordon de Q. Robin. (London: Butterworths, 1964).

601   **Surveys in South Georgia.**
      P. F. Fagan.   *Geographical Journal*, vol. 132, no. 1 (March 1966),
      p. 61-64. map.

During the 1964-65 summer a party of ten servicemen retraced Shackleton's route across the island, climbed mountain peaks, and conducted a survey of the Royal Bay area. Fagan's 'Surveying in South Georgia', *Survey Review*, vol. 19, no. 146 (October 1967), p. 159-65, is mainly concerned with the methods and equipment used, of interest only to those with a good knowledge of surveying techniques.

602   **Notes on South Georgia.**
      Rolf Böhme.   In: *Inventory of world topographic mapping vol.3:
      Eastern Europe, Asia, Oceania and Antarctica.*   London: Elsevier
      Applied Science Publishers on behalf of the International Cartographic
      Association, 1993, p. 429-31. maps. bibliogs.

The section on South Georgia provides brief information on responsible mapping organizations, mapping history, map services, and map scales and projections.

Gazetteers and place-names

603   **Gazetteer of the Falkland Islands Dependencies.**
      London: Foreign Office, 1955. 22p.

Lists 2,100 place-names, 1,000 of which resulted from the work of the Falkland Islands Dependencies Survey, the remainder coming from older British official publications, together with their latitude and longitude co-ordinates. *First Supplement*

(1958. 8p.) added 300 new names; *Second Supplement* (1959. 12p.) added another 365; whilst a second edition published in 1959 (28p.) incorporated all entries in a single alphabetical list. *First supplement to second edition* (London: HMSO, 1960. 8p.) added a further 443 new names and *Second supplement to second edition* (1961. 4p.) ninety-six more.

604   **Gazetteer of the British Antarctic Territory, South Georgia and the South Sandwich Islands.**
London: HMSO, 1962. 34p.

This is a complete list of 3,528 place-names accepted for use in British official publications. It supersedes *Gazetteer of the Falkland Islands Dependencies* (London: HMSO, 1959. 2nd ed.) and its *Supplements. First supplement to First Edition* (1964. 4p.) added 196 new names; *Second supplement* (1974. 8p.) provided another 411; and *Third supplement* (1975. 6p.) a further 269.

605   **Gazetteer of the Falkland Islands Dependencies (South Georgia and the South Sandwich Islands).**
London: HMSO, 1977. 10p.

Prepared by the Polar Region Section of the Latin American Department of the Foreign and Commonwealth Office, this gazetteer lists 763 place-names, with their latitude and longitude, which are accepted for use in British official publications. A *Supplement* was issued in 1979.

606   **The history of place-names in the Falkland Island Dependencies (South Georgia and the South Sandwich Islands).**
G. Hattersley-Smith.   Cambridge, England: British Antarctic Survey, 1980. 112p. 2 maps in back folder. bibliog. (British Antarctic Survey Scientific Reports, no. 101).

An introductory section on the origin of South Georgia names, which ranges from Captain Cook's 1772 voyage to the Combined Services Expedition to South Georgia in 1964-65, effectively constitutes a brief history of the Island's exploration. This work lists all place-names found in over 400 published and unpublished sources. They fall into three categories, each distinguished typographically in the text: 770 officially accepted names; 178 names considered superfluous by the Antarctic Place-Names Committee; and 2,950 English and foreign synonyms, cross-referenced to the officially accepted name. The information provided encompasses: latitude and longitude to the nearest minute; localities with references to the back folder maps; and details of the Islands discovery, first mapping and naming, re-mapping and re-naming and name alterations.

Flora and fauna

General

607 **South Georgia, subantarctic.**
R. I. Lewis Smith, D. W. H. Walton. In: *Structure and function of tundra ecosystems.* Edited by T. Rosswall, O. W. Heal. Stockholm: Swedish Natural Science Research Council, 1975, p. 399-423. map. bibliog.

One of the papers presented at the IBP Tundra Biome International Meeting on Biological Productivity of Tundra, held in Abisko in Sweden in April 1974, this is an overall history of the scientific investigation of South Georgia. It encompasses: environmental conditions; primary production of flora; herbivores; carnivores and insectivores; decomposition and soil processes; nutrient cycling; and interactions between terrestrial and aquatic ecosystems.

608 **Wildlife guest to the icy seas of South Georgia.**
Sally Poncet. *National Geographic*, vol. 175, no. 3 (March 1989), p. 340-75. map.

A blend of sailing adventures in rough waters and perilous seas, of natural history and wildlife conservation, of assisting in British Antarctic Survey research, and of raising a young family on board the author's yacht, this colourfully illustrated feature could only have appeared in *National Geographic*. Visits to Bird Island, Leith Harbour, the Willis Islands, Grytviken, Cape Disappointment, Cape Rosa, and King Haakon Bay are recorded.

Flora

609 **Vegetation of South Georgia.**
W. Botting Hemsley. *Nature*, vol. 34, no. 866 (3 June 1886), p. 106-07.

'The only vegetation we met with was a coarse strong-bladed grass growing in tufts, wild burnet, and a plant like moss, which sprang from the rocks' (Captain Cook's *Journal*, January 1775). By contrast the 1882-83 German expedition, which spent nearly a year on the island, gathered thirteen different flowering plants, enumerated here with their worldwide distribution pattern.

610 **The vegetation in South Georgia.**
Carl Skottsberg. Stockholm: Lithographisches Institut Des
Generalstabs, 1912. 36p. 2p. of maps. 6p. of plates. bibliog.
(Wissenschaftliche Ergebnisse der Schweidenischen Südpolar-
Expedition 1901-1908. Band 4 Botanik Lieferung 12).

Included in this wide-ranging academic paper are sections on the history of botanical exploration in South Georgia, geographical remarks, the climate and its influence on the Island's vegetation, growth forms, a list of plants (p.8-11), the origins of the flora, short notes on vegetation distribution, and plant associations. D. Philcox's 'Recent records for the flora of South Georgia', *Kew Bulletin*, vol. 16, no. 2 (October 1962), p.243-45 is an annotated enumeration of species introduced after Skottsberg's list.

611 **The W. N. Bonner (1955-61) collection of plants from South Georgia.**
S. W. Greene, E. W. Groves. *British Antarctic Survey Bulletin*, no. 2 (December 1963), p. 93-95.

Most plants in this collection were obtained in the Grytviken area with others from Cumberland Bay, Bird Island, Bay of Isles, Leith, Husvik, and Ocean and Gold Harbours. They were deposited in three herbaria: the Department of Botany of the British Museum (Natural History); Royal Botanical Gardens in Kew; and the British Antarctic Survey herbarium. W. N. Bonner was employed by the Falkland Islands Dependencies Survey as resident biologist and sealing inspector.

612 **The vascular flora of South Georgia.**
S. W. Greene. London: British Antarctic Survey, 1964. 58p. 8p. of maps. 6p. of plates. bibliog. (British Antarctic Survey Scientific Reports, no. 45).

Both a systematic account of the vascular flora of South Georgia, and an introductory exposition of the communities formed by these plants, this report includes a review of the Island's botanical history, with a chronological account of all the expeditions known to have studied its vascular plants from 1775 onwards, and notes on vascular plant collections made in South Georgia, giving their locations, size, origins, and importance. A checklist of fifty-one species is made up of twenty-four native, five naturalized aliens, and twenty-two transient aliens.

613 **The macrolichens of South Georgia.**
D. C. Lindsay. London: British Antarctic Survey, 1974. 91p. 3p. of plates. (British Antarctic Survey Scientific Reports, no. 89).

The introduction to this scientific report comprises an outline of South Georgia's physical and biological features, an account of earlier lichenological investigations, and details of collectors, collections, herbaria, and previous publications. Lindsay follows this with separate sections on the Island's physical and climatic characteristics, a systematic account of all genera and species of lichen known from the Island, lichen-rich plant communities, and a discussion on the origins of macrolichens.

614 **Postglacial pollen diagrams from South Georgia (sub-Antarctic) and West Falkland Island (South Atlantic).**
C. J. Barrow. *Journal of Biogeography*, vol. 5, no. 3 (September 1978), p. 251-74. 2 maps. bibliog.

'Six pollen diagrams are presented, five from South Georgia, and one from Port Howard, West Falkland Island. . . Many elements of the present vascular flora of South Georgia and West Falkland Island were flourishing before 9500 years BP, having in South Georgia possibly survived the last glacial (approximately 20,000-10,000 years BP). . . There are no indications that trees grew in the Falkland Islands during the postglacial (i.e. the last c.10,000 years). The distribution of peat deposits hints at postglacial coastal tussock (*Poa flabellata*) pollen deposited in the peat' (Abstract). This is an extremely well-documented study.

615 **Types of peat and peatforming vegetation of South Georgia.**
R. I. Lewis Smith. *British Antarctic Survey Bulletin*, no. 53 (June 1981), p. 119-39. map. bibliog.

This paper describes the principal peatforming types of organic deposit, and the development of peat in relation to deglaciation and plant communities distribution. There is an extensive bibliography of scholarly publications.

Fauna general

616 **Zoological observations, Royal Bay, South Georgia 1882-1883: pt. 1.**
Karl von den Steinen. *Polar Record*, vol. 22, no. 136 (January 1984), p.57-71.
Zoological observations, Royal Bay, South Georgia 1882-1883. part 2: penguins.
Karl von den Steinen. *Polar Record*, vol. 22, no. 137 (May 1984), p.145-58.

Steinen, medical officer to the Deutsche Polarkomission's South Georgia expedition in 1882-83, was also a trained zoologist. His observations are sharply drawn and have stood the test of time.

617 **Antarctic Isle: wild life in South Georgia.**
Niall Rankin. London: Collins, 1951. 383p. 2 maps. bibliog.

Fulfilling an ambition to 'find a spot in the far South where the maximum concentration of bird and animal life existed inside the smallest possible perimeter, to deposit myself in that area for an entire breeding season so that I could, if possible, keep certain individuals under observation for the whole period, and then to record what I saw' (Introduction), the author spent five months on South Georgia, from 26 November 1946 to 20 April 1947. Rankin concerns himself mainly with a study of Albatrosses, King Penguins, Elephant Seals, and the whaling industry in southern seas. He ends with a perceptive commentary on Leith, then a boom town.

618 **A naturalist in Penguin Land.**
Niall Rankin. *National Geographic Magazine*, vol. 107, no. 1
(January 1955), p. 93-116. map.

Subtitled 'Braving stormy seas in a converted lifeboat, a Briton studies the strange
wildlife of lonely South Georgia island', this generously illustrated magazine feature
tells of Rankin's experiences in photographing not only the ubiquitous penguins but
also skuas, elephant seals, leopard seals, and albatrosses. In addition he describes a
visit to a ghost whaling village at Prince Olaf Harbour, which was abandoned twenty-
four years previously.

619 **Where the albatross builds its nest.**
Lancelot Tickell. *Geographical Magazine*, vol. 41, no. 2 (November
1968), p. 144-51. maps.

Bird Island lies close to South Georgia. Tickell participated in a number of
expeditions there – he was a member of the South Georgia Biological Expedition of
1958-59 – when Peter Cordall mapped the island on a scale of 1:12,500 and research
was undertaken into the island's climate, bird and animal life during a nineteen-week
stay. During a further ten weeks on the island in the 1960-61 summer season the
Albatross' biennial breeding cycle was closely observed. From October to December
1962 a programme of fieldwork was carried out on fur-seals, ringing fledgeling
mollymauks, and on the predatory leopard seals.

620 **Ecology in the Antarctic.**
Edited by W. Nigel Bonner, R. J. Berry. London: Academic Press,
1980. 150p. maps. bibliogs.

This collection of scientific papers was presented at a meeting organized by the
Linnean Society of London in October 1979. It includes two which relate specifically
to South Georgia: J. P. Croxall and P. A. Prince's 'Food feeding economy and
ecological segregation of seabirds at South Georgia' (p.103-31) and T. S. McCann's
'Population structure and social organization of Southern Elephant Seals, Mirounga
leonina' (p.133-50). Both papers end with long lists of references.

621 **Survival: South Atlantic.**
Cindy Buxton, Annie Price. London: Granada, 1983. 237p. 2 maps.
bibliog.

Cindy Buxton has made a series of films for Anglia Television's 'Survival'
programme, including *Penguin Island* (1980), *Falkland Summer* (1981), *Stranded on
South Georgia* and *Opportunity South Atlantic* (both 1982). Together with her
assistant, Annie Price, she spent three seasons filming in the Falklands, first on New
Island and then on the totally uninhabited Steeple Jason Island (1979-80), on Carcass
Island (1980-81), and on South Georgia (14 October 1981-30 April 1982), which
included the four momentous weeks of the Argentine 'occupation', from 26 March to
25 April. However, although the backdrop of war provides an exciting final interlude,
this magnificently illustrated book is essentially concerned with filming the wildlife on
some of the Falklands' more remote islands, notably the enormous colonies of
elephant seals, albatrosses, and rockhopper, gentoo, Magellan, king and macaroni
penguins.

Birds

622 Birds of South Georgia.
Leonard Harrison Matthews.   Cambridge, England: Cambridge University Press, 1929. p. '561-92. 11p. of plates. bibliog. (Discovery Reports, vol. 1).

Notes on thirty-one species of South Georgia birds, the observations made during the 1925-27 *Discovery* investigations, and the ornithological records of previous expeditions, are included in this comprehensive scientific report. *Wandering albatross: adventures among the albatrosses and petrels in the Southern Ocean* (London: Macgibbon & Kee with Reinhardt & Evans, 1951. 133p. map) is a more popular account of Matthews' time birdwatching on South Georgia.

623 Observations on the birds of South Georgia.
S. H. Down.   Combined Services Expedition to South Georgia, 1967. 12p. map.

The 1964-65 Combined Services Expedition to South Georgia had as its main objectives the traverse of the Island along the route followed by Shackleton in 1915, and the ascent of the highest summits of the Allardyce Range. An ancillary survey programme included the compilation of a record of the location and numbers of bird colonies visited, and the collection of samples of nest debris from high altitude colonies, so that these might be examined for parasites. Many individual species are discussed here, together with short accounts of where they were observed. Tabulated information includes the date, area of observation, a grid reference to an overprinted base map of South Georgia issued by the Directorate of Overseas Surveys in 1964, and bird numbers.

624 Bird Island in Antarctic waters.
David F. Parmelee.   Minneapolis, Minnesota: University of Minnesota Press, 1980. 140p. bibliog.

Bird Island is a lonely outcrop off the north-west coast of South Georgia. Parmelee spent six weeks there as a guest of the British Antarctic Survey. His book is not intended as a scientific report but rather 'a birding experience as seen through the eyes of a field biologist and illustrated for those who observe wildlife for recreational and aesthetic purposes'. He captures quite remarkably the wildlife and scenery of this remote island.

625 Birds of South Georgia: new records and re-evaluation of status.
P. A. Prince, J. P. Croxall.   *British Antarctic Survey Bulletin*, no. 59 (May 1983), p. 15-27. map. bibliog.

Giving details of all new records of sightings, between 31 January 1977 and 30 April 1982, this checklist also summarizes the revised information now available on the status of the Island's breeding species. The total avifauna is put at thirty breeding and thirty-six visitor or vagrant species. Previous research is noted and there is a first-rate bibliography.

626   **Impact of seabirds on marine resources, especially krill, of South
       Georgia waters.**
       John P. Croxall, Christopher Ricketts, Peter A. Prince.   In: *Seabird
       energetics*.   Edited by G. Causey Whittow, Hermann Ratin.   New
       York: Plenum Press, 1984, p. 285-317. bibliog.

This estimation of the impact on the seabird community on South Georgia's marine
resources was first read at a symposium sponsored by the Comparative Physiology
section of the American Physiological Society, and held on 23-24 August 1983, in
Honolulu. A severely academic paper, it encompasses the seabird population size,
dietary composition and energy content, activity patterns, energetic costs, foraging
range, distribution of foraging effort, community food requirements and distribution,
overall food consumption, comparisons between related or similar species, and
consumption in relation to prey stocks. Five pages of references encourage further
scientific research.

627   **Observations on Albatross Island in the Bay of Isles, South
       Georgia 15-16 April 1986.**
       Angus K. Ross.   *Sea Swallow*, vol. 36 (1987), p. 25-31. map.

The Bay of Isles has long been regarded by personnel of the British Antarctic Survey
as the most interesting habitat for South Atlantic seabirds. This report concentrates
heavily on the Giant Petrel and Wandering Albatross.

Seals and reindeer

628   **The natural history of the Elephant Seal with notes on other seals
       found at South Georgia.**
       Leonard Harrison Matthews.   Cambridge, England: Cambridge
       University Press, 1929. p. 233-56. 7p. of plates. bibliog. (Discovery
       Reports, vol. 1).

Matthews reports on the distribution of Elephant Seals, their annual haul-out, breeding
habits, food and growth, returns to the sea, annual moult, mortality and natural
enemies, breathing, progress on land, swimming, numbers at South Georgia, and the
elephant seal oil industry. The other seals found there include the Weddell Seal,
Leopard Seal, Crab-eater Seal, and Fur-Seal. The author's *Sea elephant: the life and
death of the elephant seal* (London: Macgibbon & Kee, 1952. 185p. map) is a popular
account of seals and sealing on South Georgia.

629   **The fur seal of South Georgia.**
       W. Nigel Bonner.   London: British Antarctic Survey, 1968. 81p. 6p.
       of plates. 15 maps. bibliog. (Scientific Reports, no. 56).

Information presented in this account of the general biology of the fur-seal,
Arctocephalus tropicalis gazella, in South Georgia, includes a physical description;
the structure of its pelage and details of barnacle infestation; a biogeography,
taxonomy, and history of exploitation; its environment; its general, sexual and
juvenile behaviour; and a population study. The position of South Georgia's fur-seals
in relation to other members of the genus is also considered. Bonner's 'Notes on the

Southern Fur Seal in South Georgia', *Proceedings of The Zoological Society*, vol. 130 (1958), p.241-52, looks at their habitat, behaviour patterns, food, population size, and the future prospects for the herd.

630 **Population increase of fur seals at South Georgia.**
R. M. Laws. *Polar Record*, vol. 16, no. 105 (September 1973), p. 856-58.
Based on research conducted by M. P. Payne for the British Antarctic Survey on Bird Island in 1971-72, this report tells how counts of seals were carried out at weekly intervals in November and December. These were supplemented by more frequent counts in sample areas. It was found that several additional stretches of coast had been colonized since 1967.

631 **Reindeer on South Georgia: the ecology of an introduced population.**
N. Leader-Williams. Cambridge, England: Cambridge University Press, 1988. 319p. bibliog. (Studies in Polar Research).
Reindeer were first introduced to South Georgia by Norwegian whalers on at least three occasions between 1911 and 1925 presumably as a source of fresh meat for the permanent and seasonal population. Not recommended for general reading, this scientific treatise is the result of several years research, and investigates the effect of the introduction of a large Arctic herbivore on a Southern ecosystem that had not previously been exposed to grazing animals. The academic and comparative nature of this highly specialized work is emphasized by its thirty-one pages of approximately 600 citations to articles in learned and scientific journals, of which the author's 'Observations on the internal parasites of introduced reindeer on South Georgia', *Veterinary Record*, vol. 107 (1980), p.393-95, and his 'Age determination of reindeer introduced into South Georgia', *Journal of Zoology*, vol. 188 (1979), p.501-15, may stand as typical examples.

Travel guides

632 **Grytviken Whaling Station: an introduction for visitors.**
Nigel Bonner. Grytviken: South Georgia Whaling Museum, 1993. 5p.
This is a descriptive guide and tour of the Grytviken whaling station, which was the first to be established in the Antarctic, and destined to become the base of the Antarctic whaling industry. At its height the station had accommodation for 300 men and was designed to produce whale oil, seal oil, whale meat, bone meal, and frozen whale meat.

633 **Information for visitors to South Georgia.**
Stanley: Commissioner for South Georgia and The South Sandwich
Islands, 1993. 9 single-sided typescript sheets.
Scientific and tourist expeditions seeking permission to visit South Georgia are handed
this information set. It reminds them that they must report on arrival and departure and
that no overnight onshore accommodation is available. There are notes on harbours
and jetties, buoys, areas that cannot be visited, and fishing vessels. Lists of useful
names and addresses and of relevant Admiralty charts are also incorporated.

Maritime archaeology

634 **Wrecks, hulks and other vessel remains at South Georgia,
Falkland Islands Dependencies.**
R. K. Headland. *British Antarctic Survey Bulletin*, no. 65 (November
1984), p. 109-26. map. bibliog.
The coasts of South Georgia were not comprehensively charted until the *Discovery*
investigations of 1927 and onwards. Largely because of this more than fifty vessels
are known to have been wrecked or otherwise lost on or near the Island. This paper
lists in chronological order those ships whose dates of loss are known between 1796
and 1983. The annotation provided includes the ship's name, description, master,
circumstances, and a reference to a relevant source. A map of the sites is also
valuable. It was reprinted in *Falkland Islands Journal*, no. 19 (1985), p. 10-28.

635 **Ships at Grytviken.**
Nigel Bonner. Grytviken: South Georgia Whaling Museum, 1993.
2p.
Background information on the maritime history of South Georgia wrecks and hulks is
presented in this well-produced leaflet which covers: *Petrel, Albatross, Dias* and
Louise at Grytviken; *Karrakatta* at Husvik; *Brutus* at Prince Olav Harbour; and
Bayard ashore on the southern side of Ocean Harbour.

History

636 **A visit to South Georgia.**
Heinrich W. Klutschak, translated from the German by R. S.
Boumphrey. *British Antarctic Survey Bulletin*, no. 12 (May 1967),
p. 85-92. map.
Klutschak spent six months of the southern summer in 1877-78 cruising round South
Georgia in a small schooner. This early description of the island and its mountains,
climate, birds and seals, retains its interest. Klutschak's full report was first published

as 'Ein Besuch auf Sud-Georgien', *Deutsche Rundschau für Geographie und Statistics*, vol. 3, no. 11 (1881), p. 522-34.

637 South Georgia, an outpost of the Antarctic.

Robert Cushman Murphy. *National Geographic Magazine*, vol. 41, no. 4 (April 1922), p. 409-44. 2 maps.

Murphy made a year-long visit to South Georgia, sailing his brig, *Daisy*, to Cumberland Bay, westwards to the bleak and lonely Bay of Isles, and to Prince Olaf Harbour. Illustrated with thirty-nine photographs, this article describes the Island's glaciers, gales, plant life, bird and marine life, the titlark unique to South Georgia, and the sea elephant. South Georgia's history, Cook's discovery, the nineteenth-century fur-sealing industry, the whale fishery, and the scientific investigations carried out on the island, are also touched upon.

638 South Georgia: the British Empire's subantarctic outpost: a synopsis of the history of the island.

L. Harrison Matthews. Bristol, England: John Wright; London: Simpkin Marshall, 1931. 163p. map. bibliog.

Beginning with a description of South Georgia, its topography, geology, climate, and natural history, Matthews follows the early voyages which first sighted the island, studies the whaling and sealing industry, based there in the twentieth century, and considers the island's future.

639 East to South Georgia.

Kenneth Bradley. *Blackwood's Magazine*, vol. 254, no. 1534 (August 1943), p. 77-88.

These descriptive and narrative extracts from the author's diary (7-11 February 1943), kept during a voyage from Stanley to South Georgia, capture the essential flavour of life at Grytviken and Leith Harbour, and provide a graphic account of sailing round the coast to Cumberland Bay, Penguin Bay, and Dog Bay.

640 Antarctic housewife.

Nan Brown. London: Hutchinson, 1971. 190p.

The author spent two-and-a-half years on South Georgia – one of only three women on the island – accompanying her husband, a former Merchant Navy radio officer, who had been given the job of running the radio station there. Apart from journeying across the island, swimming in inland lakes and going on a whaling trip, she also found time to set up a Penguin Rehabilitation Centre where oiled-up penguins were cleaned and restored to their pristine condition. Otherwise 'their efforts to preen their feathers resulted in poisoning and death'.

641 South Georgia: a concise account.

R. K. Headland. Cambridge, England: British Antarctic Survey, 1982. 28p. map. bibliog.

In this brief account, a forerunner to his definitive study *The island of South Georgia* (q.v.), Headland includes sections on South Georgia's geography, government, history, sealing, whaling, cartography and meteorology. There are also sections on geology, glaciology, oceanography, botany, mammals, birds, fish, invertebrates, conservation, present circumstances, research and recording, communications, population and settlement, and the future.

642   The Island of South Georgia.
Robert Headland.   Cambridge, England: Cambridge University Press, 1984. 293p. 10 maps. bibliog.

With separate chapters on geography, administration, and population; discovery and first landing; early history and the first epoch of sealing; expeditions, visits and other events on South Georgia from 1882; whaling, second sealing epoch and settlement; travel and communications; physical sciences; the land, ocean and atmosphere; natural history; and military events in 1982 and the island's future, this encyclopaedic illustrated volume stands alone as the ultimate reference source for all aspects of South Georgia's history. It also contains ten appendices and an extensive bibliography. A revised paperback edition, published in 1992, has no major amendments or corrections although events since 1984 are updated in an additional note in the preface. These include a change in the islands political status in 1985 when the Falkland Islands Dependencies were dissolved into two new territories, South Georgia and the South Sandwich Islands, and British Antarctic Territory.

643   South Georgia – an island home at the Far End of the World.
John Rhind.   *Army Quarterly & Defence Journal*, vol. 117, no. 1 (January 1987), p. 48-54.

As Magistrate of South Georgia, from March to July 1984, the author was responsible for maintaining the island's civil administration and running the only surviving Falkland Islands Dependencies post office.

Sovereignty

644   Three British naval antarctic voyages, 1906-43.
A. G. E. Jones.   *Falkland Islands Journal*, no. 15 (1981), p. 29-36. bibliog.

In the first half of the twentieth century the Royal Navy made a dozen visits to the Antarctic mainly to underline British sovereignty. Jones notes that 'Comments on these voyages have been few, partly because it was seldom that anything of public interest happened on them'. However, the visit of *HMS Sappho* to South Georgia ended with an ultimatum to the Norwegian whalers at Grytviken either to lower the Argentine flag or have it shot down. It is interesting that this was not mentioned in the log-book or the official report.

645 **British letters patent of 1908 and 1917 constituting the Falkland Islands Dependencies.**
Polar Record, vol. 5, nos. 35 and 36 (January-July 1948), p. 241-44.
All subsequent British legislation is based on the text and authority of these two documents which define the boundaries of the Falkland Island Dependencies. They were first published in *Falkland Island Gazette* (1 September 1908 and 2 July 1917) and in *British & Foreign State Papers*, vol. 101 (1907-08) (London: 1912) and vol. 111 (1917-18) (London: 1921).

646 **Antarctic claims – recent diplomatic exchanges between Great Britain, Argentina and Chile.**
Polar Record, vol. 5, nos. 35 and 36 (January-July 1948), p. 228-40.
The full text is given here of the diplomatic notes sent to Argentina and Chile following naval incursions into British sovereign territory during the 1946-47 and 1947-48 summer seasons.

647 **The Antarctic problem: an historical and political study.**
E. W. Hunter Christie. London: Allen & Unwin, 1951. 336p. 5 maps. bibliog.
Providing a background to the sovereignty disputes involving Argentina, Britain and Chile in Antarctica, this comprehensive study contains a number a chapters directly relating to the former Falkland Islands Dependencies: chapter two, Southwards: the discovery of South Georgia (especially useful for the voyage of Anthony de la Roché); chapter three, Captain Cook: the discovery of the South Sandwich Islands and the first landing on South Georgia; chapter sixteen, The Falkland Islands Dependencies; and chapter seventeen, Argentina and the Antarctic. The British letters patent of 1908 and 1917, constituting the Falkland Island Dependencies, and the diplomatic exchanges of 1947, are appended.

648 **The British title to sovereignty in the Falkland Islands Dependencies.**
Polar Record, vol. 8, no. 53 (May 1956), p. 125-51.
Reprinted here is the full text of the United Kingdom's application to the International Court of Justice at The Hague, setting out the British title, and asking the Court to declare the Argentine and Chilean encroachments in British Antarctic Territory to be illegal and invalid under international law. Documents submitted include: Application by the United Kingdom relative to the encroachments of Argentina in British Antarctic Territory; Origins of the British titles, historic discoveries and acts of annexation 1643-1843; Display of British sovereignty 1908-1938; Recognition of British claims by Norway, Argentina and Chile . . . 1908; Origins and development of Argentina's pretensions to the . . . Falkland Islands Dependencies and attempted usurpation of British sovereignty; Rejection of Argentine pretensions by the United Kingdom and continued display of British sovereignty up to the present time; Argentina's persistence in her pretensions . . . and in her physical encroachments; Limited relevance in point of law of events after 1925 (South Orkneys) . . . and after 1937 (South Shetlands and Graham Land); The jurisprudence of international tribunals negatives the Argentine claims and supports the United Kingdom's titles; Acceptance

of the Court's jurisdiction; The contentions and claims of the United Kingdom
Government in the Argentine case; and a similar set of documents relating to Chile.

649   **Delimitation and administration of British dependent territories in
       Antarctic regions.**
       R. K. Headland.   *Polar Record*, vol. 28, no. 167 (October 1992),
       p. 315-21. 2 maps. bibliog.
Geographical discoveries and events, notably the Antarctic Treaty of 1959 and the
Argentine invasion of South Georgia in 1982, resulted in changes to the delimitation
and administration of the British Antarctic Territory, South Georgia, and the South
Sandwich Islands. This paper outlines the delimitation and nomenclature of these
territories from 1908 when the Falkland Islands Dependencies were designated. It is
stressed that there were never any constitutional links between the Falkland Islands
and the Dependencies.

War in the South Atlantic 1982

650   **Military action in the Falkland Islands Dependencies April-June
       1982.**
       R. K. Headland.   *Polar Record*, vol. 21, no. 133 (January 1983),
       p. 394-95; no. 135 (September 1983), p. 549-58.
The first of these two papers outlines the events in the Falkland Islands Dependencies
after the Argentine occupation of April 1982, with a brief summary of events that
precipitated the invasion. The second paper chronicles the military activities leading
to the occupation, and subsequent recapture, of King Edward Point, the administrative
centre, and the principal British Antarctic Survey station on South Georgia. Headland
was himself taken prisoner by the Argentine forces on the island.

651   **Operation Paraquat: the battle for South Georgia.**
       Roger Perkins.   Chippenham, England: Picton Publishing, 1986.
       261p. 11 maps.
Operation Paraquat was the code-name for the British reoccupation of South Georgia
which had been seized by Argentine forces on 3 April 1982. Involving the Royal
Navy, the Fleet Air Arm, the Royal Air Force, Royal Artillery, the Special Air Service
Regiment, the Royal Marine Commandos, and the Special Boat Squadron, it was a
model Combined Operation. Based on personal reminiscences, and eye-witness
accounts, this illustrated history vividly captures the hazardous events as they moved
swiftly from incipient disaster to ultimate success.

Population

652   **The first South Georgia population census.**
A. B. Dickinson.   *Polar Record*, vol. 23, no. 144 (September 1986),
p. 349-51. bibliog.

J. Innes Watson, the first stipendiary magistrate on the island, conducted a census of its inhabitants on 31 December 1909. Information obtained included the permanent shore residents, temporary residents, their country of origin, occupation, and age distribution. Of the 365 all-year-round residents all but two were whaling company employees.

Whaling and sealing industry

653   **A narrative of the life, travels and sufferings of Thomas W. Smith, comprising an account of his early life, adoption by the Gypseys, his travels during eighteen voyages to various parts of the world during which he was five times shipwrecked, thrice on a desolate island near the South Pole . . .**
Thomas W. Smith.   Boston, Massachusetts: William C. Hill, 1834. 240p.

Written long after the events recounted, 'trusting wholly to the memory, not having kept a Journal of his adventures; as the idea of publication had not until recently occurred to him', Smith indelibly portrays the early sealing industry on South Georgia (the desolate island near the South Pole) and the privations suffered by the ships' crews there.

654   **The first South Georgia leases: Compañía Argentina De Pesca and the South Georgia Exploring Company Limited.**
D. W. H. Walton.   *Polar Record*, vol. 21, no. 132 (September 1982),
p. 231-40.

This is a detailed study of the historical background, and of the leases granted to the South Georgia Exploring Company (1905), and the Compañía Argentina De Pesca (1906). It is chiefly concerned with the mineral and pasturage rights given to the Exploring Company, and with the regulations governing the Compañía's whaling and sealing operations.

655   **The history of modern whaling.**
J. N. Tonnessen, A. O. Johnsen, translated from the Norwegian by R. I. Christophersen.   London: Hurst, 1982. 798p. 7 maps. bibliog.

This translation by R. I. Christophersen is a much shortened version of the massive definitive work, *Den moderne hvalfangst historie: opprinnelse og utvikling* (Oslo: Norges Hvalfangstforbund, 1967-70. 4 vols.). Chapter ten, 'The start of Antarctic whaling 1904-1908', is a lucid and readable account of the formation of the Compañía Argentina De Pesca, the first Norwegian companies, the building of the settlement and factory at Grytviken, and of the whalers' hard and exacting way of life. There is a useful map of the whaling stations on South Georgia.

656   C. A. Larsen and South Georgia: a 75th anniversary.
Falkland Islands Newsletter, no. 39 (June 1989), p. 4-5.

Carl Abraham Larsen (1860-1924) became whaling manager of the Compañía Argentina De Pesca when it was first registered in Buenos Aires on 29 February 1904. On the first day of January 1906 the Company was granted 500 acres on South Georgia when the island's whaling industry was effectively established on a systematic basis. This illustrated feature outlines Larsen's connections with South Georgia, notably with the wooden Norwegian church at Grytviken.

657   Salvesen of Leith.
Wray Vamplew.   Edinburgh: Scottish Academic Press, 1975. 311p. map.

The firm of Christian Salvesen was founded as an unlimited private company in Leith in 1872 as shipbrokers and shipbuilders. For nearly seventy years it played a leading role in the whaling industry and in 1907 began its involvement in Southern waters, constructing a station on New Island in the Falklands. Two years later the company transferred operations to Leith Harbour on South Georgia. Based on the firm's whaling records, this industrial history is essential reading for an understanding of the economics of the industry and it also provides a detailed account of Salvesen's operations on South Georgia until their termination in 1963. There are several photographs of Leith Harbour and a map of the central part of South Georgia.

658   Logbook for Grace: whaling brig Daisy 1912-1913.
Robert Cushman Murphy.   London: Robert Hale, 1948. 290p. map.

Published here is the logbook Cushman kept of his day-to-day experiences during his voyage to the Antarctic on an American whaling and sealing vessel in 1912-13. Almost half of the book (p.138-240) is taken up by his visit to South Georgia. He notes with amazement that two officials of the Crown perform the functions of Governor, postmaster, port captain, health officer, the police, Judge and gaoler. A cruise to Prince Olaf Harbour and a vivid description of a sealing voyage, also figure prominently. Cushman's map of the Bay of Isles was published in *Petermann's Mitteilungen* in 1914 and served as the international hydrographic chart until it was superseded by that of the British Discovery Survey in 1931.

659   Report of the interdepartmental committee on research and development in the Dependencies of the Falkland Islands with appendices, maps, etc.
London: HMSO, 1920. 164p. maps. bibliog. (Cmnd. 657).

In 1917 the Colonial Office proposed an enquiry into the whaling industry, particularly with regard to the possibility of excessive hunting causing its collapse. The committee was appointed 'to consider what can now be done to facilitate prompt action . . . in regard to the preservation of the whaling industry and to the development of other industries . . . and to consider not only the economic question . . . and the scheme for the employment of a research vessel, but also what scientific investigations are most required . . . and whether any preliminary inquiries by experts in this country should be instituted'. The committee's report extended over a wide area and is arranged in twelve sections: Introduction (history, physical characteristics of the Islands, their government, scientific expeditions, scope of the inquiry); Whaling industry; Sealing; Fish, penguins and other animals; Hydrology; Meteorology and magnetism; Geology and mineralogy; Botany; Research vessels; Management and control of investigations; Finance; and Summary of recommendations (p.29-31). The most visible result of the interdepartmental committee's deliberations was the establishment of the Discovery Committee.

660   **The Discovery expedition.**
      Stanley Kemp. *Nature*, vol. 18, no. 2974 (30 October 1926),
      p. 628-32; vol. 21, no. 3055 (19 May 1928), p. 795-99. maps.

Presents an account of the *Discovery*'s voyage south, its biological and hydrographic survey of the South Georgia whaling grounds, and it plankton research programme, from February 1926 to September 1927. N. M. Mackintosh reports on the work of the Marine Biology Station at Grytviken.

661   **The work of the Royal Research Ship 'Discovery' in the**
      Dependencies of the Falkland Islands.
      A. C. Hardy. *Geographical Journal*, vol. 72, no. 3 (September 1928),
      p. 209-34.

Hardy begins with a short history of the Falkland Islands Dependencies whaling industry, an account of biological research carried out at the well-equipped laboratory in Grytviken, South Georgia, and a study of the whale in its natural environment, which revealed long-awaited information on its breeding time, gestation period, rate of growth, age of maturity, and food. He continues with a detailed outline of *Discovery*'s oceanographical work, between 1925 and 1927, notably the equipment used, and research into the distribution of different plankton forms, the movement of the ocean, the chemistry of the sea, and the nature and fauna of the sea bottom. For an account of work in the 1931-33 seasons see D. Dilwyn John's 'The second Antarctic commission of the RRS Discovery II', *Geographical Journal*, vol. 83, no. 5 (May 1934), p.380-98.

662   **Progress of the Discovery investigations.**
      Stanley Kemp. *Nature*, vol. 124, no. 3126 (28 September 1929),
      p. 483-86.

'Since the RRS Discovery returned to England . . . the oceanographic and whaling investigations which the Discovery Committee is conducting in the South Atlantic have been continued with the RRS William Scoresby and at the Marine Biology Station in South Georgia'. This is a preliminary account of the expedition's planktonic and hydrological survey of the whaling grounds.

663 **South Latitude.**
F. D. Ommanney.   London: Longmans, Green, 1938. 308p. map on
endpaper.

In no sense an official account of the work carried out by the 'Discovery' Committee
on behalf of the Falkland Islands Government, this is the author's personal record of
his time as a member of the Discovery Expedition's scientific staff to which he was
appointed in the summer of 1929. He describes his voyage to South Georgia on board
the Norwegian whaling ship *Antarctic* and the operations of the Compañía Argentina
De Pesca's whaling station in King Edward Cove and discusses the Marine Biology
Station, the British Government's offices across the harbour, Gryviken's social life,
and the ships and personnel involved in sealing and whaling on land and at sea.

664 **On the distribution and movements of whales in the South Georgia**
and South Shetland whaling grounds.
Stanley Kemp, A. G. Bennett.   Cambridge, England: Cambridge
University Press, 1932. p. 165-90. 38p. of plates. (Discovery Reports,
vol. 6).

This report is based on returns to Falkland Islands Government questionnaires issued
to whaling companies operating under licence in the Dependencies, and requesting
information on the distribution and movements of whales in the whaling areas. The
companies were asked to provide the approximate position of each whale killed, and if
whales were spotted moving, in which direction.

665 **The work of the Discovery Committee.**
N. A. Mackintosh.   *Proceedings Of The Royal Society series A:*
Mathematical and Physical Sciences, vol. 202, no. A1068 (22 June
1950), p. 1-16.

The Discovery Committee was established by the Secretary of State for the Colonies
in 1924 to carry out the recommendations embodied in *Report of the*
interdepartmental committee on research and development in the Dependencies of the
Falkland Islands (1920). This paper covers: the Committee's history; the *Discovery*
expeditions of 1925-27; the *Discovery II* and the expansion of the field; methods and
equipment; ocean surveys by the *Discovery II* in 1929-39; direct research of whales;
oceanography and whale distribution; special and subsidiary investigations;
administration and research at home; and the present and future. Several photographs
of scenes in Grytviken, South Georgia, are included.

666 **Discovery reports: issued by the Discovery Committee Colonial**
Office London on behalf of the Government of the Dependencies of
the Falkland Islands.
Cambridge, England: Cambridge University Press, 1929-66.

This long series of reports on the scientific work undertaken on the voyages of the
Discovery from the 1920s onwards at first focused on research that would assist the
regulation of the whale industry but was later extended to all scientific aspects of the
Southern Ocean. Most annually bound volumes from 1927 to 1947 carried lists of
personnel on each of the Research Stations established on the Falklands, South
Georgia, the South Sandwich Islands, and elsewhere, together with biological and

hydrological observations taken. Many of these substantial reports, which were issued separately, end with extensive bibliographies. From 1953 onwards their publication became the responsibility of the National Institute of Oceanography. A bibliographical guide to the *Discovery reports* is appended to Sir Alister Hardy's *Great waters: a voyage of natural history to study whales, plankton and the waters of the Southern Ocean in the old Royal Research Ship Discovery with the results brought up to date by the findings of RRS Discovery II* (London: Collins, 1967. 542p. maps. bibliog.).

667 Whaling stations in South Georgia.

J. G. Bannister. *Polar Record*, vol. 12, no. 77 (May 1964), p. 207-10.

Includes a table outlining the sites and periods of the whaling companies' operations in South Georgia in four columns: site of factory (Grytviken, Stromness, Husvik, Godthal, Leith Harbour, Ocean Harbour, and Prince Olav Harbour); company; dates of operation; and remarks.

668 The demise of elephant sealing at South Georgia 1960-68.

A. B. Dickinson. *Polar Record*, vol. 25, no. 154 (July 1989), p. 185-90. bibliog.

In an introduction Dickinson remarks that uncontrolled sealing for furs and oil began on South Georgia about 1786 and continued sporadically until the early twentieth century. From 1909 onwards legislation allowed licensed killing of male elephant seals which provided for a successful industry for the next sixty years. However, the industry barely survived the demise of whaling on South Georgia, coming to an end in 1968. Here Dickinson concentrates on the Japanese period of the final three seasons. Tables on the seal catches and seal and whale oil production at Grytviken, and on the value of whale products and seal oil taken there between 1923-24 and 1964-65, are included. There is also an extensive list of references, many of them to manuscript material held in the Scott Polar Research Institute.

669 A potted history of Grytviken Whaling Station.

Ian B. Hart. Grytviken: South Georgia Whaling Museum, [n.d.]. 8p.

Condensed within this skilfully-written pamphlet are all the essential aspects of South Georgia's whaling industry: the arrival of Larsen; the number of whales found; the changing nature of whaling operations; life on South Georgia; recreations; the church at Grytviken; trade-union activities and the strikes of 1912-13 and 1919; dates; details of catches 1904-65; and the total production figures of whale and seal oil, meat, and bone meal during that period.

670 The British whaling trade.

Gordon Jackson. London: Adam & Charles Black, 1978. 310p. bibliog.

The activities of Salvesen's New Whaling Company and of the Southern Whaling Company, the establishment of factories on South Georgia at Leith Harbour and Prince Olaf Harbour, and the declining numbers of whales in South Georgia waters, all figure prominently in this general history. A series of statistical tables relating to annual catches complements the text.

671 **Russians are fishing South Georgia to destruction.**
Falkland Islands Newsletter, no. 35 (May 1988), p. 8.

'Over recent years it has become apparent that the Russian method of harvesting the resources at South Georgia and Kerguelen has been to fish the stock almost to destruction and then leave the island alone for five or six years, or maybe even more, for the stock to recuperate'. Based on notes provided by Mr T. W. Boyd of Witte Boyd Holdings – long involved in the South Atlantic in monitoring for British Antarctic Survey the fishing practices of Eastern Bloc countries – this article advocates the establishment of a properly conducted fishing zone around South Georgia to avoid the industry becoming a one-ground and one-species operation.

672 **South Georgia whales and whaling: the history of South Georgia whaling.**
G. D. Moir. *Gibbons Stamp Monthly*, vol. 24, no. 9 (February 1994), p. 64-65, 67; no. 12 (May 1994), p. 62-65; vol. 25, no. 3 (August 1994), p. 60-64; no. 6 (November 1994), p. 72-75.

The February article in this mini-series concentrates on the history of the whaling industry based on South Georgia, culminating in the establishment of the whaling museum at Grytviken. The May and August articles focus on South Georgia's postal history, whilst the November article describes the six major species of whales found in southern waters: the Right Whale; the Humpback Whale; the Fin Whale; the Blue Whale; the Sperm Whale; and the Killer Whale. All four parts of the series carry illustrations of appropriate Falkland Islands, South Georgia, and British Antarctic Territory stamps.

Philately

673 **The stamps used in South Georgia.**
W. H. Lawson. *Stamp Collectors Fortnightly*, vol. 18, no. 457 (14 September 1912), p. 44.
The philately of South Georgia.
W. H. Lawson. *Stamp Collectors Fortnightly*, no. 465 (4 January 1913), p. 232.

The Post Office at Grytviken opened its doors on 3 December 1909 under the personal supervision of the Chief Magistrate. Together these two articles present a brief account of South Georgia's early postal services and of the stamps and franks used.

674   **South Georgia (Falkland Islands): notes regarding the unauthorized bisected stamp of March 1923.**
W. H. Lawson.   *London Philatelist*, vol. 33, no. 390 (June 1924), p. 150-51.

Lawson relates the circumstances surrounding the issue of bisected 2½d stamps (two at 1d each) authorized by the Acting Resident Magistrate in 1923, when stocks of the 1d stamp were exhausted.

675   **Notes on the Falkland Islands (South Georgia) provisional of 1928.**
B. S. H. Grant.   *London Philatelist*, vol. 39, no. 463 (July 1930), p. 164-67.

In this expert paper Grant examines the circumstances surrounding the Post Office on South Georgia running out of ½d and 2½d stamps in 1928. After receiving permission from Stanley 1,179 current 2d stamps were overprinted.

676   **The Falkland Islands (South Georgia) frank of 1911-1912.**
B. S. H. Grant.   *London Philatelist*, vol. 42, no. 494 (February 1933), p. 35-37.

Grant explains the circumstances of the shortage of stamps in Grytviken post office in 1911 and the consequent temporary use of an improvised rubber handstamp. He also remarks on the unsatisfactory practice whereby the postmaster there purchased his stamps for subsequent resale.

677   **The Falkland Dependency of South Georgia.**
B. S. H. Grant.   *London Philatelist*, vol. 46, no. 551 (November 1937), p. 261-65.

Besides surveying South Georgia's postal history, Grant includes in this paper brief memoirs of two eminent collectors, one of whom, Mr Louis Williams, the consul in Port Stanley for France, Chile and Argentina, a leading merchant, and owner of the Globe Hotel, was also one of the custodians of the vaults where the stamps were stored.

678   **Postal history of the Falkland Islands Dependencies.**
Richard W. Bagshawe.   Cambridge, England: Scott Polar Research Institute, 1947. 59p. map.

From 1909 to 1944 the Dependencies used Falkland Islands stamps. This illustrated postal history, reprinted from *Polar Record*, vol. 5, nos. 33 and 34 (January-July 1947), p. 45-59, looks in detail at the adhesive stamps and handstruck general postage stamps of both periods. Bagshawe appends a list of post offices and their locations in the Falkland Islands Dependencies in 1904-46.

679   **South Georgia handstamps: ghosts from the past.**
R. N. Spafford.   *Philatelic Magazine*, vol. 91, no. 10 (July 1983), p. 491, 493.

Because of the remoteness of South Georgia, Spafford found it difficult in the lingering fog of the 1982 war to discover what was happening there. However, thanks to a personal contact he was able eventually to obtain impressions of all handstamps in current use.

The press

680   **The South Georgia and The South Sandwich Islands Gazette.**
Stanley, 1985- . irreg.

In October 1985 South Georgia and the South Sandwich Islands formally ceased to be Dependencies of the Falkland Islands to become a separate territory. Prior to this all official notices and publications relating to these islands were printed in *The Falkland Islands Gazette* (q.v.) but now a separate *Gazette* became necessary. Important ordinances first published in its pages include the proclamation of a 200-mile maritime zone round the Islands (May 1993); Fisheries Conservation and Management (June 1993); South Georgia Museum Trust (May 1992); and Visitors (November 1992).

Bibliographies

681   **South Georgia: a bibliography.**
R. K. Headland.   Cambridge, England: British Antarctic Survey, 1982. 180p.

Arranged in twenty classified sections (for example, general accounts, expeditions, history, botany, glaciology and zoology), 1,344 briefly annotated entries are included in this definitive bibliography. Most were tracked down in the rich documentary resources of the Scott Polar Research Institute in Cambridge, or in the Norse Hvalfangstmuseum at Sandefjord. There is also a first-class bibliography in Headland's *The island of South Georgia* (q.v.).

South Sandwich
Islands

682 **South Sandwich Islands.**
Stanley Kemp, A. L. Nelson, G. W. Tyrrell. Cambridge, England:
Cambridge University Press, 1931. p. 135-98. (Discovery Reports,
vol. 3).

The *Royal Research Ship Discovery* visited the South Sandwich Islands at the end of
February 1930 and spent three weeks steaming at slow speed round each of the eleven
islands in the group, fixing their position astronomically, plotting their coastlines, and
exploring possible anchorages. When mist and cloud allowed, the heights of mountain
tops were determined, and soundings were continuously taken. This report describes
Discovery's itinerary and the individual islands.

683 **South Sandwich Islands – bird life.**
J. Wilkinson. *Sea Swallow*, vol. 9 (1956), p. 18-20.

This is a report of sightings by Captain Wilkinson and a volunteer team from the
ship's company of *HMS Protector*, in South Sandwich Islands waters on 15-19 March
1956, 'printed in full owing to its outstanding interest as a record of birds in a remote
group of Islands which have probably seldom been visited by a competent
ornithologist'. See also Wilkinson's 'A second visit to the South Sandwich Islands',
Sea Swallow, vol. 10 (1957), p. 22.

684 **Observations in the South Sandwich Islands 1962.**
M. W. Holdgate. *Polar Record*, vol. 11, no. 73 (January 1963),
p. 394-405. 1p. of plates. bibliog.

Topographical information and news of volcanic activity on Thule, Cook,
Bellingshausen, Bristol, Saunders, Candlemas, Vindication, Visokoi, Leskov and
Zavadovski Islands, and their terrestrial biology, is included in these observations
taken during the visits of *RRS Shackleton* and *HMS Protector* to the Islands in January
1961 and March 1962 respectively. Three tables record thirty-six known visits to the
Islands; geological and botanical collections; and the localities for rock and plant
species collected on the *Shackleton* and *Protector* visits.

685 **Pumice eruption in the area of the South Sandwich Islands.**
  I. G. Gass, P. G. Harris, M. W. Holdgate. *Geological Magazine*,
  vol. 100, no. 4 (July-August 1963), p. 320-30. map. bibliog.

In the course of its voyage in South Sandwich Islands waters in March 1962, the Royal Navy ice patrol vessel, *HMS Protector*, came across an extended pumice raft. Evidence is presented here which suggests that this material was ejected from a submarine eruption thirty-five miles to the north-west of the Islands on the axis of the South Sandwich arc.

686 **A survey of the South Sandwich Islands.**
  P. E. Baker, et al. *Nature*, vol. 203, no. 4946 (15 August 1964),
  p. 691-93. map.

A joint venture of the Royal Navy and British Antarctic Survey, the survey team landed on Leskov, Candlemas, Bellingshausen, Vindication and Visokoi Islands during a three-week voyage in 1964. This preliminary report includes sections on the land survey (C. J. C. Wynne-Edwards); geology (Baker and J. F. Tomblin); botany (R. E. Longton and M. W. Holdgate); invertebrate zoology (P. J. Tilbrook and Holdgate); and vertebrate zoology (R. W. Vaughan).

687 **Islands of ice and fire.**
  C. J. C. Wynne-Edwards. *Geographical Magazine*, vol. 37, no. 10
  (February 1965), p. 766-77. map.

Early in 1963 an underwater volcanic eruption of considerable intensity in the waters around the South Sandwich Islands aroused scientific interest in the United Kingdom. In March 1964 a scientific party led by Dr Martin Holdgate, of the British Antarctic Survey, visited the Islands in *HMS Protector*, the ice-patrol ship. Lieutenant-Commander Wynne-Edwards describes the expedition's geological, vulcanological, botanical and zoological activities. He himself was responsible for the survey work.

688 **Palaeomagnetism of some lavas from the South Sandwich Islands.**
  D. J. Blundell. *British Antarctic Survey Bulletin*, no. 9 (October
  1966), p. 61-62.

In the course of the joint British Antarctic Survey/Royal Navy survey expedition to the South Sandwich Islands in March 1964, eight orientated samples were collected from recent lava flows. A table of magnetic measurements of samples is given in this brief report.

689 **The South Sandwich Islands: 1: general description.**
  M. W. Holdgate, P. E. Baker. Cambridge, England: British Antarctic
  Survey, 1979. 76p. map. 11p. of plates. bibliog. (British Antarctic
  Survey Scientific Report, no. 91).

During a three-week voyage in 1964 a British Antarctic Survey team, with Royal Marine support, established a base camp on Candlemas Island, and made geological, botanical, and zoological studies on Zavadovski, Leskov, Visokoi, Vindication, Saunders, Montagu, Bristol, Bellingshausen, Cook, and Thule Islands, landing by helicopter from *HMS Protector*. This report includes a history of the exploration of the Islands.

690   **The South Sandwich Islands: 2: the geology of Candlemas Island.**
J. F. Tomblin.   Cambridge, England: British Antarctic Survey, 1979.
33p. 6p. of plates. bibliog. (British Antarctic Survey Scientific Report,
no. 92).

Candlemas Island is a recently active volcanic island. This scientific report includes an
introduction on its physical geography, previous visits to the island, and recorded
volcanic activity, and separate sections on its geomorphology, geology, volcanic
history, petrography, geochemistry, petrogenesis, and a comparison with other
volcanoes of island arcs.

691   **The South Sandwich Islands: 3: petrology of the volcanic rocks.**
P. E. Baker.   Cambridge, England: British Antarctic Survey, 1978.
34p. 2p. of plates. bibliog. (British Antarctic Survey Scientific Report,
no. 93).

In addition to summaries of the Island's geology and petrology, this scientific report
contains separate sections on their mineralogy, geochemistry, and petrogenesis.

692   **The South Sandwich Islands: 4: botany.**
R. E. Longton, M. W. Holdgate.   Cambridge, England: British
Antarctic Survey, 1979. 51p. 1p. of plates. map. bibliog. (British
Antarctic Survey Scientific Report, no. 94).

The authors present a record of botanical studies on Candlemas, Bellingshausen,
Visokoi, Saunders, Vindication, Bristol, Cook, Montagu, and Thule Islands. An
introductory section is concerned with previous investigations, the genera and species
recorded, distribution patterns, and the classification and general features of the
Islands' vegetation.

693   **United Kingdom – Argentina – Dispute over Argentinian scientific
base on Southern Thule Island – Further negotiations over
Falkland Islands.**
Keesing's Contemporary Archives, vol. 24 (7 July 1978), p. 29062.

On 9 May 1978 the Foreign & Commonwealth Office revealed that about fifty
Argentine scientists had established an illegal base on the island of Southern Thule
and had been in occupation there since December 1976. This report also covers
discussions on the sovereignty issue in Rome (13-15 July 1977), in New York (13-15
December 1977), and in Lima (15-17 February 1978).

Index

The index is a single alphabetical sequence of authors (personal and corporate), titles of publications and subjects. Index entries refer both to main items and to other works mentioned in the notes to each item. Title entries and the names of vessels are in italics. The numbers refer to bibliographical entry rather than page numbers.

211

N

Nabarro, D. 506
Nanina's last voyage 221
Narrative of hydrographic
survey operations in
South Georgia 595
Narrative of the life,
travels and sufferings
of Thomas W. Smith
653
Narrative of the
proceedings in a high
assembly 213
Narrative of the sufferings
and adventures of
Capt. Charles H.
Barnard 221
Narrative of the surveying
voyages of His
Majesty's Ships
Adventure and Beagle
49
National Environment
Research Council 148
National Geographic 345,
608
National Geographic
Magazine 129, 618, 637
National Institute of
Oceanography 666
National interest/national
honor 282
National Museum of
Science, Ottawa 108
National Tourism Bureau
165
Natural History 496
Natural history of an
unlikely battlefield
109
Natural history of the
Elephant Seal 628
Natural resources 27, 60
Natural vegetation of the
Falklands 118
Naturalist in Penguin
Land 618
Nature 120, 609, 660, 662,
686
Nautical Magazine 229
Naval battles of the First
World War 246

Navy List 43
Nelson, A. L. 682
Neumayer, G. 573
Neumayer Glacier 587
New Brunswick Museum
108
New Civil Engineer 334,
336
New Falklands flights on
the wild side 166
New Fortune Bay 587
New Island 57, 474, 515,
621
New Island Project 112
New Islands 40, 87
New Monthly Magazine
52, 385
New Scientist 478, 482
New voyage round the
world 38
New Zealand Department
of Agriculture 453
Newcastle, Duke of 386,
447
News from the Falkland
Islands 177
Nield, W. C. 512
Nieto, M. H. 253
1933 centenary issue of
the Falkland Islands
514
1982 Joint services
expedition to South
Georgia 581
1994 fishing agreement
490
1995 South American
handbook 165
No price on sovereignty
291
Non-Conformist Church
363
Nordenskjöld, O. 65
Norland returns from
Falklands Task Force
service 316
Norman, A. 199
Norse Hvalfangstmuseum,
Sandefjord 681
North Bay 595
Northedge, F. S. 266
Note on the geology of the
Falkland Islands 64

Notes on a collection of
fishes from the
Falkland Islands 108
Notes on the birds of the
Falkland Islands 123
Notes on the Falkland
Islands (South
Georgia) provisional
of 1928 675
Notes on the southern fur
seal in South Georgia
629
Nova Belgia 192
Nuttall, N. 291, 504

O

O'Brien, C. 56
O'Callaghan, J. 179
Oakley, D. 324
Observations in the South
Sandwich Islands
1962 684
Observations of Sir
Richard Hawkins Knt.
in his voyage into the
South Sea in the year
1593 36
Observations on Albatross
Island in the Bay of
Isles 627
Observations on the birds
of South Georgia 623
Observations on the
internal parasites of
introduced reindeer
on South Georgia 631
Observer Magazine 22
Ocean Harbour 611, 635,
667
Odd society battles on
391
Offshore oil prospects 427
Oil industry 25, 424-28
Oil riches in the Falklands
still only speculation
424
Old Falklands
photographs 30
Ommanney, F. D. 663
On Fortress Falklands
419

Q

Queen Victoria issues of the Falkland Islands 535

Quensel, P. D. 9

Quest and occupation of Tahiti 208

R

R. A. F. Harriers in the Falklands 310

R. A. F. Stanley 406

R. A. F.'s year in 1982 308

Rabson, S. 300

Racing 18

Railways of the Falkland Islands and South Georgia 436

Rankin, N. 617-18

Rare animals in the Zoological Society's Gardens 143

Rasor, E. L. 330

Ratpack war 299

Ravaged Falkland Islands 497

Rawlings, J. D. R. 310

Rea, H. 229

Realms and islands 48

Reasons for the formation of a convict establishment at the Falkland Islands 384

Reasons in writing 332

Recent Polar and Glaciology Literature 566

Recent Polar Literature 566

Recent records for the flora of South Georgia 610

Recent tree planting trials and the status of forestry in the Falkland Islands 468

Reconstruction 334-47

Reflexions on the case of Antonio Rivero 273

Regiments 405

Register of the Society of Merchants, Shipowners and Underwriters 43

Reid, D. I. 337

Reid, J. 465-66

Reid, T. G. 279

Reindeer on South Georgia 631

Relation du voyage de la Mer du Sud 39

Religion 353-64
see also Churches

Remarks on the Government of the Falkland Islands 236

Remember the Darwin 437

Rendell, P. 26, 377

Rennie, G. 350

Reply to reflexions on the case of Antonio Rivero 273

Report on the British barque Lady Elizabeth 190

Report on the economy of the Falkland Islands 414

Report of the interdepartmental committee on research and development in the Dependencies of the Falkland Islands 659, 665

Report on the scientific results of the Scottish National Antarctic Expedition 475

Representing the islanders over fifty issues 545

Reptiles 7

Research problems in studying Britain's Latin American past 267

Resolution journal of Johann Reinhold Forster 1772-1775 570

Resolution to the Shackleton Valley controversy 578

Return of the Great Britain 181

Revello de Torre, J. 558

Revenge at sea 245

Rhind, J. 643

Richards, P. 428

Richards, P. A. 592

Richmond, Duke of 213

Ricketts, C. 626

Right Whale Bay 595

Rio Gallegos 292

Ripon, Marquis of 368

Rivero, A. 273

Roberts, G. 514

Robertson, J. 451

Robin, G. de Q. 600

Robinson, G. S. 151

Robinson, P. 331

Robinson, W. 90-91, 93

Robson, G. 399

Rochford, Earl of 209, 212

Role of the Falklands lobby 545

Roman Catholic Church 360-62

Roper, P. 160

Rosenberg, A. A. 488

Ross, Sir Jas C. 113, 233

Ross, M. J. 233

Ross in the Antarctic 233

Rosswall, T. 607

Rough, D. A. 440

Rowland, K. T. 180

Roy Cove 62

Royal Air Force 308, 310, 319, 406-08, 438, 651

Royal Air Force yearbook 1983 308

Royal Anglian South Georgia Expedition 584

Royal Artillery 312, 651

Royal Bay 80, 574, 580, 593, 616

Royal Botanical Gardens, Kew 464-65, 611

Map of the Falkland Islands

This map shows the more important towns, settlements, islands, and other features.

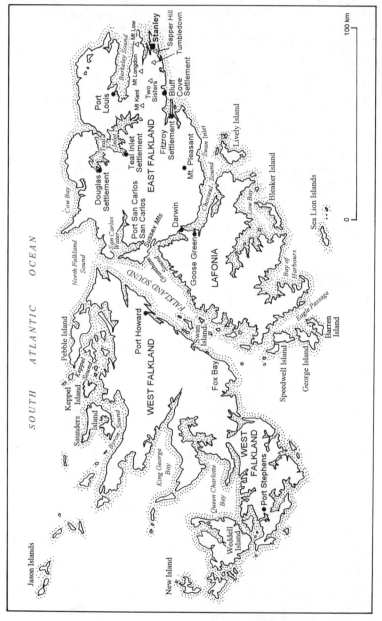

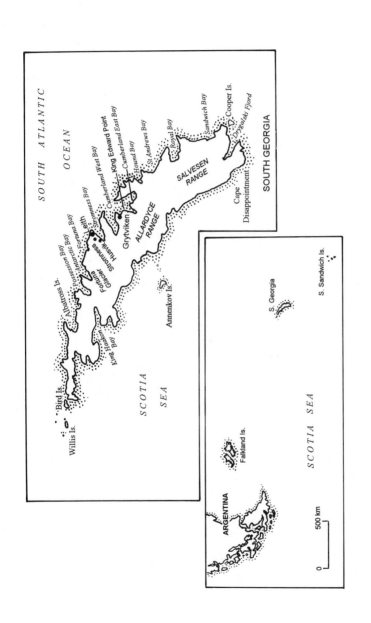

ALSO FROM CLIO PRESS

INTERNATIONAL ORGANIZATIONS SERIES

Each volume in the International Organizations Series is either devoted to one specific organization, or to a number of different organizations operating in a particular region, or engaged in a specific field of activity. The scope of the series is wide-ranging and includes intergovernmental organizations, international non-governmental organizations, and national bodies dealing with international issues. The series is aimed mainly at the English-speaker and each volume provides a selective, annotated, critical bibliography of the organization, or organizations, concerned. The bibliographies cover books, articles, pamphlets, directories, databases and theses and, wherever possible, attention is focused on material about the organizations rather than on the organizations' own publications. Notwithstanding this, the most important official publications, and guides to those publications, will be included. The views expressed in individual volumes, however, are not necessarily those of the publishers.

VOLUMES IN THE SERIES

1 *European Communities*, John Paxton

2 *Arab Regional Organizations*, Frank A. Clements

3 *Comecon: The Rise and Fall of an International Socialist Organization*, Jenny Brine

4 *International Monetary Fund*, Anne C. M. Salda

5 *The Commonwealth*, Patricia M. Larby and Harry Hannam

6 *The French Secret Services*, Martyn Cornick and Peter Morris

7 *Organization of African Unity*, Gordon Harris

8 *North Atlantic Treaty Organization*, Phil Williams

9 *World Bank*, Anne C. M. Salda

10 *United Nations System*, Joseph P. Baratta

11 *Organization of American States*, David Sheinin

TITLES IN PREPARATION

British Secret Services, Philip H. J. Davies

Israeli Secret Services, Frank A. Clements